THE ULTIMATE ~~OXBRIDGE~~

INTERVIEW GUIDE: LAW

UniAdmissions

Published by *RAR Medical Services Limited*
www.uniadmissions.co.uk
info@uniadmissions.co.uk
Tel: +44 (0) 208 068 0438

THE ULTIMATE OXBRIDGE INTERVIEW GUIDE: LAW

LEILA SYMONDS

GRACE DAVIS

DR TOBY BOWMAN

DR. ROHAN AGARWAL

EDITED BY
DR. RANJNA GARG

UniAdmissions

About the Authors

Leila is a law tutor and student, currently reading Law at **St Anne's College, Oxford**. She is an expert in Law interviews and the LNAT – and has a particular interest in Roman law.

Grace has recently completed her undergraduate in **PPE at Hertford College, Oxford**, and her masters in The History of Political Thought and Intellectual History at UCL/QMUL. She enjoys tutoring to teach more students about the intersection between Politics and Philosophy which she has found myself especially interested in over the course of her academic career. Having been the only person from her high school to have gone to Oxford, Grace has a particular interest in helping students to fulfil their potential and study at Oxbridge.

Toby is an academic researcher and publisher, who has supported students through the Oxbridge admissions process for nearly a decade. Since the completion of his DPhil in the History of Technology at Green Templeton College, Oxford, he has worked on research projects examining the impact of immersion on virtual reality technology adoption, and maintains a teaching presence at Oxford and with Oxbridge candidates. He also works as an examiner for Oxford's HAT exam, and as a civilian consultant to the NASA Ames Research Centre's Human Factors division in California. In his spare time, Toby creates digital art and music, and is an avid player of games.

Rohan is the **Director of Operations** at *UniAdmissions* and is responsible for its technical and commercial arms. He graduated from Gonville and Caius College, Cambridge and is a fully qualified doctor. Over the last five years, he has tutored hundreds of successful Oxbridge and Medical applicants. He has also authored ten books on admissions tests and interviews.

Rohan has taught physiology to undergraduates and interviewed medical school applicants for Cambridge. He has published research on bone physiology and writes education articles for the Independent and Huffington Post. In his spare time, Rohan enjoys playing the piano and table tennis.

CONTENTS

The Basics 10

General Interviews 16

Subject Interviews 95

   Law 97

   PPE & HSPS 195

   History 304

Reading List 352

Final Advice 353

Preface

Oxbridge interviews are frequently the source of intriguing stories. You'll frequently hear tales of students who were asked seemingly obscure questions e.g. "Why do we have two nostrils but only one mouth?", or impossibly difficult ones e.g. "How many grains of sand are there in the world?"

If taken in context, both of these are very fair Oxbridge interview questions. The first would naturally lead to a discussion concerning the evolution of sensory organs and the pros/cons of having multiple mouths e.g. reduced risk of infections vs. inability to eat and speak simultaneously etc.

The latter question would test a candidate's ability to breakdown an initially very large problem into more bite-sized chunks in order to manage it e.g. surface area of the Earth, percentage of the Earth covered by land, percentage of land covered by sand, average depth of sand and so on.

Oxbridge interviews are not about testing your knowledge. Instead, they are about testing what you can do with the knowledge you already possess. Remember, once you're at university, you will rapidly assimilate a great deal of new information (so much so that you will start to wonder what all the fuss A-levels were about).

This is the main reason why it's not particularly useful for interviewers to ask purely knowledge based questions e.g. "What is the normal plasma concentration of magnesium?". Knowledge of isolated facts is neither necessary nor sufficient for a successful Oxbridge interview. Instead, it is the application of some basic facts to novel situation that is the hallmark of success.

One of the best ways to demonstrate this is to discuss my interview experiences at Cambridge when I applied to study Medicine several years ago.

Interview One:

This was my first science interview and the interviewer was delighted when he found out I studied physics at A2. His opening question was "What have you read recently?" I explained I'd been reading about the new drug Rosuvastatin – a statin that was being recommended for everyone above a certain age (regardless of their actual cholesterol levels). The follow-up questions were what you would expect e.g. "How do statins work?" (Ensure you know the basics of any topic that you voluntarily bring up), "What are the risks/benefits of giving them to everyone?"

This led to a discussion on how I would convince someone that this drug was useful for them, followed by how I would convince someone that blue light was more damaging than red. I struggled with this for a while, bouncing ideas back and forth (with each of them sequentially shot down) until I finally stumbled onto Einstein's $E=hf$. This led to a discussion about why the sky is blue and sunsets can be a myriad of colours. All of this culminated in the classic- "What colour is the Sun in reality?" (Hint: It's not yellow, orange or red!). This is the question that tabloids would take out of context to make the interview seem like an array of bizarre questions when in fact this was perfectly reasonable giving the preceding questions.

This interview serves as a perfect example of a non-scripted interview, i.e. one where the interviewer was happy to bounce ideas between us and forced me to think about concepts in ways I never had. I'm certain that if I had offered a different answer to the initial question about my reading, the discussion would have gone along a significantly different route.

Interview Two:

My second interview was more scripted – the interviewer had a pre-set agenda with corresponding questions that he wanted to discuss. Given that this person is known to ask the same interview questions annually, I've refrained from including specifics in order to not spoil the plot for everyone and to unfairly put future applicants at an advantage (or disadvantage!).

After going through my **BMAT essay** very briefly, he asked me to draw a graph on his whiteboard. This was no easy task. I spent fifteen minutes struggling with this graph due to its unusual axis. Like many candidates, I made the mistake of learning about excessively complex topics like the Complement Membrane attack complex and ignored much core A-level topics like human physiology. This meant that I wasn't completely sure about a basic fact that was required for the graph. This was a tough interview and at the end of it, I was certain I had flunked it. This was compounded by the fact that other candidates were bragging about how they had got the correct graph in only thirty seconds.

When you're in the waiting room with the other candidates, it may appear that many of them are far smarter than you and know a lot more. Again, remember that the entire point of an interview is to assess your ability to apply knowledge.

People get nervous and unconfident whilst waiting for interviews. One of the ways they try to feel more secure is by exerting their intellectual superiority. In this example (although there were some exceptions), the students who tended to arrive at the answer very quickly were unsuccessful. This is likely because they had previous knowledge of the question from their school/extra reading. Although this allowed them to get the correct answer quickly, they were unable to explain the intermediate steps that led them to it, i.e. they *knew* the topic but didn't *understand* it.

Learning Points:

As you can see, I made lots of errors in my interview preparation. Please learn from them. Good students learn from their mistakes but *great* students learn from others' mistakes.

1) **Don't be put off by what other candidates say** in the waiting room. Focus on yourself – you are all that matter. If you want to be in the zone, then I would recommend taking some headphones and your favourite music.

2) **Don't read up on multiple advanced topics in depth**. Choose one topic and know it well. Focus the rest of your time on your core A-level syllabus. You are not expected to know about the features of Transverse Myelitis, but you will be expected to be able to rattle off a list of 10 cellular organelles.

3) **Don't worry about being asked seemingly irrelevant questions** that you'll often hear in the media. These are taken out of context. Focus on being able to answer the common questions e.g. "Why this university?" etc.

4) **Don't lose heart** if your interviews appear to have gone poorly. If anything, this can actually be a good sign as it shows that the interviewer pushed you to your limits rather than giving up on you as you clearly weren't Oxbridge material.

5) **Don't give up.** When you're presented with complex scenarios, go back to the absolute basics and try to work things out using first principles. By doing this and thinking out loud, you allow the interviewer to see your logical train of thought so that they can help you when you become stuck.

Good Luck!

Dr Rohan Agarwal

THE BASICS

What is an Oxbridge Interview?

An interview is a personal 20-30 minute session with one or two members of academic staff from Oxford or Cambridge. The interviewers will ask questions and **guide the applicant to an answer**. The answers usually require a large degree of creative and critical thought, as well as a good attitude and a sound foundation of subject-specific knowledge.

Why is there an Interview?

Most of the applicants to Oxbridge will have outstanding grades, predicted exam results, sample course work and personal statements. Interviews are used to help **determine which applicants are best-suited** for Oxbridge. During the interview, each applicant has a unique chance to demonstrate their creativity and critical thinking abilities- skills that Oxford and Cambridge consider vital for successful students.

Who gets an Interview?

At Cambridge, any applicant who might have a chance at being accepted to study will be called for interview. This corresponds to approximately **90%** of applicants. At Oxford, a slightly smaller **40-80%** of applicants are interviewed (applicants are shortlisted based on their admissions test results and UCAS form). No one is offered a place to study without attending an interview.

Who are the interviewers?

The interviews are conducted by a senior member of staff for the subject you've applied to; usually this person is the **Director of Studies** for that subject. There may also be a second interviewer who takes notes on the applicant or also asks questions. Interviewers describe this experience as just as nerve-wracking for them as for the applicants, as they are responsible for choosing the right students for Oxford and Cambridge.

When is the Interview?

Interviews are held in the **beginning of December** and some applicants may be invited back in January for a second round of interviews at another college. There are usually multiple interviews on the same day, either for different subjects or at different colleges. You will normally be given 2 weeks' notice before your interview- so you should hear back by late November, but it is useful to **begin preparing for the interview before you're officially invited**.

Where is the Interview?

The interviews are held in Oxford and Cambridge **at the college you applied to**. Oxford applicants may have additional interviews at another college than the one applied to. Cambridge applicants may get 'pooled' – be required to have another set of interviews in January at a different college. If you are travelling from far away, most Oxbridge colleges will provide you free accommodation and food for the duration of your stay if you wish to arrive the night before your interview.

Very rarely, interviews can be held via Skype at an exam centre- this normally only applies to international students or for UK students in extreme circumstances.

How should I use this book?

The best way to gain the most from this book is to let it guide your independent learning.

1. Read through the **General Interview** section.
2. Read the **Subject Interview** chapter for your subject.
3. Read the chapters on PPE, HSPS, and History for more experience.

Finally, work your way through the past interview questions – remember, you are not expected to know the answers to them, and they have been included here so that you can start to appreciate the style of questions that you may get asked. **It is not a test of what you know – but what you can do with what you already know.**

Oxbridge Tutorials & Supervisions

Hopefully, by this point, you're familiar with the unique Oxbridge teaching system. Students on the same course will have lectures and practicals together. These are supplemented by college-based tutorials/supervisions. A tutorial/supervision is an **individual or small group session** with an academic to **discuss ideas, ask questions, and receive feedback** on your assignments. During the tutorial/supervision, you will be pushed to think critically about the material from the course in novel and innovative ways. To get the most out of Oxbridge, you need to be able to work in this setting and take criticism with a positive and constructive attitude.

The **interviews are made to be model tutorials/supervisions**, with an academic questioning an applicant and seeing if they can learn, problem-solve, demonstrate motivation for their subject. It is by considering this ultimate goal of the interview that you can start to understand how to present and prepare yourself for the Oxbridge interview process.

What Are Interviewers Looking for?

There are several qualities an interviewer is looking for the applicant to demonstrate during the interview. While an applicant may think the most 'obvious' thing interviewers are looking for is excellent factual knowledge, this is already displayed through exam results. Whilst having an excellent depth of knowledge may help you perform better during an interview, **you're unlikely to be chosen based solely on your knowledge**. The main thing an interviewer is looking for is for the applicant to demonstrate critical thought, excellent problem-solving skills and intellectual flexibility, as well as **motivation for the subject and suitability for small group teaching**. It is also important for them to see that the applicant is willing to persevere with a challenging problem even if the answer is not immediately apparent.

How to Communicate Answers

The most important thing to do when communicating your answers is to **think out loud**. This will allow the interviewer to understand your thought processes. They will then be able to help you out if you get stuck. You should never give up on a question; show that you won't be perturbed at the first sign of hardship as a student, and remain positive and **demonstrate your engagement with the material**. Interviewers enjoy teaching and working with students who are as enthusiastic about their subject as they are.

Try to **keep the flow of conversation going** between you and your interviewer so that you can engage with each other throughout the entire interview. The best way to do this is to just keep talking about what you are thinking. It is okay to take a moment when confronted with a difficult question or plan your approach, but ensure you let the interviewer know this by saying, *"I'm going to think about this for a moment"*. Don't take too long- if you are finding the problems difficult, the **interviewers will guide and prompt you** to keep you moving forward. They can only do this if they know you're stuck!

The questions that you'll be asked are designed to be difficult, so don't panic up when you don't immediately know the answer. Tell the interviewer what you do know, offer some ideas, talk about ways you've worked through a similar problem that might apply here. If you've never heard anything like the question asked before, say that to the interviewer, *"I've never seen anything like this before"* or *"We haven't covered this yet at school"*, but don't use that as an excuse to quit. This is **your chance to show that you are eager to engage with new ideas,** so finish with *"But let's see if I can figure it out!"* or *"But I'm keen to try something new!"*. There are many times at Oxbridge when students are in this situation during tutorials/supervisors and you need to show that you can persevere in the face of difficulty (and stay positive and pleasant to work with while doing so).

Types of Interviews

There are, at Cambridge and for some Oxford subjects, several different types of interview that you can be called for. **Every applicant will have at least one subject interview**. Applicants to some courses may also have a **general interview**, especially if they are applying for an arts subject. Either way, you will be asked questions that touch on the course you are applying to study. It may be useful to **look at your interviewers' teaching backgrounds and published work** as this could potentially shed some light on the topics they might choose to discuss in an interview. However, there is absolutely no need to know the intricacies of their research work so don't get bogged down in it. Interviews tend to open with easier and more general questions and become more detailed and complicated as you are pushed to explore topics in greater depth.

Using the Practice Questions

This book contains over loads of practice interview questions. **They are all actual questions that successful Oxbridge applicants were asked in their interview**. However, it is important you take these with a pinch of salt.

They are taken out of context and only included to give you a flavour of the style and difficulty of real Oxbridge interview questions. Don't fall into the trap of thinking that your interview will consist of a series of irrelevant and highly specific knowledge-based questions.

> OXBRIDGE INTERVIEWS ARE **NOT** ABOUT YOUR KNOWLEDGE
>
> THEY ARE ABOUT WHAT YOU CAN DO
> WITH THE KNOWLEDGE YOU ALREADY POSSESS

Thus, it does little benefit to rote learn answers to all the practice questions in this book as they are unlikely to be repeated. Instead, follow our top tips, take inspiration from the worked answers and put in some hard work – you'll be sure to perform well on the day

GENERAL INTERVIEWS

A general interview is a get-to-know-you session with senior admissions tutors. This is your chance to demonstrate a passion for Oxbridge; that you have understood the Oxbridge system, have a genuine interest in being a student, and could contribute to Oxbridge if you were admitted. These are more common for arts and humanities applicants, but all applicants should nevertheless be prepared for a general interview.

- This will be less specific than the subject interview. The interviewers will focus more on your personal statement, any essays you may have submitted or have completed on the day of the interview and may discuss your SAQ form if you are applying to Cambridge.

- One of the interviewers may not be a specialist in the subject you've applied for. Don't be put off by this – you aren't expected to have any knowledge of their subject.

- Ensure that you have read your personal statement and any books/journals that you've claimed to have read in your application. You will seem unenthusiastic and dishonest if you can't answer questions regarding topics and activities that you claim to know about. Remember that it is much better to show a good understanding of a few texts than to list lots of texts that you haven't properly read.

- Read and re-read the essays you have submitted. Be prepared to expand on the ideas you have explored in them. Remember, that the interviewers may criticise what you've argued in your submitted essays. If you believe in it, then defend your view but don't be stubborn.

- You will normally be asked if you have any questions at the end of the interview. Avoid saying things like, *"How did I do?"* – Instead use this as an opportunity to show the interviewers the type of person you are e.g. *"How many books can I borrow from the library at one time?"*

What type of questions might be asked?

The three main questions that are likely to come up in an Oxbridge interview are:

- *Why Oxford/Cambridge?*
- *Why this subject?*
- *Why this college?*

You may also get asked more specific questions about the teaching system or about your future career aspirations. This will also be the time for discussing any extenuating circumstances for poor exam results and similar considerations.

To do well in a general interview, your answers should show that you understand the Oxbridge system and that you have strong reasons for applying there. Thus, it is essential that you prepare detailed answers to the common questions above so that you aren't caught off guard. In addition, you should create a list of questions that could potentially be asked based on your personal statement or any submitted work.

Worked Questions

Below are a few examples of how to start breaking down general interview questions- complete with model answers.

Q1: How did you choose which college to apply for?

This question is a good opportunity to tell the interviewer about yourself, your hobbies, motivations, and any interesting projects you have undertaken. You can demonstrate that you have read about the College thoroughly and you know what differentiates your College from the others. The decisive factors can include a great variety of different things from history, alumni, location in the city, community, sports clubs, societies, any positive personal experiences from Open Day and notable scholars.

This is a warm up question – an ice-breaker – so just be natural and give an honest answer. You may not want to say things like, *"I like the statues in the garden"*. The more comprehensive your answer is, the better.

Good Applicant: I chose which college to apply for based on a number of factors that were important to me. First of all, I needed to consider how many other students at my college would be studying the same subject as me; this was important to me as I want to be able to engage in conversation about my subject with my peers. Secondly, I considered the location of the college as I wanted to ensure I had easy access to the faculty library and lecture theatres. Thirdly, I am a keen tennis player and so looked for a college with a very active tennis society. Finally, I wanted to ensure that the college I chose would feel right for me and so I looked around several Cambridge colleges before coming to my conclusion.

This response is broken down into a set of logical and yet personal reasons. **There is no right answer to this question** and the factors which influence this decision are likely to be unique for each individual. However, each college is unique and therefore the interviewer wants to know what influenced your decision. Therefore, **it's essential that you know what makes your college special** and separates it from the others. Even more importantly, you should know what the significance of that will be for you. For example, if a college has a large number of mathematicians, you may want to say that by attending that college, it would allow you to discuss your subject with a greater number of people than otherwise.

A **poor applicant** may respond with a noncommittal shrug or an answer such as, *"my brother went there"*. The interviewers want to see that you have researched the university and although the reason for choosing a college won't determine whether or not you get into the university, a lack of passion and interest in the college will greatly influence how you are perceived by the interviewers.

Q2: Why have you chosen to apply to study at 'Oxbridge', rather than another Russell Group university?

This is a very broad question and one which is simply designed to draw out the motives and thinking behind your application, as well as giving you an opportunity to speak freely about yourself.

A **good applicant** would seek to address this question in two parts, the first addressing the key features of Oxbridge for their course and the second emphasising their own personality traits and interests which make them most suited to the Oxbridge system.

It is useful to start off by talking about the supervision/tutorial system and why this method of very small group teaching is beneficial for studying your subject, both for the discussion of essay work and, more crucially, for developing a comprehensive understanding of your subject. You might also like to draw upon the key features of the course at Oxford and Cambridge that distinguish it from courses at other universities.

When talking about yourself, a good answer could take almost any route, though it is always productive to talk about which parts of your subject interest you, why this is the case, and how this ties in with the course at Oxford/Cambridge. You might also mention how the Oxbridge ethos suits your personality, e.g. how hard work and high achievement are important to you and you want to study your chosen subject in real depth, rather than a more superficial course elsewhere.

A **poor applicant** would likely demonstrate little or no knowledge of their course at Oxford/Cambridge and volunteer little information about why studying at Oxbridge would be good for them or why they would be suited to it. It's important to focus on your interests and abilities rather than implying that you applied because Oxbridge is the biggest name or because your family or school had expected you to do so.

Q3: What do you think you can bring to the college experience?

This is a common question at general interviews and **you need to show that you would be a good fit for the College** and that you are also really motivated because you have researched the college's facilities, notable fellows and alumni, societies and sports clubs etc. You can mention that you have looked at the website, talked to alumni and current students.

This question also gives the interviewer an excellent opportunity to learn about your personality, hobbies and motivations. Try to avoid listing one thing after the other for 5 minutes. Instead, you should try to give a balanced answer in terms of talking about the College and yourself. You should talk about your skills and give examples when you had to work in a team, deliver on strict deadlines, show strong time-management skills etc. You should also give a few examples from your previous studies, competitions or extracurricular activities (including sports and music).

Q4: *Tell me about a recent news article not related to your subject that has interested you.*

This can be absolutely anything and your interviewers just want to see that **you are aware of the world in which you live** and have a life outside of your subject. You could pick an interesting topic ahead of time and cultivate an opinion which could spark a lively discussion.

Q5: *Which three famous people would you most like to be stuck on a desert island with?*

This is a personal question that might be used by your interviewers as an 'icebreaker' – you can say absolutely anyone but try to have a good justification (and avoid being melodramatic). This is a really **good chance to show your personality and sense of humour**. This is also a good question to ease you into the flow of the interview and make yourself feel more comfortable.

Q6: *Do you think you're 'clever'?*

Don't let this one faze you! Your interviewers are not being glib but instead want to see how you cope with questions you may not have anticipated. You could discuss different forms of intelligence, e.g. emotional vs. intellectual, perhaps concluding that you are stronger in one over the other.

Q7: What experiences do you have which suggest to you that you'll cope well with the pressures of Oxbridge?

The **interviewers want to hear that you know what you're signing up to** and that you are capable of dealing with stress. If you have any experience of dealing with pressure or meeting strict deadlines, this would be a good opportunity to talk about them. Otherwise, mention your time management skills and your ability to prioritise workloads. You could also mention how you deal with stress, e.g. do you like running? Yoga? Piano? Etc.

Q8: Why are you in this room right now?

There are hundreds of potential responses to this type of question, and the interviewer will see this as a chance to get to know your personality and how you react to unusual situations.

Firstly, **take the question seriously**, even if it strikes you as funny or bizarre. A good response may begin with: "There are many reasons why I am in this room. There are lots of smaller events and causes that have led up to me being here". You might choose to discuss your desire to attend Oxbridge, the fact that you have travelled to the college to take your interview. You might choose to discuss the interviewer or college's taste and budget when it came to selecting the chair you are sitting in, as that determined why and how you have come to be sitting in that particular chair, rather than any other chair. You might then simply mention that you were invited by the interviewer to take a seat.

A weak response to this type of question would be to dismiss it as silly or irrelevant.

Q9: Let's say you're hosting a small private party, and you have a magical invitation which will summon anyone from time and space to your dining table. Who's name do you write on the invitation?

This is a fairly straightforward question to get in a general interview, so use it to show your personality and originality, and to talk about something you are really passionate about.

If you are asked a question like this, give an answer that is relevant to your application. This is not the time to start talking about how you are a huge fan of Beyonce and would just love to have dinner together! You should also avoid generic answers like "God".

If you would love to meet Obama and know more about him, consider what that would be like. Would he be at liberty to answer your questions? Might you not get more information from one of his aides or from a close friend, rather than the man himself? As this is a simple question, try to unpick it and answer it in a sophisticated way, rather than just stating the obvious.

Q10: What was the most recent film you watched?

This question seems simple and appears to require a relatively short answer. However, a good candidate will use a simple question such as this as an opportunity to speak in more depth and **raise new and interesting topics of conversation**: "What I find particularly interesting about this film was…. It reminded me of….. In relation to other works of this period/historical context, I found this particular scene very interesting as it mirrored/contrasted with my previous conceptions of this era as seen in other works, for example… I am now curious to find out more about… This film made me think about…etc."

Whilst it is extremely important to respond accurately to the questions posed by the interviewer, do not be afraid to **take the conversation in the direction led by your personal interests**. This sort of initiative will be encouraged.

Q11: How do you think the university will evaluate whether or not you have done well at the end of your degree, do you think that this manner of assessment is fair?

This question invites you to show your potential and how diverse your interests are. There are three aspects of this question that you should consider in order to give a complete answer: "end of your time here", "measure" and "your achievements". You may want to discuss your hobbies and interests and potential achievements regarding various aspects of university life including academia, sports, student societies, jobs, volunteering etc.

Then you may want to enter into a discussion about whether there is any appropriate measure of success. How could you possibly compare sporting excellence to volunteering? Is it better to be a specialist or a generalist? This ultimately comes down to your personal motivation and interests as you might be very focused on your studies or other activities (e.g. sports, music). Thus, multiple things would contribute to your success at university and your degree is only likely to be one way to measure this. Finally, it might be a great closing line to mention that getting your degree might not be the "end of your time here".

Q12: Tell me why you think people should go to university.

This sounds like a very general question at first but it is, in fact, about your personal motivations to go to university. You don't need to enter into a discussion about what universities are designed for or any educational policy issues as the interviewer is unlikely to drive the discussion towards this in a general interview.

The best strategy is to **discuss your motivations**- this could include a broad range of different things from interest in a certain field, inspiring and diverse environments, academic excellence, opening up of more opportunities in the future and buying time to find out more about yourself etc. As it is very easy to give an unfocused answer, you should limit yourself to a few factors. You can also comment on whether people should go to university and whether this is good for the society.

Q13: I'm going to show you a painting, imagine that you have been tasked with describing this to someone over the phone so that they can recreate it, but you only have a minute. How would you describe the painting in order to make the recreation as close to the original as possible?

This question is very common and surprisingly difficult. **You can take a number of approaches**. Ensure that you have a concrete idea of the structure you will use to describe the painting. For example, you could begin with your personal feelings about it, then the colours and atmosphere the painting creates, then the exact objects, then their respective position and size. It does not matter which approach you take but this question is designed to test your way of organising and presenting your ideas.

You could also comment on the difficulty of the task and argue that human language limits you from adequately describing smell, taste, sound, and vision. Modern language applicants may have read about Wittgenstein, in which case, they can reference his works on the limitations and functions of language here.

Q14: Which person in the past would you most like to interview, and why?

This is a personal question but try to **avoid generic and mainstream answers**. Keep in mind that you can find out much more about a particular period or era by speaking to everyday citizens or advisors for politicians or other important figures. It is much more important to identify what you want to learn about and then set criteria to narrow down the possible list of persons. This question opens the floor for developing an analytical, quasi-scientific approach to your research.

Q15: What's an interesting thing that's been happening in the news recently?

Whilst this question may be asked at a general interview, it's a good idea to come up with something that is related to your course. Instead of going into technical detail with an interviewer who may be from a completely different discipline, it is better to give a brief overview of the article and then put it into a broader context.

For example, an economics applicant may want to discuss the most recent banking scandal. A physics applicant may want to discuss a recent discovery.

A **good** candidate might say something like "That's a great question, there are lot of really interesting things which have happened recently. For me I think the most interesting one is the confirmation of increased magnetic movement in muons at the Fermi National Accelerator in America.

This is mainly interesting for two reasons, I think that it as always interesting when you have examples of the standard model of physics perhaps not working as it should. It's seemed like there have been problems with the way we understand everything working for some time now, but actually being able to perhaps find a new force, and write new laws of physics is incredibly exciting! The other reason this in particular is interesting is because it shows some of the strengths and weaknesses of the scientific process. Even though this magnetic movement has been detected in multiple experiments for over twenty years, it is still not something which we can consider confirmed, because this movement has not been confirmed to the five-sigma level of certainty needed to announce an actual discovery. This rigour helps ensure that we don't have incidents like the Pons and Felischmann Cold Fusion scandal, but does also mean that we will have waited more than two decades to start re-writing the textbooks at the point that this can be confirmed, assuming of course that it ever is. Events like this one really show how thorough and reliable scientific work can be, but also that in areas like theoretical physics things can be very slow to change."

The answer should not be a complete analysis of the issue but an intuitive and logical description of an event, with a good explanation of why it is interesting to you, personally. They really want to see here your enthusiasm for the topic of the article in question (and hopefully the topic of your chosen course) as well as your ability to reflect in a mature way on its most general themes.

Q16: Can people be entirely apolitical? Are you political?

In general, you should avoid expressing any very extreme views at all during interviews. The answer, *"I am not political"* is not the most favourable either. This question invites you to **demonstrate academic thinking in a topic which could be part of everyday conversations**. You are not expected to present a full analysis of party politics and different ideologies. It doesn't matter if you actually have strong political views; the main point is to talk about your perception of what political ideas are present and how one differs from the other.

With such a broad question – you have the power to choose the topic- be it wealth inequality, nuclear weapons, corruption, human rights, or budget deficit etc. Firstly, you should **explain why that particular topic or political theme is important**. For example, the protection of fundamental human rights is crucial in today's society because this introduces a social sensitivity to our democratic system where theoretically 51% of the population could impose its will on the other 49%. On the other hand, it should be noted that Western liberal values may contradict with social, historical and cultural aspects of society in certain developing countries, and a different political discourse is needed in different countries about the same questions. Secondly, you should discuss whether that topic is well-represented in the political discourse of our society and what should be done to trigger a more democratic debate.

Q17: One of the unique features of the Oxbridge education is the supervision system, one-on-one tutorials every week. This means a heavy workload, one essay every week with strict deadlines. Do you think you can handle this?

By this point, you should hopefully have a sound understanding of the supervision/tutorial systems. You should also be aware of the possibility of spending long hours in the library and meeting tight deadlines so this question should not be surprising at all. It gives you an opportunity to **prove that you would fit into this educational system very well**. Firstly, you should make it clear that you understand the system and the requirements. On average, there is one essay or problem sheet every week for each paper that you are reading which requires going through the reading list/lecture notes and engaging with wider readings around certain topics or problems. Secondly, you should give some examples from your past when you had to work long hours or had strict deadlines etc. You should also tell the interviewer how you felt in these situations, what you enjoyed the most and what you learned from them. Finally, you may wish to stress that you would *"not only be able to cope with the system but also enjoy it a great deal"*.

Q18: If you had to live in the world of a book you have read, which book would it be, and whose role would you take?

This question is an ice-breaker- the interviewer is curious to find out what type of novels you read and how thoroughly you are reading them. You want to show that you are capable of thinking on your feet, talk them through why you've chosen their particular world, does it have advantages which outweigh its pitfalls. For example, if you say you like Robin Hood, it is a world in which you could carry out noble deeds in an idyllic setting, but you also have to deal with poverty, homelessness, and a brutal regime. If you would like to live here, then tell them why. As for the character, centre in on who you want, for instance Robin himself, explain his situation briefly as becoming an outlaw, resisting the authorities, and aiding the poor and his fellow men. Would you like to take his role because you would like to do the things he did, or do you feel that you could 'be' him differently, or even better? Would you be able to learn or grow from entering your chosen world, and being a certain character - think of what course you are applying to, and see if there are particular skills which you think this experience could teach you, empathy, if you're applying for medicine, or social responsibility, if you're applying for economics & management, as examples.

The main point is to be able to **give a very brief summary of the character and the world in which they live in**, (especially if you choose a less well-known work), and have a good and interesting justification for choosing them.

Q19: Do you think that we should give applicants access to a computer during their interviews?

This is a classic open question for an insightful debate. The most important thing to realise here is that **Oxbridge education is about teaching you how to think** in clear, structured and coherent ways as opposed to collecting lots of facts from the internet.

Internet access would provide each candidate with the same available information and therefore the art of using information to make sound arguments would be the sole decisive factor. On the other hand, the information overload can be rather confusing. In general, a braindump is not helpful at the interview as it does not demonstrate in-depth understanding and analysis of any problems. At the end of the day, it comes down to the individual candidate, i.e. what would you look up on the Internet during the interview? Would you want to rely on unverified knowledge? How reliable is that information on the internet? How could you verify this information?

Q20: What was your proudest moment?

This is another chance to highlight your suitability for the course, so try to **make it as subject-relevant as possible**. *"I felt proud to be awarded first place in a poetry competition with a sonnet I wrote about…"* (if you're applying for English). *"I recently won the Senior Challenge for the UK Mathematics Trust.", "Achieving a 100% mark in my AS-level History and English exams – an achievement I hope to emulate at A2"*.

Of course, it's not easy to pick one moment and this is not a question you might have expected. You could also argue that you can't really compare your achievements from different fields e.g. your 100% Physics AS-level and football team captaincy, but be careful. You should always try to settle on one in the end, this will show the interviewer that you are able to answer the questions you are given, even if they are very challenging, which is a vital skill. A useful tip here is to talk them through your thought process, there are several competing moment which could be your proudest, and you need to work out which one was the best. Try separating out the ones which impressed others versus those which were more personal to you, and decide on one which, overall, was the most impactful. This way, you have talked through a number of impressive things with the interviewer, but you have shown critical thinking skills and attention to detail in providing a definitive answer.

Q21: Would you ever use a coin-flip to make a choice, if so, when?

This question can be quite tricky and aims at revealing how you make decisions in your life, your understanding of abstract concepts, rationality and probabilities. You should begin with answering the question from your perspective, you can be honest about it but give a justification even if you never want to make decisions based on luck. Try to **give a few examples when tossing a coin could be a good idea**, or would cause no harm. Then you can take the discussion to a more abstract level and argue that once all yes/no decisions are made by tossing a coin in the long run, the expected value should be fifty-fifty so you might not be worse-off at all and you could avoid the stress of making decisions (although this is very simplistic).

You could also reference the stock markets where high returns may be purely luck-dependent. On the other hand, **rational decision-making is part of human nature** and analysing costs and benefits would result in better decisions in the long-run than tossing a coin. In addition, this would incentivise people to conduct research, collect information, develop and test theories, etc. As you see, the question could be interpreted to focus on the merits of rigorous scientific methodology.

Q22: If you had omnipotence for a moment, but had to use it to change only one thing, what would it be?

This question tests your sound reasoning and clear presentation of your answer and the justification for it. There is no right or wrong "one thing" to choose. It is equally valid to choose wealth inequality or the colour of a double-decker bus if you argue it well! It should be noted that if you've applied for social sciences, it is a better strategy to choose a related topic to show your sensitivity to social issues.

Firstly, you should choose something you would like to change while demonstrating clear thinking, relevant arguments. Secondly, you are expected to discuss how, and to what extent, you would and could change it. Again, a better candidate would realise that **this is not necessarily a binomial problem** – either change it or not – but there may be a spectrum between these two extremes. Once you've identified the thing you'd like to change, talk them through why. A good way to make sure you always do this is by thinking aloud, and walking the interviewer through the way you would reach this conclusion yourself.

Q23: Oxford, as you know, has access to some very advanced technology. In the next room we actually have the latest model of time machine, if we gave you the opportunity to use it later, when would you go?

This is a question where you can really use your imagination (or draw on History GCSE or A-level). **You can say absolutely any time period** in the past or the far future but you must have a good reason for it which you communicate to the interviewer. This doesn't necessarily need to be linked to your subject.

For example, *"I would love to see a time when my parents were little children and see where and how they grew up. I'd ideally like to stay for some time to gather as much information as possible. This would be really valuable to me as I'd get to see them when they were people without children, just as they themselves were developing, and could give me opportunities to better understand them. I think understanding ones parents is often a good way to help you understand yourself. The pursuit of self-understanding never stops, but this opportunity would give me a unique chance to improve that."*

Choosing something personal or creative will make you stand out and you are more likely to get interesting questions from the interviewer if you are able to involve them in an intriguing conversation. It is also fine if you choose a standard period like the Roman Empire or a time which has not yet come to pass, say the year 4000, if you have a good reason.

Q24: Should interviews be used for selection?

This question may appear slightly inflammatory on the surface, considering that you are answering it in an interview, to an interviewer who likely believes in the merit of interviewing for selection. However, remember that the interviewer is interested in your opinion, and will not take offence providing you respond in a measured way, providing examples/evidence. Another important thing to remember for any question that addresses interviews and/or selection, is that what you are currently sat in is not the only form of interview, and what you are being selected for is not the only form of selection. As a result, you could wildly disagree with interviews for selection in most situations, but agree with them in the situation you are currently sat in, or vice versa.

"One up-side to using interviews for selection, is that it forces the interviewee to think on their feet (providing the questions aren't known to them in advance), which can demonstrate their real-world knowledge of a subject and is likely to bring out more honest answers about themselves. One down-side is that an interview is quite a short and high-pressure situation, as a result, an interviewee could easily make a number of mistakes or say something inappropriate and tarnish the interviewer's opinion of them. By extension, interviews rely somewhat on the opinion of the interviewer, therefore, are prone to bias."

This would be a good answer, as it addresses one for and one against aspect, justifying each point with an explanation. However, a great answer would be one that takes this further, and considers interviews' appropriateness for different types of selection.

"In some situations, the ability for an interviewee to make a mess of the interview due to the short time they are with the interviewer, and the pressure they are under, is a bad thing. This is in the same way that an entire year's work boiling down to one exam is often criticised as a way of measuring someone's academic ability. However, if the interview is for something that requires working in that situation, such as a politician who will be subjected to questions and interviews throughout their job, then an interview is a great way to measure their suitability."

By considering the appropriateness of an interview in different scenarios, you are not only demonstrating your breadth of consideration, but also your ability to remove yourself from your own head and think outside of your current situation. This question could, however, specify a type of interview and/or a particular thing being selected for. In this case, make sure you stick to that specific concept. You may address an alternative concept for comparison, but always bring the conclusion back to the question's specific elements.

Q25: Would you ever choose to go to a party rather than write an essay for university?

At first glance, this might feel like a trick question. As an interviewer, they are likely a practicing academic at the university and could well be a subject tutor you could end up having! However, it's important to remember two things. Firstly, tutors are human too and like to have fun occasionally. Secondly, all universities have 'parties' that are sanctioned by the university or an individual faculty, therefore, it's perfectly fine to want to go to parties! There are a couple of distinctions to make when constructing an answer for a question like this, and they hinge on the importance of each element.

In isolation, you might consider it impossible to argue that a party is in any way important. However, there are lots of ways in which it could be. This could a big, once in a lifetime faculty ball, it could be a party for a close friend's birthday, it could have valuable networking opportunities, or it could simply be a party you really could do with as you're feeling a bit down at that moment. The other aspect of this question is, of course, the essay. When picking something over something else, you should be considering the importance of each thing in isolation to the current situation, rather than just the concepts in general. For example, if the essay is due tomorrow and the party is a small get-together down the hall which is going to result in you not sleeping properly and not being able to finish the essay in time, then it would be quite difficult (although not impossible in the 'right' circumstances) to argue that you would pick the party over the essay.

Under some circumstances, the party might be a well-deserved break from your work, and not directly impact your ability to submit the essay by the deadline. For example, if an essay is due at the end of the following day and the party is that night, it might initially seem sensible to finish the essay first and relax after. However, you won't be able to go to the party tomorrow afternoon once you've finished the essay, as it won't be going on then. So, in that case, it would make sense to go to the party and then finish the essay the following afternoon before the deadline (providing you have enough time to do so). This sort of decision-making is more likely to go approved by an interviewer if the party has some kind of important element (e.g., a big, one-off organised event or a birthday party), but even if not, it is important to be able to back your decisions. As long as you are completing the work to a high standard and on time, it's also important that you enjoy yourself!

Q26: Who do you think has the most power: Biden, Merkel or Adele?

Answering a question like this first rests on your knowledge of each person. You don't need to know a great deal about them, but it is important you know what their role is. If you don't know that, make sure you ask the interviewer! Once you have established who each person is, you need to address any words in the question that have multiple interpretations. In this case, that word is 'power'. In order to answer the question, you need to decide how to measure power. As with all of these types of questions, you are welcome to pick one definition and go with it, or address the fact that there are multiple definitions and briefly approach each one individually. You can always make a comparison/conclusion at the end of the latter to potentially pick the 'best' definition for that particular situation.

When defining power, there are two key starting points. The first is how many people are aware of what each person says or does. This is probably the easiest to answer.

"If you consider power to be the potential of each person's words or actions to affect others, then the most influential would probably be Adele. Her music and name are known worldwide so, while she is probably not known by as many people in the US as Biden is, her reach is more global and likely through to a younger audience. More people will have heard her, and responded in any number of different ways, even turning off the radio is affecting others. However, as Biden progresses through his presidency and makes more headlines, that could easily change!"

Due to the simplicity of this definition, in this case, it is probably best to address at least one other definition of influence. One alternative definition is how much those who hear what that person says or sees what they do, will change their thoughts or long-term actions based on it.

"If defining power as how much people will change their actions or thoughts based on the actions and words of that person, then the most influential person is probably Biden. As the Amercian president, the majority of the US population will be brought into his words and actions, even if it is to vehemently disagree with them!"

You could go on to explore whether power can be just as valid when someone disagrees with the words or actions of an influential individual, or how many more people would someone need to affect a little bit to make them more powerful than someone who influences a smaller number of people a lot. The important thing is that you explore your thought processes aloud, and see them through to a conclusion each time. The conclusion doesn't need to be right, as with a concept like this it is hard to be 'right', it just needs to be some kind of decision (even if that decision is there is a tie!).

Q27: What would you say was "your colour"?

With a question as basic and seemingly abstract as this, there are two ways you can approach it. The first is to delve into the question in-depth and explore each concept and its origin. The alternative is to answer the question succinctly and give a clear reason for your conclusion. Below is an example of the latter.

"I believe that red is a colour that represents me best as it is my favourite colour. I think it came about as my favourite colour because my parents' car when I was a child was red, as was the front door on the first house I remember living in, so I always associated red with my family and home".

That would be enough detail to give a valid answer. You have given the basis of the reason (that it is your favourite colour), and then discussed the origin of that reasoning. Alternatively, you can choose to explore the question in much more detail. The first concept to approach when doing this, is the idea of representation. Is this self-representation, how others would represent you, or perhaps how you relate to what the colour typically represents in society. Below is an example of a succinct approach to all three of those concepts, something you could state after outlining the three concepts aloud.

"For myself, the colour green represents me best because it is my favourite colour, I own lots of green clothes and decorations in my room and would love to have a green house! If other people had to choose, I'd say they would pick blue because I spent a lot of time in rivers in my parents' canoe, and enjoy spending time in the sea on holiday. If I had to be represented by a societal norm, I would day that red best represents me because I have a fiery temper."

While, in the real interview you would probably approach each of these in a bit more details, this gives a basic outline of how you would separate the three concepts. You don't have to address every concept in your answer but, as usual, it is always good to outline all the concepts in the beginning to demonstrate to the interviewer that you are thinking comprehensively. Remember, when you are addressing multiple concepts in an answer, it is all too easy to drift away from the origin of your thoughts. Bring it back each time by answering the actual question at the end of each of your thought processes, in the context that thought process has been discussed in.

Q28: What shape is man? What shape is time?

On the surface, this question seems impossible to answer because it is simply too abstract. There is no shape that fits the shape of a person, and time isn't a physical concept. However, this is a test of how you address something seemingly impossible to answer. There is no wrong way to answer this question, providing you actually answer it! The important thing to remember is to get started with answering it quickly, the longer you spend pondering the wider concept, the more difficult it will be to get started!

Addressing each question individually is important and something you need to conclude on so, as a result, it is easy for you to separate two concept discussions by addressing one per question. When considering the first question, you can start by providing the obvious answer, and follow-on by delving into the concept more deeply.

"There is no named shape that is the shape of a person, so you would refer to 'man' simply as being 'man-shaped'. We refer to things in this way all the time, so not having a named shape to represent something shouldn't limit you. One important differentiator is that 'man' is not an exact shape, as every person is different. Therefore, if your definition of shape must be precise such as a square having four equal length sides with four ninety-degree corners, then that would not be possible to apply to 'man'. However, a shape like an oval doesn't have explicit parameters, so is closer to the idea of a shape which could define 'man'."

There are clear caveats to this answer, such as an oval having the strict rule of no straight edges and being entirely symmetrical, but the consideration of two different types of existing shape definitions is a great way to start the discussion. When moving that discussion on to consider time, it becomes even more abstract. You could open the discussion with the fact that time is not considered a physical concept, thus it would be inappropriate to allocate it a shape. However, you then open the discussion around space-time, where time can be considered represented physically. An interviewer may not choose to entertain such a discussion, as it is not exactly psychology related, but making sweeping and abrupt statements like that are best avoided anyway. A better way to open the discussion might be to explain that time is often considered a circle (history repeating itself, the circle of life etc.). While it would be inappropriate to state that time is a specific shape, acknowledging these ideas demonstrates your ability to think conceptually and compare it to real societal discussion.

Q29: Do things have to have specific names?

When answering why, the first thing to consider is 'what's in it for the user'. In this case, what is gained by naming things.

"One reason why things have names is to avoid having to describe them every time we refer to them. Once you have learned what the name refers to, conversations can be had much more quickly, and more easily across different languages. Rather than having to learn all the terms that describe a thing, you would only need to learn the name of that thing in order to tell a person about it in a different language."

You can centre the entire discussion around this idea of what we gain from something, but it is important to broaden your horizons a little if you want to make the discussion as interesting and engaging as possible. You may consider a few gains we make by naming things, but the next step is to consider the origin of naming things and the reason for the concept. The first reason is that we gain something from doing it, so it justifies the effort of coming up with and learning the names, However, another example which would explain the origin of naming something is that we want to take ownership of it. By giving something a name, it can be recognised by that name and associated with one person as its 'owner'. This could be considered the origin of naming, whereby everyone would have a different name for the few things they considered to be there. Gradually, through communication, perhaps we established it would be easier to have a unified naming process, such that there were fewer names to remember. This could have led to the origin of possessive pronouns, to go with these unified names.

None of this is necessarily true, and would be almost impossible to prove either way due to how long-ago naming things came about as a concept. Discussions of this type do, however, demonstrate your ability to consider both the value and the origin of a concept or action and link them together. The importance of a question like this, is to evoke a discussion of the abstract that you can tie together into a coherent conclusion. As such, it is vital that regardless of the content of your discussion, you conclude with an actual answer. This is welcome to be a brief touch of each of the discussion points you have made, as it is often impossible to make an explicit decision on which is 'right', but it needs to be clear and concise.

"I believe things have names because it was a way of identifying them as our own, which developed into a way of communicating what they were between people who didn't know of each other's possessions. It stuck as a concept, because it enabled shorter discussions through not having to fully describe a thing each time it was mentioned."

Q30: Do you read any international publications, do you think there is a value to doing so?

This question requires honesty above all else. This doesn't mean you couldn't implicitly overstate quite to the extent that you read a particular publication, but you absolutely should not discuss something you haven't actually read. Many of the interviewers you will speak to will ask this question because they are very well read, thus could easily pull you up on a particular publication. As a result, you need to have actually read an international newspaper or publication to answer this question. It would be best if you have read at least one of each, but if you have only read one, open with that.

What the interviewer will be looking for is your critique of the publication. It would be a bonus if it is psychology-related, but don't think it to be necessary. The important thing is that you recognise and address the context under which the publication is written, and how that might influence what they write about and how they write about it. When critiquing an academic paper in an essay, these are the sorts of things a tutor will be looking to see, and it is what the interviewer wants to assess your ability on at this stage. This isn't to say that you should construct your entire discussion of the publication around this critiquing, but it is definitely something you should include.

"I read [American Newspaper] online quite regularly, and tend to focus on the 'social issues' section of the paper. It is interesting to read about American social issues because some of them are so similar to our own, whereas others are so distinctly different. One article I read in the most recent version [don't be this specific if you're not sure it was] highlighted the ease with which someone could buy a gun as a non-American citizen, meaning that someone who's history is unknown to American authorities could enter the country and buy a weapon with bad intentions. I wonder whether gun culture contributes to xenophobia and racism, as the risk that someone coming into the country with bad intentions poses, is potentially much higher than if the same thing happened where guns weren't accessible to the public."

While this is a very simplistic discussion of a point and you would want to delve into some more detail and evidence in the real interview, it demonstrates how you can bring a psychology them to a seemingly unrelate article. The next stage in your discussion would be to critique the paper itself. With gun culture being alien to a UK resident (if indeed you are one), you could consider your views on the topic to be biased. You could also make a suggestion to rectify that, by discussing the article with an American person or someone who is in favour of guns being legally accessible to the public. This last bit is important as it is key to consider how you can broaden your views in a practical way. If the context is right, you can link it to how you might do this during your time at university.

Q31: Can you hear silence?

There are two elements that can be considered in almost any question which touches on biology in a psychology interview. The first is the biological element, and the second is the concept that we experience/express as a result or in anticipation of that biological effect. In this case, there is the biology of hearing something, and the interpretation of that into neural signals. In this case, how you explain the biology is very much dependent on your biology knowledge. Unless it is something you have mentioned in your personal statement or in the interview, the interviewer won't expect you to have comprehensive knowledge of the biology behind hearing. However, they will expect you to have a general understanding that sound travels in waves, and those waves are interpreted into neural signals (which we 'hear') by bones in your ear.

When considering this from a biological perspective, then you can be pretty conclusive in your statement that we cannot hear silence. If there are no sound waves, then we do not 'hear' anything from our environment. However, this doesn't mean that we don't interpret the silence as something other than nothingness, from the neural signals we receive. Without making any sweeping statements about the complicated biology around neural signalling, it would make sense to assume that neurons aren't ever 'silent'. Things in biology are rarely as cut and dry as being 'off' or 'on', so you could use that train of thought in the following discussion.

"I imagine that neurons are never at a point when there is no transmission of chemical between them. It is more likely to imagine they have a 'resting rate' of transmission, which is then greatly increase when 'active'. As a result, even when there is no noise, you might assume there are still some signals being sent between neurons related to hearing. In order to create a silent environment, humans have gone to great lengths to create sound-deadening material. Therefore, one could assume that silence is not something you would come across in a natural setting. If the human hearing system has not evolved to consider true silence, when faced with it, its reaction will likely be to 'hear' the 'resting rate' of signals that would normally never be reached due to ambient noise. With that in mind, while you cannot actually hear silence because there are no sound waves to hear, the experience of true silence is likely to manifest as some kind of ambient sound."

Making one point per statement in a discussion like this enables you to create an argument that is easy to follow. This is beneficial for three reasons. Firstly, the interviewer can take note of every point you have made. Secondly, the interviewer can see you are proficient at organising your thoughts. Thirdly, the interviewer can be invited to target a new discussion (even if that is to disagree with you) at any one of your points. The more discussion the better!

Q32: You mentioned having good thinking skills in your personal statement, can you tell me how many golf balls can you fit in a Boeing 787 Dreamliner?

This question is testing a few things, all related to your thinking process, despite its seemingly pointless nature. The first thing it is testing is the comprehensiveness and commitment of your subject consideration. What the interviewer will be looking for is you to exhaust all aspects of the question, in order to work towards the answer. Part of this is considering the physical nature of the objects in mind. The two elements in this question are the plane, and the golf balls. To consider the physical size of the plane, it might be best to get some clarification from the interviewer if you don't know the size of the plane. The number will be very different between a double-decker transatlantic plane compared to a private jet! If you know the size, make sure you state it out loud, it doesn't really matter whether you are right or not, just that the interviewer knows what you are working from. When discussing the golf ball, make sure you also give the rough size you are working from.

The next step has two options. The first is to take a mathematical approach, based around volume. The other is to consider all the places you could put a golf ball on a plane (overhead storage, under seats, in cockpit etc.). Depending on your maths confidence, the choice would be yours. Don't worry if the maths you do isn't exactly right, just make sure you talk through each step out loud and ensure that the number you come out with at the end seems believable. If working through the different places a ball could go, try to attribute a number to each one (e.g., 300 golf balls in each overhead storage area, 300 passengers so 100 areas, 30000 total golf balls in overhead storage), and make sure you write it down! It's far too easy to get caught up in the line of sums, without being able to add them together to an answer at the end!

Once you reach a point of concluding, ensure that your answer appears believable and answer the question! Don't let yourself tail off at the end of your last consideration and not actual provide a number. It doesn't matter (within reason) what that number is, as long as the methods you used to get to it made sense.

Q33: How would you work out the number of flights passing over London at this moment?

This question is testing just one thing, that being the degree to which you can work through a large series of thoughts, considering all possible options. While it is vital that you give a numerical answer, the value of that answer (within reason) doesn't really matter, what matters is how you got to the answer. When beginning this question, it might be helpful for you to outline some parameters. If you know how many airports London has (6), then you can start from there. There will definitely be more than 6 planes over London as they will be coming and going from each airport. So, from your starting point you can work out a realistic maximum.

If you know anything about airport scheduling then absolutely discuss it, any colourful insights into your life will be memorable for an interviewer. However, most people won't have that kind of insight so will be starting from scratch. It would be safe to assume that there is a gap of at least two minutes between planes landing, in order that they can taxi off of the runway. At the speed planes travel, they could probably traverse London in 15 minutes or so. Considering of the 6 airports, there are maybe 10 runways, assuming planes are always nose to tail coming in and out, you could sum 7 planes per 'queue' times the 10 runways, making a total of 70 planes.

It doesn't matter if this is entirely wrong, it may be hugely more than this or hugely fewer. The important thing is the steps taken to get to that value. If you want to extend your discussion, you can go on to review the number you have reached. If you look up at the sky at any given time, you can only see a couple of planes at most, and your view extends quite a few miles in every direction. As such, you might choose to assess that 70 seems like too many, and perhaps halve your answer. If you add in the explanation that maybe there is a 4-minute gap between landings, rather than the originally assumed 2, the numbers would add up. Being comprehensive and explanatory in your thought processes is vital and will be most well received by an interviewer.

Q34: How many deliveries are made in the UK every day?

As with any numerical question, the value is your method, not the answer. However, you must give an answer to 'complete' the process. To reach any kind of answer to the scale that this will be will take some considerable calculations. If you have any prior insight (such as knowing how many they delivered last year, or how many your local post office receives), then outline and apply it aloud. Each bit of information you can bring to inform your calculation will not only likely make it more accurate, but also impress the interviewer that you have such niche knowledge and have thought to apply it.

When starting your calculations, it can be helpful to set parameters. You can assume that not every person in the UK receives something every day, so the number is likely going to be less than the total UK population (if you know it accurately, great, if not it can be generally helpful to know it's around 70 million people). Your next point of consideration is that commercial mail exists as well. While much of mail is sent via email now, businesses still account for a lot of the mail sent each day. As such, you may choose to reconsider your original 70-million limit, to account for commercial mail.

None of the assumptions and considerations you make matter in their accuracy to reality, only in their abundance and degree of thought. Within reason, in a question like this, the more times you reconsider a particular point, the greater depth of understanding it demonstrates to the interviewer. When you have made all the considerations you think are reasonable (it can be helpful to write them down to keep track), make sure you conclude with an actual value. Once you have a value, it can often be insightful to reflect upon that relative to a reasonable assumption you might pick out of the air. If this calculated value and the 'random' value are distinctly different, perhaps spend a moment discussing why that might be, relative to the calculations and considerations you have just undertaken.

Q35: Have you been to this college before?

This question is unusual, in that it is not testing anything in particular. It is far more of an exploratory question which seeks to bring out your experience of university and the college, as well as your expectations for it going forward. When answering any question based on your experiences, it is important to be honest. You can embellish the truth in part if you wish, but always ensure that the core of what you're saying is true. The interviewer will probably expect you to have visited Oxford at least once before the interview (unless you are an international student), but it is not a problem if you have not.

If you have not ever visited the college before, the interviewer will want to know what attracted you to it, and that will likely be the next question. As a result, your considerations should immediately be looking towards why you were interested in the college, as soon as this initial question is asked. The best way to approach that, is to describe in what context you have seen the college (e.g., through the university website) and what it was that you liked about what you saw/read.

If you have visited the college before, the first thing to outline is under what context. If it was a family trip to Oxford and you looked around as a tourist, it is fine to focus on the 'tourist things' that you liked about the college e.g., the architecture. If you visited quite recently (during the time you might be expected to have been thinking about university) or as a school trip, where the focus was a little more on the academic side, then make sure you address some of the 'non-tourist- aspects too. It is fine to talk about the grounds and the architecture, but having done some reading around the library, subject foci and alumni/faculty members will go a long way.

This is one of the few questions where it wouldn't really be fitting to conclude by answering the question. Answering the question should be the very first thing you do, everything that follows is simply an extension of that. One key thing to make sure is that you don't end up talking too far into the subject. It may be that the interviewer was simply asking this as a yes/no question, precursory to a more in-depth question. With that in mind, try to read the interviewer's body language to see if they were expecting you to take the reins on the discussion!

Q36: Do you think that Oxford/Cambridge will suit you?

This question is testing two main things. The first is your understanding of (and, by extension, your reading up on) the university, and your self-awareness. You want to ensure that the overriding message of this answer is 'yes', as that is the whole reason you are applying. However, don't be afraid to touch on some elements that may not be 100% positive. For example, if you feel like you don't have much in common with the stereotypical student of the university, you can say that! However, what is important is to express your realisation that the stereotype isn't the reality.

If you want to go down this route of discussion, the safest is way to is to describe your experiences once you have arrived. By the time you have gone into your first interview, you will have had quite extensive contact with some other prospective students. More than likely, you will have found some people with things in common with yourself, take that on board I your discussion. The more recent the experience and the more truth behind it, the better! If this process of meeting your fellow interviewees has squashed some doubt about whether you would fit in, that's a fantastic result and you should definitely share it!

The next part is to make sure that you have read up on the university, and to make that clear! If the university is very research heavy, match that up to your own academic interests! The same goes for if they have a particular department that is of interest to you. Don't be afraid to add a little more personality to the discussion, perhaps the location is convenient for you in some way, but make sure your answer hinges on the more impactful content.

"After my undergraduate degree, I would really enjoy pursuing a PhD in psychology. I'm not sure exactly what I would want to specialise in yet, but the opportunity to be surrounded by practicing academics to discuss that with is invaluable. In addition, I'll be able to stay on my undergraduate campus for my postgraduate studies, and have access to some incredible research facilities and equipment. In addition, the university is only 45 minutes' drive from my home town, so I'll be able to visit there easily for birthdays and other special occasions!"

Remember, this question is about why the university is the right fit for you. You could easily be asked why you are the right fit for the university, and you would have to phrase your answer slightly differently. To explain why the university is the right fit for you, you should be assessing why the features of the university fit into your life and personality. If you're answering why you're the right fit for the university, then that answer is the other way round!

Q37: What do you think you'll be doing in a decade? How about in two decades?

No interviewer will expect you to have an actual plan for the next 10 or 20 years of your life. Instead, what they're looking for is an understanding of how you gaining your degree might set out a path for you in life. This is far more about understanding your options than it is deciding which one you are going to pursue. It is important to distinguish the sections of your answer between the 10 and 20-year mark. Remember if you wanted to do a PhD, you wouldn't likely finish that until around 8 years from the point that you're in this interview. As such, if that was your plan, you wouldn't be far into post-doctoral research/your first 'proper' job in the first 10 years. It is important to articulate details like this, even if you haven't definitely decided you want to do a PhD. Any understanding of your options in this way demonstrates to the interviewer that you have considered these things.

If you are more concerned with the industry you want to go into than any postgraduate studies, then discuss how you might want to pursue success there. At the 10-year point, if you have spent 6 years of that in an industry, what would you like to have achieved. You have the classic milestones such as being a team leader, running your own project, owning your own home, or any other 'standard' aspirations. However, you should try and add in some things which are unique to you and your preferred industry. If you wanted to go into marketing, something that is quite common for psychology graduates, then it would be great to aspire to have one of your projects on national television, or up in the store of a 'household name' business.

It is, however, important to remember that the interviewer is likely to be an academic, and is likely to (be it potentially implicitly/subconsciously) want you to aspire to do the same thing. As a result, you should consider how you 'tune' your answer to appease those who are listening to it. I would never expect a tutor to reject an applicant on the basis that they didn't want to pursue studies beyond undergraduate, however, it is easier to engage with someone on a topic they are interested in. The more engaged you are with the interviewer, the more likely they will remember and the better a conversation they will have with their peers after you are gone. This isn't a hard and fast rule, but it is human nature to frame memorable things in a positive light (unless of course it was objectively bad!). in sum, you want to approach this question with honesty, but make sure that you consider your audience!

Q38: What is your favourite activity outside of school?

This is a question which 'assesses' your personality outside of academia. It's great if you have genuine hobbies which are subject-related, but most people don't and no interviewer will expect you to. What they are looking for is ways in which you unwind, what environments you choose to put yourself in (rather than those which are thrust upon you!), and how competitive you are. If every hobby of yours involves playing a competitive, spectator sport to a high level, then the interviewer can deduce that you are outgoing, competitive and have an interest in exhibiting your skills. This is very different (although by no means better/worse) than someone who's hobbies are all quiet activities to pass the time that you engage with alone.

As you discuss your interests, remember that the interviewer will likely be comparing their stereotypical view of someone who has these interests, alongside their experience of you in this setting. If you are describing yourself as confident and outgoing through the activities you like to do, but are aware that you have been shy in this setting, it could be a good thing to highlight that! Having a high level of self-awareness is a great sign of emotional intelligence and will only be another point in your favour!

When talking about your interests, it is always beneficial to highlight any achievements you might have made in them. This doesn't mean you should tune the entire conversation into a list of your achievements (as that wasn't the question!), but it can be useful to highlight where you have committed yourself and gained success. In addition, spend some time on the less usual hobbies. This is the perfect opportunity to inject some real personality into the interview and, you never know, the interviewer might even share an unusual hobby of yours which you can engage on!

Lastly, it can be a good idea to describe how you are going to continue pursuing those hobbies through university. The interviewers don't want someone who is going to drop everything and become a sheep when they arrive on campus, they want someone who is going to bring something new to the table! As a result, whether it's simply a hobby you'll keep up in your own time, or a club that you'd want to set up in your college, make sure you outline how you'll go about keeping these things up! Make sure these are realistic and measured against the amount of commitment you will need to bring to your academic studies, but by all means dream big!

Q39: How will your fellow college residents see you?

There are a few ways in which you can contribute to college life as a student. One, which could be easily overlooked when considering college life specifically, is simply being a friendly and approachable person. When talking in the context of college life, it's easy to forget the things that make you a contributor to a pleasant society in general. When it comes to college-specific things, it's good to open with some more general points, with some demonstration that you have read up on college-specific things as well.

What this means is first considering what makes a good contributor in any small community. You could contribute by applying your skills in a particular sport (or otherwise) to the college team, you could apply your academic ability and commitment to success to enhance the college's academic rankings. You could even include something like experience in party-planning or finances to contribute to the college ball (should there be one). The next step is to introduce some college-specific things, to demonstrate that you've done some reading around the college, and to highlight your specific suitability.

An easy (although predictable) one would be if the college has any particularly successfully (or perhaps even unsuccessful, although that would be more difficult to find out!) sports teams. You could highlight this if you have an interest/skill in any one of those, and highlight that you would be keen to join in. Some of the less predictable things would be societies outside of sport, or whether your college has a chapel and you'd like to be involved in that. There is a wealth of different things which a college could be interested in having someone contribute to, it's just a case of matching one up from your research to something you're interested in. The important thing to remember is that it doesn't have to be something you have dine already, it could be trying something totally new!

Lastly, you want to make sure you can contribute to the college after you leave. Something that many people wouldn't consider is going on to be a respectable and successful person in your industry, adding to the college's notable alumni. As with any question that requires you to speak well of the college/university, it is a fine balance between selling yourself as an admirer of the college, and seeming over the top or fake. Strike the balance well by practicing talking around these kinds of subjects, you'll soon develop a way that works for you.

Q40: Why do you think we structure the course in the way that we do?

This question doesn't try to hide what it's assessing at all. One of the big indicators of someone who is committed to the application process (and, by extension, the university) is how much preparation they have done for the interviews. The first thing you should have looked at when deciding which course to choose, is what the actual course content in. There are two sides to a course decision, the first is how it will help you get to the next stage if your education/career (if you have planned that far ahead!), and the other is whether it will interest you while you study. The latter can only be answered by exploring and reading around the course content.

When talking about the course structure, it is best to keep the objective details to a reasonable level. You don't want to sound like you're simply reciting a list of modules, nor do you want to risk getting muddled and saying something that is objectively wrong. You are much better off making a point which you have come to the opinion of through your reading, and then evidencing it in the discussion thereafter.

"I can see from reading up on the course that it focusses a lot on social psychology in the first two years. This was one of the things that attracted me to it, as I think undertaking a social science independent study in third year would be really interesting. The focus on social psychology seems to come from the disproportionately high number of modules which approach topics in the field, when compared to subjects like perception."

Above is a bit of a clunky answer, but one that demonstrates you've read around the course content and are very happy with what you have read (which is arguably the most important bit!). You could construct an answer in a more coherent manner, by opening with the number of modules on one particular subject, highlighting that it appears to be a particular focus of the course, and then finishing with why that is a good thing for you. However, when opening with the number of modules on a course, it sets up the answer to feel too over-prepared. Your preference between them is, of course, your own and either will make a good structure to answer a question like this.

As aforementioned, the most important bit is to highlight why the course content works for you. Make sure to not have that as the conclusion of your answer, because that isn't the question, but always make sure it is included.

Q41: What would you say was your single greatest weakness?

Answering this question well is very difficult. There are two ways in which you could go wrong. Neither of these ways would necessarily be terrible, but they are best avoided if possible. The first way is to give an answer that is simply a positive attributed in disguise. An example of this would be 'admitting' that you can sometimes be too much of a perfectionist or be too detail oriented. These are things which would certainly be bad traits under certain circumstances, but the combination of the fact that in a lot of cases they are good and that they have been presented as 'sometimes' being an issue, makes them far too weak as answers.

The other way in which you could answer this question in a non-ideal way is to overshare on your weaknesses. The interviewer doesn't want to hear that as soon as there's a test around the corner you have a complete meltdown and only just drag yourself through. If your weakness has something to do with an event you'll face at university, you're best-off underselling it slightly (only if it's really bad of course!). if this is the case, it would also be beneficial to explain what you're doing, and will continue to do, to work on that weakness. Self-awareness of a real weakness is a great sign of the potential for personal growth, but the growth only comes if you actually act to solve the problem!

In an ideal scenario, you will have a genuine weakness that you are working on fixing, that doesn't really have anything to do with university. That way, you can have an honest conversation with the interviewer, without it having any chance of jeopardising their view of you as a competent student. However, this isn't normally possible and you will likely have to talk around a weakness that could affect you as a student.

As a result, you want to focus on what you are doing to rectify this weakness, and the timeline over which you are acting. The latter is very important, no interviewer will expect you to start university as a perfectly formed student, but they would be very keen to see some kind of commitment from you to have worked on that weakness prior to starting your course. It might be that you know you're a slow typist, so you're going to take a touch-typing course over summer. Or it could be that your handwriting is bad quality, so you're going to spend your last few months at school comparing your handwriting every week and looking to see an improvement over time.

There's any number of things you could list as a weakness, just remember that it needs to be honest (and an actual weakness!) but something that is fixable (or at least manageable) in a sensible time-frame.

Q42: You have mentioned a number of personal strengths in your statement, which is your greatest?

Answering this question involves just as much care as answering what your biggest weakness is. It is far too easy to list a generic skill like 'essay-writing' and explaining how it will benefit you in your degree because that is something you will spend a lot of your time doing. The key to answering this question well is finding a balance between bragging and being too modest. If you undersell your strengths, it demonstrates a lack of confidence and perhaps an indication that you might not be as good as you appeared on paper. Oversell your strengths, and it suggests a lack of self-awareness and an arrogance towards your own ability.

To balance this answer properly, you want to find a couple of strengths to 'warm-up' with, that are related to your main strength. Alternatively, you can find one main strength that is backed up with 'auxiliary' strengths. Here is an example of the former, followed by the latter.

"Leading up to my GCSE's, I spent a lot of time doing creative writing in my spare time. I was able to apply those skills and experiences to my English work, as well as my longer answer questions in other subjects. Through all that, I've built up a keen interest and strong ability to write engaging texts on a wide range of topics, making me a good essay-writer. I would say this is my biggest strength in academia."

"My biggest strength in academia is essay-writing. I enjoyed writing through school and wrote lots of stories as a child. By the time I got to my GCSE's my experience and developed proficiency enabled me to excel in English, and at the longer-answer questions in other subjects. I have continued this success into my A-Levels, securing a really good grade in English."

Both of those answers highlight the same strength, but present it in a different way. The latter is for those who are more comfortable 'selling' themselves, the former for those who struggle more with that. One important thig to note is that moth answers highlighted this as being a strength in academia. If you are going to pick that, it is totally fine, but I would open with a statement that highlights it. The interviewers know that you are more than what you can do at school, so will often be looking for non-academic strengths to answer a question like this. If you highlight in the beginning that it is specifically an academic strength, then it prompts them to ask if you have considered a non-academic one too. If you have, feel free to explain that you opened with the one you did because it is your biggest strength, and then explain your other one.

If you want to go ahead and discuss a non-academic strength, of course feel free to do so! It is often easier to add personality in this way, but is sometimes harder to evidence how you have been strong. However, if you use a similar structure, you should be able to present it as a convincing strength.

Q43: How will your experiences from the Duke of Edinburgh scheme benefit you during your time at university?

This is a question that many interviewers will be keen to ask, if you have something like a Duke of Edinburgh mention on your CV/in your personal statement. It may sound a little like they are trying to belittle the achievement by asking it in a sarcastic way, or to try and trip you up. Rest assured that is not the case, they are simply interested to see how you view the skills you have acquired through the program, and how you would apply them to the entirely different environment of studying for a degree.

The key to answering this question well, while it seems obvious, is picking out genuinely applicable skills and experiences. This means valuing relevance over and above the extent of your experience/skill. If you try to shoehorn a skill to fit your university studies, just because it was a large focus of your scheme, your answer will come across ill-fitting. It is important to be prepared for a question like this because it is quite likely to come up, if it is something you have discussed in your personal statement or have on your CV, and it is something quite difficult to come up with off the cuff.

To establish will skill to select, it is best to consider what you have actually done compared to what you will be doing in your degree. If you spent time orienteering and doing crafts, that's not something that fits the bill, however big a part of the scheme it was or how much you enjoyed it. However, if you spent one of the nights up on your own, devising a plan of action and getting everything ready for the following morning, that is something that can be very easily applied to your degree.

"On the last night before our long walk, our team remained very disorganised and we still hadn't got a route fully together, or decided exactly what we needed to pack. I decided, rather than have a frantic rush in the morning, to work into the evening and night to prepare the map route and set up a packing list for each of our team. I had to do this on my own as the rest of my team were getting early nights, so had to rely on my own intuition and conviction behind my decisions. Even though I was tired the next day, I was happy that we were able to set off with a clear route and could have all of our things packed without having to think about whether anything important was missing. I think having to work late, on my own and being able to make those independent decisions has prepared me for the independent projects I will have to take on in my degree."

You could easily have continued the explanation further, regarding the applicability of skills and experience to situations in degree studies, but this demonstrates how you can apply the experience of one isolated event, better than you could trying to apply an irrelevant experience. Remember that the relevance is so much more important than the abundance. It is much easier to oversell how big a deal the event was, than oversell how applicable it is to your degree!

Q44: Why choose Oxford or Cambridge, if you know that other universities are less competitive, and may mark your work much more generously?

There are two ways to approach this question. You can answer successfully discussing one or both. The first point you could make is that you may not actually do better elsewhere. You will likely have spoken in that interview, previous interviews or your personal statement, about how the environment of your chosen university will give you the drive to push forward and excel. At a university where perhaps that drive is not present to the same degree, you may not be pushed in the same way. This is a tricky answer to phrase, as you don't want to come across like you are unable to self-motivate, but if you feel like it applies to you then convincingly portraying that self-awareness will be received well. However, if you don't feel confident discussing that, or it doesn't apply to you, then there is the bulk of the answer to approach.

When answering the main part of this question, you need to consider the value of the university beyond the grade on your degree. If you are confident in yourself that you can achieve a first class result regardless, then that's great. It wouldn't necessarily be the best structure to lead with that, as it would be easy for that to appear arrogant. However, it is a good way to round off your answer, if you are confident talking about that. Approaching the value of the university is all about understanding what it will bring you along the way. If you want to be an academic at that university, then the grade relative to any other university is not really relevant. If you want to learn about your field in the most all-encompassing way possible, then the grade you get is not really relevant to that part of the experience.

However, it is important to acknowledge that as something you have considered. Expressing that awareness will be well-received by an interviewer. The key is to balance it against the personal points you are making. You may wish to make those points after acknowledging your concern around the topic, or you may wish to save it until the end, rounding it off as something that has been weighed up and dismissed based on your conclusion. Most importantly, you should demonstrate that you have the self-confidence to know you can do well in any environment, and not feel the need to establish a different one.

Q45: Cambridge is very intense; do you think your current approach to time management will be sufficient?

There are lots of ways in which you can say you will manage your time. However, the interviewer is going to have heard them all before. The way to make your answer convincing and stand out, is to give evidence of where you have learned these techniques and where you have successfully applied them. It would be a good idea to pick a few techniques for organisation, stress management and timekeeping (although there will. Be some overlap with organisation), and prepare some examples for when these techniques have worked for you in the past. While it would likely make your answer too convoluted if you tried to do this for every technique, it can inject some personality into the answer if you talk about where you learned one of the techniques, particularly if the story is interesting!

"One challenge I am sure that I will face is having to prioritise work. In this sort of situation, it's important to manage explicit deadlines, as well as the importance of each piece of work. During sixth form, I have been a private tutor. Having to manage marking my students' work and completing my own has been very challenging at times. I have mostly chosen to prioritise my students' work, as I have already had discussions with my teachers and they are happy to be lenient with my deadlines, providing they are not exams or coursework!"

By giving a real and honest example of a difficult situation, you'll connect with the tutors a lot better than if you try to make something up on the spot. Once you have explained the situation and experience, as above, it is then important to explicitly apply this to your degree experience.

"From this experience, I am confident talking to tutors and asking them for help with my schedule. In order to stop myself getting too stuck, I would make sure I reach out to a tutor when in need, and ask them to extend my deadline. I would make sure that I am prioritising the work that leads on to future work, so that I don't fall behind on a series of pieces."

By demonstrating your understanding of how you might prioritise something, this gives the interviewer further evidence to suggest what you are saying is something you actually have had to do. In addition, you are showing the confidence to stand up for your decisions, even if that means asking for help.

Q46: What have you read in the last 24 hours?

As with any question that asks you directly about an event, honesty is the best policy. However, it is completely realistic to assume that you may not have read anything on the morning of your interview, or the night before apart from your interview preparation notes. With that in mind, consider this question to be asking more 'what have you read very recently', rather than specifically this morning. That is, unless you have the confidence to be fully honest when, by all means, be exactly that! If you are going to be entirely honest, just ensure that you're not wandering down the road of oversharing. Remember, while the interviewers are friendly and they want to have a pleasant conversation, they are still assessing you! Saying something like "I've actually not read anything in the last 24 hours, I've been a little busy, but just the other day I read some of *The Count of Monte Cristo* in my spare time" is a good way to remain honest while still giving the interviewer something to play off, and giving you something you can explore in depth.

You should make sure you discuss a text you have read recently, and ensure that your discussion is realistic. The interviewer is not going to believe that you have spent your entire morning reading the full works of a particular psychologist, or a novel from cover to cover! The best approach to picking a text is to have read something very recently in preparation for your interviews, and discuss that! If the text is relevant to your interviews, then there's no real reason to spend a lot of time highlighting its relevance. However, if the text is a little more unusual, then by all means explain its relevance to the interviews.

If you choose to discuss a text that has nothing to do with interviews, that's fine too! The interviewer will appreciate the fact that you're reading for pleasure, not just for work! However, the text you discuss should either have an element of psychology, or an element of personality to it, for maximum impact in the interview discussion. The more you can recall about what you read, the better. That's not to say you should go about reciting it verbatim, but it enables you to discuss its content with confidence. If you open with a single point about the text after a brief description of its context, the interviewer may ask you to expand or continue, in which case that gives you the starting point from which to begin your full discussion. If they don't respond in any way to your initial point, try to make you second point psychology related. It may be that they are simply interested to know what you have read recently; in which case they may not pry beyond your initial description. Don't worry either way, all interviewers are different in the way they will want to explore what you have read and how you interpret it.

Q47: What would you say was your greatest personal challenge in life? How did you handle it?

This question is supremely personal, and you should make your answer as such. In an ideal world, you will have had a challenge which comes to mind immediately and you will have no need to prepare any thought on it at all. However, in most people's lives, there are a large number of small challenges, rather than one outstanding one. In this case, the thought you should put into this question is regarding how you overcame one of those challenges. The interviewer is looking to understand a bit more about your background, and build knowledge on how you deal with difficult situations. If you have a challenge that was not quite as big as your biggest ever challenge, but you handled getting over it in a much better way, then that might be your better bet to pick!

As with any of these personal questions, depending on your confidence, you may choose to be 100% honest. It may be that the biggest challenge you have faced was one that you did not overcome well, one that may have beaten you. That is completely fine, as long as you talk about what you learned from that experience. It is no good discussing a difficult situation that wasn't handled well, and then simply going on with your life as if nothing happened! The interviewer will be looking for honesty, self-awareness, self-reflection and the ability to better yourself after a setback. It will be very common for you to come across aa seemingly impassable challenge in your degree, so the interviewer wants to know what experience you have dealing with that kind of situation.

If there is an element of independence to your overcoming of the challenge, highlight that it might be that due to not having the support you might have had in other situations, you didn't handle the challenge as effectively as you might have otherwise. That's fine, but highlight what you learned from the experience and how you would go about approaching it differently next time! It is vital that there is at least an element of self-reflection in your answer. It might be that the challenge happened very recently, and you haven't had enough tie to process it and become better at tackling situations like it. It might be that your biggest challenge was preparing for this interview! If this is the case, then make sure you reflect on that. Don't be afraid to put yourself on the spot to evoke some more honesty out of your answer.

There are three stages to a good answer in this question; situation, specific challenge (and why it was challenging) and what you did/would do next time to overcome it.

Q48: Do you think that the impact of a good teacher can stretch beyond the walls of a school? Who do you think was your best teacher?

Of course, it doesn't matter who your best teacher was, it certainly doesn't need to be the one who is teaching you the subject you're applying for! What matters is how you have assessed them to be your best teacher, and the extent to which you understand how they have influenced you. A poor answer is one that doesn't address any of these elements in any detail, as follows.

"My favourite teacher was my year 9 maths teacher. She inspired me to do better in maths and got me from really struggling at the beginning of the year, to being almost top of the class by the end, and really enjoying it!"

A better answer, is one that considers each element of the question in some detail, with a degree of reflection into why you have the thoughts that you do. Below is an answer that does this.

"My favourite teacher was my year 9 maths teacher. She inspired me to do better at maths by simply letting me get on with it, my teachers in years before had always tried so hard to engage me in the lesson when working on the board, and as a shy student I just shrank away and disengaged from the lesson. As soon as I was left to my own devices, I realised I could do it when I wasn't put on the spot! Since then, my confidence grew a lot and by the end of the year I was asking to go through things on the board! I'm not sure how she knew to treat me differently than my previous teachers, but she definitely had more patience. Maybe she saw that my homework was always right but my classwork wasn't and put the pieces together to work it out!"

This answer demonstrates a real insight into why a teacher treated you how they did, and what the result of it was. It also implies that you are a good independent learner (which is always a bonus to slip into an answer!). When you are discussing why a teacher has treated you a certain way, it is important not to consider any of your own assumptions to be fact. Remember, the interviewer is likely also an educator, and they may see that your assumptions which you have made out to be fact, are likely wrong. It is, however, important that you outline what your views on how they treated you are, as even just the fact you are considering the reasons behind teachers' actions is a great way to better understand yourself and how you work best.

Q49: What are your long-term plans in life?

This question is incredibly open, and doesn't need to be answered like a 'where do you see yourself in x years' question. You can answer this question entirely unrelatedly to academia and work if you like. If your goal in life is to own your own home and have a family, say that! The important thing is to ground it around how this degree will help you get there. It could be something as simple as the degree with unlock doors in the job market that you wouldn't normally have been able to enter, or it could be that the degree will teach you how to work hard and independently, which will help you achieve things in later life. Whatever angle you approach it from, it is a great idea to include a piece about your degree studies.

However, you want to be honest with these plans as a question as open as this is a perfect opportunity for you to discuss something memorable to the interviewer. Maybe you have always wanted to be a clown, so working a job which pays well will enable you to go to clown school at the weekends and learn! It doesn't really matter what it is, as long as it's honest. If you start talking about something because you think it will be memorable, rather than because it is the truth, the interviewer will likely see right through you, so don't!

It is totally fine to have 'boring' aspirations, everyone's life is their own! If your aspirations in life are somewhat mundane, make that part of the explanation!

"I know it seems pretty mundane, but what I'd really like is to have a house, family and a stable job by the time I am thirty. This degree will teach me the skills I need to do well in the working world, unlock access to a job that I will enjoy, and enable me to earn the money I need to own my own home."

It isn't the most personality-injected answer, but if the above answer is honest then it is totally fine to go down that route! Obviously, if you have an honest ambition that is a little more whacky then discuss it, but don't feel like you have to make something up to be memorable! Honesty is the best policy, but try to make a link between whatever you're discussing and your degree studies. It doesn't have to be forced if it really doesn't work, but ideally you want your long-term plans to be tied into your degree, to some extent!

Q50: If you had to name your three greatest strengths, what would you pick?

This is a very open question. Because of this, it would be best to make at least one of these skills something to do with your degree and another something very personal to you. Beyond that, the floor is yours! When answering, for each skill you should explain what that skills is, where it originated, and how is has/will be useful to you. When talking about how it will be useful, that's where the degree studies bit comes in! Below is an example of how to outline one of these three skills.

"One of my top skills is my ability to type very fast and very accurately. I started typing pretty young because my mum worked from home and I used to use her keyboard to type fake emails while she was on her lunchbreak. I had to touch-type to a degree because I wasn't tall enough to see over her desk! When I started school, I used to get into accidents a lot so spent a few terms in various casts. Whenever that happened, I had to do all of my schoolwork on a laptop. Since starting sixth form, I've done all of my work on my laptop and have really honed my typing skills. These will definitely come in handy when writing essays, as I can much more easily and accurately write down citations!"

This answer brings some personality as it describes the origin of the skills, from an amusing childhood story to current working conditions in sixth form. If you are lucky to have a skill with such an extensive back story, then absolutely discuss it, even if perhaps you wouldn't consider it one of your top three skills! The clearest way to explore these three skills is to tell them as three individual stories, if you outline the skills first and go into the stories after, it will be too easy to get muddled and lose track of where you are. It would be great if you had skills which spread across a variety of disciplines. For example, in addition to the skill explained above, you could have one which relates to your social skills (e.g., recognising when someone is upset, even if they're trying to hide it) and one which relates to your physical ability (e.g., your proficiency at a certain sport). Of course, it would be all too convenient if that were the case, so don't try to bend the truth too much to get it to fit this model. It is better to be honest in a question like this, providing your answers have some degree of interest and relation to your subject!

Q51: How much should you charge to wash all the windows in London?

This question is not looking for an exact answer; instead the interviewer is inviting you to take them through your thought process as you make an estimate. Ultimately the tutorial experience is all about reasoning through often ambiguous or tricky problems, and this is an opportunity to demonstrate that you can do this.

A standard applicant might estimate the total surface area of windows in London, the average surface of windows washed per hour, and the hourly labour costs of window washing and use these to provide an answer. What will set a **good candidate** apart from a standard one is the quality of reasoning behind the numbers they come to. In this specific question, you would want to recognise that residential and commercial buildings, flats, and houses all have different numbers and sizes of windows. You may also want to consider other factors, such as London being a distinctly urban area, and windows potentially needing to be washed on both sides. Remember, these are just some possible considerations; there are all sorts of factors you could bring into the discussion.

For example, let us assume that there are 8 million people in London, and the average household is 2.5 people. This would mean that there are about 3.2 million households in London. You might then assume that the average number of windows across all residential and commercial buildings works out at 7.5 windows per household, and that the average surface area is 80cm by 50cm. To account for washing windows on both sides, you would multiply by 2 to give you the total surface area. Multiplying various decimals live might seem a bit daunting; feel free to round numbers where appropriate (and explain to the examiners why you are doing this). So in this example, you would calculate 3 million x 8 x 0.8 x 0.5 x 2 which would be about 19.2 million square meters of window.

From there you could discuss per hour labour costs, and the estimated surface area of windows you could wash per hour. Again, nuance is the key to making your answer stand out. Factors you might want to consider include (but are not limited to): skill required in window washing, cost of materials, cost of living in London, competition within the London window washing market, or whether the labour market is seasonal. Introducing these considerations offers you the opportunity to show not only that you are logical and rigorous, but also creative. To conclude this example, let us say you assume a wage of 10 pounds per hour, and 50 square meters of window per hour. This would give you a total cost of 3.84 million pounds.

A **weak answer** may have a very similar structure to a strong answer but lack the justification for numbers chosen. Other pitfalls to avoid include making simple calculation errors, and failing to use common sense when estimating numbers. For example by assuming that a population of 8 million people in London means that there are 8 million households. Avoid the temptation to be funny (e.g. answering "I have better things to do than wash windows"); this will not go down well.

Q52: How many piano tuners are there in Europe?

Although questions like this might seem initially daunting, the goal here is not to accurately estimate the number of piano tuners in Europe but rather to demonstrate clear, well explained reasoning.

In other words, a **good applicant** will offer sensible numbers backed up by a brief explanation as to how they chose these figures. For example, you could estimate that there are 750 million people in Europe, about 2.5 people per household, and therefore a total of 300 million households. Then by assuming that something like 1 in 50 households have a piano, you would estimate the number of pianos in Europe as around 6 million. Factors to consider when selecting these numbers could include how popular an instrument the piano is, or the cost of a piano. From there you could ascertain the number of piano tuners by dividing the average number of times people need their pianos tuned in a year by the number of pianos a piano tuner is able to tune in a year. When creating these numbers you could consider factors such as how long it takes to tune a piano, or how many days a year a piano tuner works (these are just a few examples, feel free to introduce your own ideas). For example, you could estimate that it takes a piano tuner 2 hours to tune a piano and they work about 8 hours a day, five days a week, for 50 weeks a year. This would amount to 1000 pianos per tuner per year. So, to carry out 5 million piano tunings you would need about 5000 piano tuners in Europe. Great answers could also introduce interesting considerations such as the potential impact of the increasing popularity of electric keyboards, and whether technological changes have led to an oversupply of trained piano tuners. Answers that contain deeper exploration like this help a candidate by showing nuanced, creative and forward-looking thinking.

A **poor applicant** will be thrown by the ambiguity of this kind of question and may just guess a number, or fail to use common sense or basic general knowledge; e.g. not offering even a rough idea of the population of Europe, or merely asserting the number of pianos tuned per year rather than estimating it logically. More generally, students should avoid the temptation to waffle when uncertain. What differentiates a weak from a strong answer, at least in part, is that the strong candidate will adopt a systematic and deductive approach to answering the question.

Q53: India introduces a new population control policy to address the gender imbalance. If a couple has a girl, they may have another child. If they have a boy, they can't have any more children. What would be the new ratio of boys to girls?

Obviously, the nature of this answer may vary substantially between applicants – a political scientist and a mathematician are likely to give very different answers. However, the essential thing is to be able to clarify and justify the assumptions that you are making when you answer this question.

For example, a **good quantitative candidate** might decide to discount any parental preference for one gender or the other, and assume that there is perfect compliance with the policy. From there, the candidate would note that every birth has a 50% independent probability of resulting in a girl and a 50% independent probability of resulting in a boy. This would mean that half of all families stop at one child, and the rest go on to have another child which also has a 50% chance of being a girl. Putting aside practical considerations, this process could repeat infinitely - although the probability of an unbroken chain of girls converges towards zero. The big thing to note here is that with each pregnancy the probability resets to 50/50. However, even when offering a quantitative answer the candidate should still acknowledge practical limitations (e.g. having infinite children is not possible).

By contrast, a **good humanities candidate** may choose to focus on questions of citizen preferences, and the state's ability to enforce policies. You could draw on your real-world knowledge to consider instances where similar policies have been implemented. For example, sex selective abortion is illegal in China and the number of children per household is restricted, yet there is still a gender imbalance. A weaker answer might use this evidence to simply conclude that the policy in India would be ineffective; a stronger answer would acknowledge that the policy would have some impact, but could use the example of China to argue that this may not be enough to make the gender balance 50/50.

More broadly, a **weaker answer** is likely to contain some of these elements but fail to identify key assumptions, or make implausible assumptions (e.g. parents having infinite numbers of children). Candidates who choose to use examples should also be wary of relying on anecdote rather than reasoning. For example, a weaker answer may use the example of China to discuss the effects of birth control policies on sex ratios, but simply argue that because sex ratios remain imbalanced in China they will do the same in India; it would be more useful to explore the similarities and differences between the two countries and their policy environment, rather than making a blanket correlation.

Q54: Why are manhole covers round?

As with many of the more unusual questions you may be asked, the key here is not to find the answer, but rather to demonstrate the ability to engage with ambiguous questions and reason logically. The key advice for questions such as this is to always try to tackle the question head on, engage with the hypothetical, and ask yourself why this specific question is being asked. This should hopefully help you to avoid the sort of woolly and non-committal answers that questions such as this often provoke.

A **strong candidate** would focus on the core of this question: what is distinctive about the circular shape (as opposed to, say, a square)? A good candidate will also avoid the trap of getting hung-up on the empirical question of whether all manhole covers are round – there is no need to go beyond an acknowledgement of this doubt. Focusing instead on the unique features of circles would allow the candidate time to offer a range of explanations as to why manhole might be round. Possible explanations could be that you do not need to worry about the orientation of a circle when replacing it back on to the hole, circles can be rolled which is useful since a manhole cover is usually heavy and made out of metal, or that round manhole covers are less likely to fall down the manhole. A great candidate will be able to specifically link this answer back to the purpose of a manhole. For example, the cover being easy to roll is likely to be important if you only have one person working on the manhole, or when a manhole is deep and so preventing things (people, or the cover) falling down the hole is very important.

A **weak answer** could take several forms. Candidates who attempt to debate whether manholes are all round, are unlikely to meet with much success. Although under certain circumstances disagreeing with the premise of a question can be a fruitful tactic, this rarely tends to be the case when the premise is a factual claim. Other weak approaches include offering a vague answer such as `tradition` or `culture`. Answers such as this one fail to engage with the core of the question; a good warning sign is that your answer could apply to a broad range of other questions. If this is the case, your answer is probably lacking in specificity.

Q55: How many times per day does a clock's hand overlap?

There many ways of getting the answer other than the one provided below; however, more important than the specific method is walking through the steps in your reasoning clearly and logically. This does not just demonstrate your thinking process to the interviewer, but will also help you to avoid making silly mistakes by jumping to an answer too quickly. If you find it hard to structure your thoughts in your head, consider taking a minute to write down your thought process on a piece of paper.

A **good answer:** On a 12-hour clock face the hour hand completes two full circles in a day, and the minute hand does a full rotation every hour; i.e. 24 rotations in a day. Having established these facts, one approach is to visualise the first time the two hands cross. If you start from midnight with the hands in the same position you would need to wait for at least one full rotation before they intersect. Since the hour hand is moving from midnight to 1am the intersection would be at roughly 1:05 (it would actually be a bit later since the hour hand would actually be at the 1 when the minute was at the 12). Now we know that the two hands cross at approximately 1.05 we can visualize the next overlap which would be when the hour hand is at about 2 and the minute hand is at about 10 minutes past (again the numbers are not quite exact). What you might notice here is that the overlaps happen at about 65 minutes intervals. There are 14400 minutes in a day (60 x 24), so if you divide 14400 by 65 you get a little over 22. Therefore the total number of overlaps would be 22.

As noted above, a **weak answer** may occur due to simple calculation error or trying to jump to the answer too quickly. For example: "The minute hand goes around the clock 24 times in a day, so it presumably crosses the minute hand once each time. So that would be 24." Many candidates may slip up on this question by choosing a seemingly obvious answer. The larger lesson to draw from this is that if a solution seems obvious, ask yourself whether it is likely that the interviewer would get any value from seeing you solve this problem. Not only the content, but also the brevity may be a warning sign that your answer is on the wrong track.

Q56: You are given 7 identical balls and another ball that looks the same as the others but is heavier than them. You can use a balance only two times. How would you identify which is the heavy ball?

Although questions like this may seem somewhat intimidating the best way to approach them is to start by slowly working step by step. You do not necessarily have to start with the correct method, but try to work towards it and rule out less useful approaches as you go.

A good candidate might start by noting that they do not know how much heavier the heavy ball is. From this information they can deduce that placing 3 balls on one side of the scale and 4 balls on the other may not give us precise enough information. Instead, for a more accurate approach we must start by placing an equal number of items on each side. If one places three balls on each side, then whichever side is heavier must include the heavy ball. However, if the balance is equal then the heavy ball must be the ball that was not placed on the scale. From here a candidate could deduce that either they had solved the problem, or they would need to repeat the experiment with the three balls on the heavy side of the balance. In this instance, the candidate would compare two of the balls from the heavier side and set the third ball aside. If either of the two balls on the balance was heavier we would have our answer, or if they were equal, the remaining ball that the candidate had set aside would be the heavier ball.

By contrast, **a weaker candidate** may use a process of trial and error instead of taking a step back, drawing conclusions from their thinking and using these new conclusions to inform their next move. Note that not all strong candidates will immediately come to the solution; the difference between the strong and the weak candidate is that a strong candidate will be able to course-correct as they go and spot the nature of their error, whereas a weak candidate may not be able to identify where they made a mistake.

Q57: What is your favourite number?

This question is a great opportunity for you to demonstrate enthusiasm for your chosen subject. For example, as a mathematician you may find a specific number theoretically interesting, as a historian you could pick a specific date, or as a biologist you might pick a number that represents an interesting phenomenon in the natural world (e.g. rate of bacterial reproduction). When answering the question, take care to pick something that you genuinely find interesting and can talk about at length, rather than something you think will sound impressive. Make sure the interviewer remembers you for the whole content of and justification for your answer, not just the opening line.

Although personal stories are unlikely to harm you, choosing your grandmother's birthday, a football player's jersey number or the numbers you always pick for the lottery is unlikely to strengthen your application. The important thing to remember when confronted with an unexpected question is to take a step back and think about how you can direct the conversation to something that will bolster your case for admission.

Finally, although it is important to draw in interesting content about your subject, a good candidate will also answer the question. A **weaker answer** might use the answer as a springboard to offer a prepared answer on an unrelated topic. For example, cite a historical date and then simply talk about their interest in that historical period. By contrast a **strong answer** might talk about the role numbers play in memory, or the importance of quantification in history. These answers are stronger because they focus on the core of the question and justify why the number is a relevant feature of the answer, rather than the number being an afterthought. Directly engaging with the question is important as it shows that you are responding authentically and in the moment, rather than seeming like a poor listener or an overprepared candidate.

Q58: Who am I? (Always read up on your interviewers!)

This is a good opportunity for a candidate to demonstrate they have thought about their college choice and know who the tutors in their subject area are; this is a chance to show that you are thoughtful and engaged with your chosen degree subject.

Good answer: 'You are Professor X, you work in the field of [biomedical science, economics, etc]. I think more specifically you work in the subfield of [human anatomy/microeconomics] and some of your research looks at [cerebral cortical development/auction theory]. I was really excited about applying to this college because, as I mentioned in my personal statement, I am particularly interested in [the role of cortical development in conditions such as dyslexia/the application of auction theory to public goods tenders].'

This is a good answer because it shows that the candidate has serious academic reasons for applying to a college, and has begun to develop interests within their subject area. Of course, this is contingent on these interests being real. Do not bring up research if you do not understand it; this is likely to lead to embarrassment! There are other ways to answer this question. For example, a tutor might state on their college webpage that they love working with undergraduates, or you may have seen them give an inspiring talk at an Open Day. These are also valid things to bring up about a tutor, as they have chosen to put this information in the public domain.

A **weak answer** could go in a lot of different directions. For example, the student might attempt to move in an excessively abstract direction (e.g. what is the nature of identity?) - this might be OK if you are in a philosophy interview, but less so for subjects like maths. Alternatively, the student may simply not know who the interviewer is. You will typically be interviewed by fellows at the college, so you should have the opportunity to have a look at their research. Additionally, you are normally told who your interviewers will be prior to the interview, which should give you an opportunity to look them up.

Q59: Is there any question that you wished we had asked you?

This question is a great chance to highlight an aspect of your application that you would like to talk about. For example, you may have written about a specific book on your personal statement that you think you can speak about further in an interesting manner, or you might have written an extended essay which demonstrates your interest in and understanding of a specific subject. Thanking the interviewers and expressing enthusiasm about the content can also be a nice touch. However, it is inadvisable to simply state your desire to go to Oxbridge, or launch into abstract declarations of your love for the subject. These should be demonstrated through actions not words; over the top displays of emotion are more likely to make an interviewer uncomfortable than convince them to admit you.

More commonly, however, what will differentiate a strong from a weak answer is not the topic but rather the manner in which you talk about it. For example, a **strong answer** should highlight an aspect of your application in a concise manner that directly underscores your commitment to the subject and shows intellectual maturity. However, you do need to make the case as to why you want to discuss this; it should not come across as simply a desire to introduce impressive things you have done. Ways to avoid this include explaining why a given activity demonstrates your curiosity about your subject, or perhaps an interest in the process of academic research.

A **weaker answer** could come in many different forms. Any answer that strays into boasting or flattery is unlikely to make a favourable impression. If you genuinely do not have any topics you would like to discuss it is fine to admit to this; interviewers know that the interview experience can be stressful and not all candidates (even strong ones) will relish the prospect of further interview questions!

Q60: What are you looking forward to the least at this college?

This is a question where you can be honest to a certain extent, but must remain balanced. **Poor answers** are likely to fall into one of two extremes; the 'fake problem' or the 'too blunt'. Interviewers are unlikely to believe the candidate who claims that they are least looking forward to a choice of modules because they wish they could choose everything (is that really the worst possible thing you could think of?). As a result, this attempt to avoid admitting to any negative or undesirable opinion risks coming off as insincere. However, veering too far in the opposite direction is also inadvisable. Saying you are worried about the workload before you have even arrived is likely to raise red flags and make interviewers wonder whether you will be able to cope with the pace of Oxbridge.

By contrast a **good answer** will strike a balance between sincerity and oversharing by stating a genuine concern - but ideally one that does not relate to academic concerns. For example, you could quite reasonably express concerns about financial stability, being able to find a common cultural community, or other similar considerations. If these are genuine concerns, they are things a college will be interested in knowing so that they can try to help solve them. If you are struggling to find an appropriate concern, while not ideal it is OK to say that you will miss your cat, home cooking, or that you are mostly very excited about going to university and so do not yet have anything you are very worried about.

Ultimately, this sort of question serves two functions for interviewers: it helps them to decide whether students are applying for the right reasons (academic work not college balls), but also to make sure that they are aware of applicants concerns. Colleges really do want to make themselves accessible and friendly places, so this is a time when it can be appropriate to raise a concern or question that may have been bothering you.

Q61: Who has had the largest influence on your life?

Questions such as these should be answered in a way that is first and foremost plausible, and secondly makes the case for you as a candidate. Ways you can make that case include demonstrating that your interest in your chose subject is deep and long-standing (i.e. you didn't apply on a whim and you have specific subject interests).

Weak answers may come from candidates too eager to impress interviewers with their passion for their subject. Very few people are likely to believe that Marie Curie has had more influence on your life than a family member, or caregiver. It is important to remember that seeming genuine is just as important as seeming intelligent (if not more so). Other ways candidates can provide weak answers include being too laconic, or unreflective. Failing to relate the answer to your current subject interests, while not something that is likely to be penalised, might be a bit of a missed opportunity.

Explanation is the key to a **good answer**. For example, you might quite plausibly be able to say that your mum has been the biggest influence on your life, briefly discuss non-academic ways in which she has influenced you and then discuss how she has had a role in your intellectual development. Maybe she encountered problems when finding work that made you want to become an economist to better understand the labour market. Perhaps at a certain point she stopped being able to answer your questions about the world, and as a result you wanted to become a biologist. Ultimately, the connection you make will depend on both your subject and your chosen person. Of course, sometimes a connection to your degree will not be obvious, and that is fine. It is better to have a natural seeming answer than forcing a subject matter connection where none exists, and running the risk of seeming disingenuous.

Q62: If you were me, would you let yourself in?

Although some people might feel a temptation to answer 'no' to stand out, this is not the time for being wacky. Instead, treat this as an opportunity to advocate for yourself while also addressing any perceived weaknesses you might have. Each candidate will vary in the traits that make them distinctive, so answers will differ substantially between candidates. However, a **strong candidate** should start by considering qualities that Oxbridge might look for in a candidate, and then assess themselves against this framework. Not only does this directly answer the question, but also demonstrates to the interviewer that the candidate is a structured and rigorous thinker.

For example, you might start by defining a 'good' candidate as having both a deep interest in their subject, and academic aptitude. You might then illustrate your interest in your subject by referring to your personal statement and extra-curriculars. This could include addressing any weakness (e.g. mixed GCSE results) with reference to a mitigating or balancing factor (e.g. a strong focus on science subjects, and strong predicted A-levels). Any suggestion that a weakness is either acceptable or irrelevant should be backed up by a plausible explanation; if you believe that an explanation will simply sound like an excuse, it may be better to not raise it at all.

A **poor candidate** may have woolly reasoning or be unable to explain what makes them distinctive - many candidates will have excellent marks and a good personal statement. It is also inadvisable to speak negatively about other candidates (even in broad brush terms). For example, I am X unlike all of Y who are the same. You can make points about your own distinctiveness without coming across as mean-spirited or negative. Remember that these interviewers will have to teach you; they do not just want to know you are clever, they also want to know that working together will be an enjoyable experience.

Q63: What do you think my favourite colour is? Why do you say that?

Although many questions offer the opportunity to demonstrate your interest in your subject, in certain circumstances you may have trouble doing so naturally. Again, answering the question and demonstrating good listening skills is key. In situations such as these, rather than offering a tangential and canned answer, think of critical thinking strengths you can highlight through your answer. In this instance, good deductive reasoning and clear communication can help you demonstrate to your interviewer that you are a clear and logical student who will fare well in tutorials.

A **good answer** may discuss how a favourite colour might influence someone's clothing or room decoration choices. This would not be simple reasoning, such as "people will wear their favourite colour", but would introduce nuance by considering limitations to the evidence that they are using. For example, if you really like bright pink or bright green you might not wear that colour in a professional setting, or just limit it to somewhere inconspicuous such as a tie, or a pair of socks. Importantly, although a good answer will consider limitations to reasoning it *should* come to a conclusion. A candidate who twists themselves in knots of uncertainty will come across as a messy thinker who is not able to weigh competing pieces of evidence. By all means acknowledge weaknesses in your logic or contradictory evidence, but you should offer a guess.

A **weak answer** might suffer from a lack of nuance; or conversely a candidate may be so aware of the limitations of their reasoning that they offer a long-winded reply that ultimately comes to no conclusion. Other pitfalls include coming across as combative or annoyed by a seemingly irrelevant question. Although the interview experience can be stressful, being polite and upbeat is key; these are people you will have to work with.

Q64: What is a lie? How do I know what you just said isn't a lie?

In questions that ask you to offer definitions of complex concepts, a great way to start is by using examples to explore your initial intuition. Interviewers are unlikely to expect you to have a ready-made definition; many of these concepts are the subject of intense academic debate! What *is* important, however, is showing that you are a creative thinker who can course-correct and explore their own thinking in a structured manner.

For example, a **strong candidate** might start with a definition such as "a lie is a statement that is knowingly false", and then use specific examples to test whether this definition fits across a range of contexts. For example, what does it mean to lie to oneself? What is the role of intent in the definition of lying? Are 'white lies' still lies? These are just a few examples of questions a candidate might raise, and there are no definitive right or wrong answers. Instead, the important feature of a good answer is that a candidate can navigate from the intellectually abstract definition to a concrete situation with fluency, demonstrating both strong conceptual thinking and an ability to drive their own intellectual process. The use of examples is a great way to do this because it allows you to ground your answer in everyday experience and may help you to tease out weaknesses or contradictions in your thinking. Again, coming to a conclusion (or at least a specific definition) is critical to a good answer. You can certainly acknowledge weaknesses or uncertainties, but a good candidate should be able to weigh evidence and come down on a side.

By contrast, a **weaker candidate** is likely to be less reflective about the quality of their own answer, and perhaps rush to a conclusion (or be unwilling to come to one at all). One mistake that candidates often make is thinking that an interview is a debate; that they are obliged to stick to and defend their original statements. In fact, it is often a great idea to let your position evolve if you change your mind. Tutors are looking for people who are open-minded and intellectually flexible.

Q65: If you could keep objects from the present for the future, what would they be?

Rather than taking this as a whimsical or warm up question, use this as an opportunity to highlight your passion for your subject. This will naturally vary from candidate to candidate, but the broad lesson is that even seemingly off the wall questions can be used to strengthen your case for admission.

A **good answer** from an historian might, for example, highlight their thoughts about the importance of sources to future generations of historians. A biologist may be interested in species preservation and want to keep a patch of the Amazon. In instances where material objects might be less relevant to your subject (e.g. as an economist, or a theoretical physicist), you could show creativity by suggesting an item emblematic of a phenomenon you find interesting (e.g. promotional material from the sharing economy, or the computer used to carry out complex calculations).

A **weaker answer** could take many different forms, but failing to relate your answer to your subject or poorly justifying your choice are common errors. Many weak answers use the same examples as stronger ones, but simply fail to fully explain why they selected the item. For example, a biologist simply saying "I would preserve a tree in the Amazon because I think that the biodiversity in underexplored areas of the rainforest is enormous, and I think deforestation might eradicate our chances to access this knowledge" does not fully demonstrate that the candidate understands what they are talking about. Their answer remains very general and does not specify what sort of information they are concerned about preserving. A candidate in this position could easily strengthen their answer by drawing on examples of findings they have read about, thus demonstrating that their example is not a vague concern about the environment but rooted in specific knowledge indicative of a deep curiosity about their subject.

Q66: What is more important – art or science?

As with many abstract questions, a **good answer** will offer clear reasoning, an acknowledgement of alternative positions, and an explicit conclusion. For example, you may believe that *generally speaking* science is more important than art because science is central to material improvements in people's well-being. You might then acknowledge some weaknesses in this position, e.g. that this is not true of all science (certain forms of pure mathematics have no known practical application), or that art can be critical to social or moral progress. Finally, do offer a rebuttal (e.g. physical life is the basis of all other values and so although art is important, medical advances are necessary to enjoy art). These are just a few examples of arguments that could be raised, and a compelling case could be made on either side.

A **weaker answer** may offer the same general reasoning as the strong answer, but simply fail to offer much justification. Another common trap is listing the advantages and disadvantages of both disciplines but failing to explain how you weigh these different considerations. This is a question that may arouse strong feelings in many candidates who want to demonstrate their interest in their chosen subject; however, you should be careful about coming across as brow beating, or arrogant. Even if you – as a scientist – believe that art can only exist because of scientific progress, there are ways to explain this view without seeming dismissive of something that many others value enormously. The same applies to humanities students who believe that life only has meaning due to art – beware of sounding pretentious! Once again, always remember that your interviewer may tutor you in the future, so coming across as friendly and open-minded is just as important as seeming clever. Launching into a tirade is more likely to make you seem unreflective than passionate.

Q67: If you could have one superpower, which one would it be? Why?

Seemingly random questions can often be used as an opportunity to talk about your interest in your subject. One way of answering this question would be to think of a problem that you face in your field, and select a superpower that would help you resolve it. Obviously, omniscience might do this, but probably also makes for a less interesting answer.

As with other questions of this variety, what will differentiate a good answer from a weak answer is not the topic chosen, but rather the explanation given. For example, a historian could talk about their desire to time travel; but what would distinguish a good answer from a weak or commonplace one would be the justification. For example, a **weaker candidate** might simply say "I am interested in Napoleonic history so I would love to be able to observe the Battle of Waterloo". While the candidate may talk specifically what they would like to see and demonstrate strong understanding of Napoleonic history, enthusiasm for historical facts is not the same as showing a scholarly approach.

By contrast, a **strong candidate** might discuss their desire to go to a specific period and then relate this to an interest in collecting oral history sources. In an answer such this, the student not only explains their reasoning and relates it to a specific personal interest, but they also display good knowledge of the problems scholars of their subject might face. All of this suggests a mature thinker who would do well at university.

Although a time travelling historian might seem like an obvious example, similar answers can come from a variety of disciplines. A physicist might want to be able to observe unobservable events, a biologist might want eyes with the power of microscopes. Ultimately this sort of question is very open to interpretation and the strength of the answer will lie in the justification.

Q68: Would you ever go on a one-way trip to Mars? Why/why not?

As ever, you should treat every question as an opportunity to highlight why you would be a good candidate for admission. Even questions such as this, which may appear to be utterly random, can often be related back to your chosen subject. However, it is also fine to inject human concerns into your answers; it is always important for your reply to seem natural.

For example, a **good answer** from a biologist might talk about their desire to know more about microbial life on Mars, and their interest in the findings of the Mars Curiosity Rover, but ultimately conclude that they would rather rely on earth-based study than abandon their family. The student expresses enthusiasm for their subject, but also sets out quite reasonable limits on what they are willing to sacrifice for science. This honesty may come across as more credible than the candidate who claims that they would be willing to abandon their family and friends. A word to the wise: if you do raise specific examples (e.g. microbial life) then be certain that you can talk about them in more depth if probed. For non-STEM candidates, a clear relationship to your subject may be harder to draw; but creative thinking should allow you to find one. For example, historians might draw parallels with prior explorers of the globe, and philosophers could establish an ethical framework for evaluating such a choice. However, even if you cannot think of a link to your subject, remember to offer clear reasoning and a conclusion.

A **weak answer** could fall into any of the pitfalls mentioned above. Although it is fine to answer that one would indeed take a one-way trip, making sweeping claims such as "I love physics so much I would abandon my family and live alone on Mars" may ring somewhat hollow. Other weak answers may simply fail to grasp the opportunity to relate their thinking back to their subject. While this is unlikely to actively harm the your chances, it would be a missed opportunity.

Q69: Does human nature change?

Questions which ask candidates to discuss abstract concepts are a great opportunity to demonstrate to your interviewer that you are a structured thinker, who can engage with high level concepts and not get muddled. To answer this question well, the candidate needs to explore what people mean by the term 'human nature'. The candidate may also want to explore what is meant by the term 'change', and under what circumstances their answer might vary.

A **good candidate** might, for example, discuss whether the use of the term 'nature' implies some unchanging essence. There are a variety of strategies a candidate could adopt to do this effectively, including looking at examples of when people use the term 'human nature' and what they tend to be explaining when they do this. Alternatively, the candidate may want to provide a direct definition of human nature (e.g. the basic motivations of all homo sapiens). Strong candidates will also seek to define the parameters of their answer. Rather than simply providing a yes or no conclusion to their answer the candidate may offer a qualified response, e.g. "Yes, human nature can change over time, but a single individual cannot change their nature". While this is just an example, answers such as these show to the interviewer that the candidate has thought deeply about their answer and is able to generate a rigorous conceptual framework on the fly.

Weaker answers are likely to fall into one of a few different traps. Some candidates mistake conversations such as these for a debate and try to defend their instinctive initial answer; however, this can often come across as intellectual inflexibility, or arrogance. Showing willingness to engage with new ideas and revise your own when confronted with (reasonable) criticism can be a strength. Other candidates struggle with the lack of structure provided by this question and will throw out a range of possible considerations but be unable to draw them together into any coherent answer. Taking a minute before answering the question to jot down some thoughts can be a good way to give your answer more structure.

Q70: Define 'success' in one sentence.

This question, like many of the more abstract questions asked, is an opportunity for the candidate to showcase the quality of their thinking when confronted with an unfamiliar topic. Beyond simply showing clear and logical reasoning, candidates can also excel by using this question as an opportunity to emphasise their passion for their subject through their choice of examples.

For example, **a good candidate** might start with an initial definition that is further refined as they reason out loud. One way to do this would be work through a few examples to test whether the definition of success they came up with holds true in each case. An answer would be enhanced if the examples the candidate chooses not only draw on their subject matter expertise, but are also a little unusual. For example, an art historian could, of course, discuss whether Van Gogh (who died in penury) can be considered a success; but this is an example even a non-subject specialist might come up with. By contrast, selecting an artist from a period the candidate mentioned in their personal statement would allow them to demonstrate that their interest has real depth to it.

As with many with many of these abstract questions, a **weak answer** to this question is likely to be caused by a lack of structure, or under-explanation. A good answer and a weak answer may start off with the same definition; but where the quality of the answers will diverge is in the explanation of how a candidate came to that answer. A weaker candidate may offer examples of success as evidence, whereas the good candidate will use examples to pick out specific features of what could and could not be called success. Returning to the Van Gogh example, the strong candidate might point to the tension between the lack of recognition during his lifetime and his subsequent acclaim, and then examine whether or not we would call him a success if he had been famous during his lifetime and then forgotten. By contrast, the weaker candidate's exploration may be limited to noting that 'success can happen outside of your lifetime'.

Q71: Is there such a thing as truth?

Applicants can adopt one of two strategies to answer this [...] ever, students can draw examples from their own subject to illustrate their answer; for example, mathematicians might want to talk about proofs, and historians might want to talk about source reliability. Alternatively, students can take this as an opportunity to simply show clear reasoning, and good verbal expression. The best applicants may be able to combine these two approaches.

A **good candidate** might start with a simple answer that they explicitly state they plan to refine. An example of such an answer would be "I think there is such a thing as truth, and I will define truth as a statement that describes a situation that exists or has existed in the world". From there, the candidate might use situations which appear to be truthful but do not cohere with this definition to examine whether it is possible to come to a meaningful definition of truth. For example, they might examine whether statements which are mildly inaccurate can be called truth and whether it is possible to make truly accurate statements (e.g. can we say that 'the cat jumped on the table five minutes ago' is a lie, if the cat jumped on the table 6 minutes ago?). Good candidates will also note that certain domains might have 'truth' and others might not. For example, do moral or aesthetic statements have truth value?

A **weaker applicant** is likely to offer a less thoughtful answer. The weakest answers are likely to be characterised by brevity: "Yes, because I can say that this chair is here, and it is. That's a true statement". Although you may believe this to be true, it is always worth fleshing an answer out by exploring where you could be wrong. Less obviously weak answers are likely to suffer from a lack of structure. It is very possible for a candidate to raise a few interesting thoughts but fail to explore them comprehensively or organise them well. While intellectual promise is helpful, without clear explanation a candidate's answer may simply be interpreted as scattershot.

Q72: You are shrunk down so you're the size of a matchstick and then put into a blender with metal blades. It is about to be turned on – what do you do?

This question can be used to demonstrate all sorts of different skills, from creativity to analytical thinking, and could even show how you are able to apply subject knowledge to an unusual problem. The physicists, biologists, and engineers out there may want to ask clarifying questions about the scenario to gain more information, such as the density of the shrunken human body. If you can explain why these questions are relevant and how they influence your answer, then ask away – it is often an excellent way to engage.

For those for whom there may be no obvious subject connection, a **good candidate** could simply work through the problem by breaking it down into component pieces. As with any non-traditional question there is no single correct way of doing this. For example, certain candidates might identify that there are two solutions: break the machine or avoid the blades. They could then discuss which of these two solutions would be more likely to succeed and then select that solution. Other equally successful candidates might consider whether someone is trying to blend them intentionally - and if not, how someone so small might be able to attract the attention of the person about to turn on the blender. Candidates are, of course, also expected to show basic common sense; just because a situation is fantastical does not mean that they can posit absurd solutions. Candidates should try to consider realistic features such as the centrifugal force of the blades, or strength of the machine relative to someone the size of a matchstick.

Weaker candidates are less likely to be let down by the content of their answers, than by the lack of enthusiasm, intellectual curiosity, or flexibility that they demonstrate. Note that even the good candidate may not find a satisfying solution to this (rather strange) problem; but what they will do is explore a variety of ideas, and demonstrate the ability to evaluate their own thought process while remaining engaged with the interview.

SUBJECT INTERVIEWS

Subject interviews are where subject-specific questions are asked to test critical thinking and problem-solving skills. These interviews are very likely to follow the format of tutorials/supervisions. You will be interviewed by one or two senior academics from the college you applied to. They will be experts on the subject you've applied for and will ask academic questions around a central theme. **The questions are intended to be difficult** so as to push you and test your critical thinking abilities in a learning situation. You are not meant to know the answers, but to use your existing knowledge to offer creative and original thoughts to address the questions.

Here are some general tips to keep in mind:

- Apply the knowledge you have acquired at A-Level and from your wider reading to unfamiliar scenarios.
- **Stand your ground if you are confident in your argument**- even if your interviewers disagree with you. They may deliberately play the devil's advocate to see if you are able to defend your argument.
- However, if you are making an argument that is clearly wrong and are being told so by the interviewers - then concede your mistake and revise your viewpoint. Do not stubbornly carry on arguing a point that they are saying is wrong.
- Remember, making mistakes is no bad thing. The important point is that you address the mistake head on and adapt the statement, with their assistance where necessary.
- The **tutors know what subjects you have studied at A-Level** so don't feel pressured to read EVERY aspect of your subject.

In the chapters that follow, each subject is discussed in detail — including common types of questions and model solutions to previously asked interview questions. This book is not intended to be an exhaustive list of all that you need to know for your Oxbridge interview (if that's even possible!). Instead, it is designed to guide your learning by exposing you to the style and difficulty of questions that might come up and how to best approach them.

LAW

A law applicant may be asked legal questions or questions from a related subject, including history, politics, or current affairs with a legal slant. None of the questions asked of you will assume any previous legal knowledge, as the interviewers understand that applicants will likely not have studied law before. Be prepared to explain why you want to study law and show through extra-curricular reading or activities how you've fostered this interest.

The interview will usually consist of a large question with many smaller sub-questions that the interviewer will ask in order to guide the applicant to an answer. The main question may seem difficult, impossible, or random at first, but take a breath and start discussing with your interviewer different ideas you have for breaking down the question into manageable pieces.

The questions are designed to be difficult to give you the chance to show your full intellectual potential.

For law, the questions will usually take one of a few possible forms based on highlighting the skills necessary to 'think like a lawyer'. Five main question types are:

- Observation-based questions ("tell me about...")
- Practical questions ("how would you decide if...")
- Statistical questions ("given this data...")
- Ethical questions ("are humans obligated to...")
- Questions about proximate causes (mechanism; "how does...") and ultimate causes (function; "why does…"), usually both at once.

Questions also have recurring themes which appear in many questions because they are central to jurisprudential thinking: the workings of the English legal system, problems of access to justice, the centrality of morality in legal development, the future of the legal profession, the impact of international treaties and legal institutions, looking carefully at words and drawing fine distinctions, building up an argument and applying that to examples.

WORKED QUESTIONS

Below are a few examples of how to start breaking down an interview question, complete with model answers.

Q1: In a society of angels, is the law necessary?

Applicant: Well, an angel could be defined as someone who is always inclined to do what is good, just, and moral in any situation. If I thought that the sole purpose of the law was always to achieve what is good, just, and moral, I might conclude that in a society of such creatures, law would not be necessary as angels would already be achieving this goal on their own. Why don't I continue by giving my own definition of the purpose of the law in society, taking account of the law's function as a social coordinator and as an international arbitrator? Perhaps I should also add a brief of what it means for something to be necessary and apply that definition to my discussion at hand. I may even expand this discussion further and think about what a society without any laws would look like, or indeed, if such a society would be at all possible.

This shows that <u>the question can be broken down into sub-parts</u>, which can be dealt with in turn. At this point, the interviewer can give feedback and help make any modifications necessary. In the case of the above interview, the applicant will realise that the function of the law is not just to promote what is good, just, and moral, but also to act as a method of social cohesion. The details are unimportant, but the general idea of breaking down the question into manageable parts is important. The interviewer is not looking for an expert in legal philosophy, but someone who can problem-solve in the face of new ideas.

A <u>poor applicant</u> may take a number of approaches unlikely to impress the interviewer. The first and most obvious of these is to say "I don't know anything about societies of angels" and make no attempt to move forward.

Q2: What are the advantages and disadvantages to a non-written constitution?

This question is looking to see if you understand something of the nature of the <u>British constitution</u> and whether you can lay down pros and cons of an argument, with a conclusion that comes down on one side or the other of the debate.

Perhaps begin by defining what is meant by a written and a non-written constitution and try to give examples of countries with each (e.g. the UK and the USA). A constitution could be defined as a legal contract which states the terms and conditions under which a society agrees to govern itself, outlining the functions, powers and duties of the various institutions of government, regulates the relationship between them, and defines the relationship between the state and the public.

Problems of a non-written or uncodified constitution – firstly, it is difficult to know what the state of the constitution actually is, and secondly, it suggests that it is easier to make changes to the UK constitution than in countries with written constitutions, because the latter have documents with a 'higher law' status against which ordinary statute law and government action can be tested. Is the problem then more with the perception of our constitution than the legal status of the constitution itself?

Are they really so different? The American constitution may be elegantly written and succinct, but it can be amended or reinterpreted or even broken as the times demand, in the same way that the UK's unwritten constitution can be. Furthermore, even a written constitution is supplemented by unwritten conventions and most countries' constitutions embody a mixture of the two. This line of argument could lead you to conclude that the issue here is really only with semantics as <u>there isn't any real difference in governance</u>.

This question could lead to a discussion of the ways the UK constitution allows for laws to be made – e.g. "should judges have a legislative role?"

A poor applicant would not attempt to address both written and non-written constitutions, instead, sticking staunchly to whatever they have read on either subject.

Q3: How would you clarify the meaning of the words intention and foresight?

The question is looking for your ability to give <u>accurate definitions of two principles central to criminal law</u>. Intention could be defined as an aim or a plan, whilst foresight could be defined as the ability to predict what will happen. Thinking about the way these subtly different definitions might be applied in a legal context, we see that one might foresee that doing X will lead to the death of B but that consequence was not necessarily intended.

This intuitive distinction is mirrored in <u>criminal law in the UK.</u> There are two different types of intention: direct intent which exists where the defendant embarks upon a course of conduct to bring about a result which in fact occurs, and oblique intent which exists where the defendant embarks on a course of conduct to bring about a desired result, knowing that the consequence of his actions will also bring about another result.

A particularly topical example of the application of this distinction in practice can be seen discussing "the doctrine of double effect". This doctrine is only really applied in medical cases. Consider this example – a doctor who administers a lethal dose of painkillers to their terminally ill patient in order to relieve their suffering also foresees that such a dose will kill the patient. Should this doctor be guilty of the murder of her patient? Ultimately, the doctrine says that if doing something morally good has a morally bad side-effect it's ethically OK to do it providing the bad side-effect wasn't intended. This is true even if you foresaw that the bad effect would probably happen.

A poor applicant would fail to distinguish the two and would fail to see how these definitions are applied in modern criminal law.

Q4: Does a computer have a conscience?

Intuitively, we want to answer this question with a resounding "no" as it seems obvious that only living things can have consciences. Computers are creations of man and therefore merely act according to our needs, having little or no agency of their own. A poor applicant would only be able to articulate this very basic intuitive response and would be incapable of digging further.

In fact, the answer depends entirely upon which definitions you choose to give to the key terms in the question. Conscience could be defined as a moral sense of right and wrong which is viewed as acting to a guide of one's behaviour.

A computer is an electronic device which is capable of receiving information and performing a sequence of operations in accordance with a predetermined set of variables. Given these two definitions, it could be possible to program a computer with a conscience.

You could discuss the <u>distinction between having a conscience and being 'sentient'</u>-the former being a form of moral compass, whilst the latter is merely the ability to perceive or feel external stimulus. Do you think "artificial intelligence" is possible? Is it dangerous? If a computer does have a conscience, what might this mean for data protection laws?   Freedom of expression? Ownership? Would this mean that computers should have rules protecting them from abuse, e.g. Computer Rights?

Q5: What is justice?

It might be good to begin with a succinct <u>definition of 'justice'</u> like 'behaviour or treatment which are just' with 'just' meaning 'equitable, fair and even-handed'.

You might then want to expand on this initial definition. Perhaps an exploration of what justice means in the context of criminal law which might go as follows:

Firstly, custodial sentences are used for their deterrent effect. Secondly, decisions on the form and duration of the sentence focus upon the crime itself rather than looking at how the punishment will best rehabilitate the offender, appease the victim, and benefit society as a whole. This judicial inflexibility which we see in the sentencing of criminals reflects a right-wing conception of justice based on the maxim 'an eye for an eye'.

You might put forward that an alternative conception of justice might achieve fairer results - perhaps one which takes a <u>utilitarian approach</u> to punishment. Such a conception would necessitate finding the best possible outcome for the largest number of people.

However, the counter argument to this would be that this approach would not allow for the idea of <u>'moral forfeiture'</u>, the principle that in committing a crime, you give up some of your rights. This contextual approach gives us a taste of just how difficult it really is to define justice, even in such a narrow context.

We often hear the term 'social justice' which is another context in which the term is applied. The concept in this context is very difficult to reconcile with justice as vengeance in the criminal context. Social justice too has several definitions; one might be socioeconomic equality amongst all members of any given society, whilst another might be more meritocratic and insist upon greater social mobility and fairness in general. We see that, upon examining this wider application of the idea of justice to non-criminal contexts, that the conception of justice itself is made even more difficult to define.

To conclude, we have proven that our initial definition of justice was not sufficient. The concept seems to defy any coherent definition as it is so broad and subjective.

Q6: Should the aim of the law be to make people happy?

One might argue that the aim of the law is to generally make everyone's lives better. Indeed, improving the quality of citizens' lives is the explicit focus of much of the policymaking and regulatory work done by many governments around the world. If we accept this, the next question would be 'what does better really mean?' One account could be that to make someone's life "better" we should render that person more able to get what they want. Another account might be that the quality of someone's life depends on the extent to which they do well at the things that are characteristically human to do. This difficulty in defining what it might be to make any one person's life better and therefore making them happy is one difficulty with placing this as the law's overarching aim – happiness is internal – how can we accurately know what anyone is feeling, and therefore truly know how well the law is working?

Perhaps one way to combat this problem could be to develop a <u>method of measuring subjective happiness</u> – a type of well-being analysis. How might we do this? Well, we could introduce a system of weekly online surveys which would be answered by a representative portion of society on how happy they were able to make particular administrative decisions. Over time, such large masses of data would allow us to accurately pinpoint just what really makes people happier and just how the law can shape itself to better achieve this.

Q7: Which laws are broken most frequently? Are they still laws?

Millions of people who declare themselves law-abiding citizens actually commit seven crimes on average per week. The most common offences are things like speeding, texting while driving, dropping litter, downloading music illegally, or riding bicycles on the pavement. Many of these more common 'minor crimes' are committed so regularly that they have almost become legal, which might be the reason so many people aren't fazed when they do break these laws.

<u>Are these 'minor laws' still laws?</u> You might argue that a law is a law even if it's not followed. The definition of a law, as a law, lies in the process by which it is enacted, i.e. the legislative process. This line of argument would lead you to believe that all laws are of the same importance because they become law by the same process.

However, you might not necessarily think that is the case. For instance, most people would think that killing someone would be much worse than accidentally dropping your train ticket and therefore littering. This would suggest that there is a hierarchy of laws, and therefore, that some laws are more important or that some laws are more immoral. This would lead you to conclude that 'minor laws' are still laws, but merely a lower class of laws, perhaps because the repercussions of infringement in these cases is lesser or the infringement is seen as less immoral and therefore are less thoroughly enforced.

Q8: After you have been to the hairdressers and had all of your hair cut off, do you still own your hair?

Intuitively, we believe that when our hair is attached to our heads, we do own it. The law supports this and if someone were to cut off your hair without your consent, you would be entitled to compensation.

However, where you have <u>consented to your hair being cut</u> off, the situation is very different and there is very little precedent to go on. You might argue that if you hadn't expressed an interest in maintaining your ownership of your hair once it had been cut off, it would be for the hairdresser to dispose of as he saw fit, in line with common practice in a hairdressers. You might think that the hairdresser's use of your hair would be of no consequence to you, but what if he sold it on eBay? What if it was used in an art exhibition to make a political point with which you disagreed? Would you then have a claim to your hair in these cases?

This question might lead on to a discussion about whether or not we own our own bodies. Surprisingly perhaps, we <u>have no legal right to decide what happens to us when we die</u> – instead, we can only express preferences and there are some things that the law will not let us do (e.g. leave your body to be used as meat for the dogs in Battersea Dogs' Home). We may contrast this with the approach the law takes to our other possessions after we die – in the case of all other property, your wishes are absolute. This contrast would suggest that we do not have the same legal relationship with our bodies as we do with our toasters, our cars, or our pocket-watches- but the really interesting question is – *should we?*

Q9: Should prisoners have the right to vote?

The European Court of Human Rights has ruled that Britain's blanket ban on voting for all convicted prisoners is a breach of their human rights. Allowing only some prisoners to vote would be ok, states the Court, but refusing the vote to all convicted prisoners is unacceptable.

Prison is generally considered to serve three key purposes; 1) to protect the public, 2) to serve as a deterrent, 3) to rehabilitate. Most prisoners have not committed crimes that warrant a life sentence. Most will eventually be released from prison. It's in everyone's interest that once out of prison, they do not commit any further crimes, but instead, become useful members of society. That involves reform whilst still in prison, and rehabilitating offenders to think - and act - more positively about their civic duties and responsibilities. One of the most important contributions a citizen can make to society is to take part in democracy and vote – removing a prisoner's civic duty does not, therefore, seem to accord with the aims of putting them in prison in the first place.

Alternatively, one might argue that all citizens of a country have implicitly agreed on a set of rules that gives them, and those around them, certain rights. It is the duty of every citizen to protect this framework and to respect the rights of others. If a person is in prison, it is because they broke the rules, and hence, in a way, forfeited their rights. The citizenship of prisoners can be seen as temporarily suspended along with all their rights.

Human rights do not mean that someone cannot be suitably punished or imprisoned for a crime once fairly tried and convicted. Human rights means that all humans deserve them, and the State protects them from abuse of their basic civil rights. If the State can be allowed to abuse humans – any humans, for any reasons or excuses – then how can we justify laws against humans abusing other humans? How the State behaves must be reflective of how we want all humans to behave.

<u>Human rights are meant to be universal</u>, which means the rights apply to all humans without exception; to you and to me; even to criminals and foreigners, and even to those humans we do not like. Once we take basic rights away from one human, we start to erode the basic protections for all humans.

Q10: Should 'immoral' or 'evil' laws be obeyed?

Note: if candidates are unsure of what the question means, interviewers can share Victorian jurist Dicey's famous example: should Parliament legislate for all blue-eyed babies to be killed, the law would still be a valid law but citizens would be 'mad' to obey it.

This question requires candidates to take a step back and consider the purpose and basis of the law. A good candidate would be able to make some comment about <u>legal normativism versus legal positivism,</u> but this is not essential. It is more important that they can engage with concepts and ideas, not get bogged down in technical terms.

A sensible place to start would be a discussion on why people obey the law -- out of a sense of moral obligation independent of the law (e.g. if I think stealing is wrong, I will not steal regardless of what the relevant statute precisely says), versus wishing to adhere to social norms (i.e. not being "looked down upon" or shunned by one's peers for being involved with illegal activities), versus actually fearing legal sanctions (e.g. avoiding recreational drugs while travelling in the Far East because I fear the death penalty being applied to me as a 'trafficker'). This should lead to strong candidates taking a step back and addressing to what extent morality should be the basis of law in a liberal society.

Candidates are free to proceed in a number of ways. It is only essential that they show that they have thought about the topic and have read some appropriate material. However, they must highlight that such 'immoral' laws would attract political criticism, and be conscious of the fact that political and legal mechanisms must work in tandem to <u>protect basic constitutional values and civil liberties</u>.

Q11: Given that juries consist of untrained people who do not have to give reasons for their decisions, are juries inherently inefficient and unreliable?

Candidates may not be aware of precisely what role juries play in the British justice system. It may be necessary to simply state that juries decide questions of fact but not law, which are used in certain more serious criminal trials, and jury members are picked at random from <u>all adults on the electoral roll</u> (except for members of certain professions, such as solicitors or MPs).

Candidates must be aware of the fundamental constitutional significance of trial by jury, an institution dating back to the time of the Magna Carta: being tried in front of a body of one's peers is purported to be central to democracy as they are held to be fairer and more objective than a single judge, as the jury is drawn from members of all strata of society, and thus, better able to understand the lifestyle of the ordinary man (as opposed to the white, middle-aged, male and upper-middle-class views of most judges). Juries can also play a role in repudiating repugnant, undemocratic laws. Not having to give reasons, the jury may refuse to convict if they believe the law was enacted to be overly harsh.

Candidates should also be aware that jury trials are expensive and inefficient. A balance between these two competing factors is necessary, and being able to provide sensible reasons for their preference is all that is needed.

However, <u>strong candidates</u> should question whether unelected juries ought to have a de facto power to ignore the legislation of the elected parliament if they think the law is repugnant. They should also consider whether or not jury decisions are even reliable.

Q12: Is the British monarchy antiquated and undemocratic? What reasons are there for either keeping or abolishing this institution?

This question is general and superficially familiar to any British applicant. However, it is one which hints at the complex, <u>uncodified nature of the British constitution</u>.

Candidates should know that a large range of powers are vested in the Monarch nominally. However, the Monarch does not exercise these powers independently as a matter of convention: there is no legal requirement that the Monarch must take the advice of the Prime Minister in, for example, giving Royal Assent to any Act duty passed by the elected Parliament. However, it would be unthinkable that she would refuse such advice, and, if she were to exercise such powers arbitrarily, it is likely that legal sanctions would be enacted to severely curtail the Monarch's power or to abolish the Monarchy altogether. There must be an awareness that what is right and wrong in law is not what is right or wrong generally and that the law is not the sole control of behaviour in society.

It would not be wrong for candidates to discuss the advantages or disadvantages of constitutional monarchy vs. republicanism in general, but they should not waste time discussing something not strictly pertinent to the question asked.

Strong candidates must frame their answer with reference to the tension between the theoretical anachronisms and empirical modernity which exist in the British constitution. A balanced approach is crucial, or, minimally, one which at least acknowledges the popularity (and therefore quasi-democratic mandate) of the Monarchy, and the importance of the Monarch as <u>uniting numerous Commonwealth countries</u> (e.g. Australia, New Zealand, Canada and the Bahamas), and how the removal of the Monarch in the UK would force citizens of many other countries to change their constitutional arrangements, possibly against their will.

Q13: Should publications like Charlie Hebdo be free to circulate uncontrolled? What kinds of restrictions on the media are compatible with freedom of speech?

If candidates are unfamiliar with the Charlie Hebdo killings, they would be told that Charlie Hebdo is an 'irreverent' French magazine which published inflammatory cartoons of the Prophet Mohammed. Outraged by these 'blasphemous' cartoons, Muslim extremists stormed the Charlie Hebdo office and killed a number of cartoonists. Many reacted with horror and immediately highlighted the importance of the freedom of speech. However, a smaller number of voices, while decrying what had happened, also highlighted the importance of responsible journalism.

Obviously, this is connected to ideas about <u>Freedom of Speech</u>. More generally, this raises fundamental questions about the nature of rights, and how rights are balanced against one another, as well as how the rights of the individual need to be balanced against the rights of the community.

A sensitive, nuanced approach would consider the overtones of Islamophobia which have tainted discourse on this case. In contrast, many simply speak about 'the right to offend' and the 'terror of extremism' with reference to this case.

A candidate who is able to think laterally may talk about how, in the UK, one's personal reputation is strongly protected by the <u>UK's vigorous defamation laws</u>. In contrast, offending or defaming an entire religion does not have such protection. Some consideration should be made of the role and position of religion in a secular, liberal society.

Q14: In the UK, the age of minimum criminal responsibility is 10, but the age of sexual consent is 16. A 15-year-old boy caught kissing a 14-year-old girl on the mouth could thus be convicted of various sexual offences. Is this satisfactory?

This question mixes together two anomalies in British criminal law. England has one of the youngest minimum ages of criminal responsibility in the Western world (it is 12 in Canada, Scotland, France, Germany, and Ireland), and the UN has recommended that all countries raise the age of minimum criminal responsibility to 12. Further, England has one of the highest minimum ages of consent for sex: it is typically 12 to 14 in Western Europe (but 18 in most of the US).

A <u>good candidate</u> must talk about whether or not the low age of criminal responsibility and high minimum age of sexual consent is justified. However, a strong candidate must interact with the question and be aware of the 'double whammy' effect these laws have.

One tension that must be identified is that the <u>law must be reasonable and realistic</u>. If the law were to criminalise activities which one is unlikely to be arrested for (which is inherent to the clandestine nature of underage mutually consensual sex), it may bring the law into disrepute.

Candidates must have a balanced view, however, and acknowledge how a high minimum age for sexual consent can protect the vulnerable and how a low minimum age of criminal responsibility is politically popular separately, but the interaction between the two can be problematic. It may be helpful to talk about how law is influenced by culture and the 'traditional' British attitude towards law and order and openness about sex.

Ultimately, a successful candidate must interact with the question and come to a sensible, thoroughly-considered opinion. A range of conclusions are acceptable, namely that the law should <u>protect the young from harmful overly-early sexualisation,</u> and because a 10-year-old facing a charge will not go to an adult jail (the emphasis being on rehabilitation). It could be suggested that the minimum age of criminal responsibility should be raised for the sake of compliance with international norms and the rights of the child, acknowledging their psychological immaturity and the sheer iniquity of charging children in an adult court. Also, that the age of sexual consent could be lowered so that the law should keep up with current societal norms, or some other combination of reform and consistency.

Q15: What are the fundamental differences between US and British Law? What are the implications of this?

It would be unfair to expect any technical knowledge from the candidate, so this need only be answered in general terms.

Primarily, we are concerned with the fact that the US has a <u>codified constitution</u>, and that there is, therefore, a clear separation of powers and the legislature, unlike in the UK, is not 'sovereign'. This means judges have the power to overturn unconstitutional legislation, and that in the US, the supreme source of authority is the constitution, not the will of Congress.

Another pertinent point is that the UK is a constitutional monarchy, but the US has a President. Though the <u>monarch nominally has vast discretionary</u> powers, these are never exercised by the monarch per se. In contrast, the elected President can and does use his considerable powers. This can be linked to the earlier point about the UK's uncodified constitution and that constitutional conventions play an important role in the UK.

A further point that can be mentioned is that the US is a federal system with each state having equal and defined powers, whereas the UK uses a devolution system where full power nominally remains with Westminster, not, say, the Scottish Parliament.

All these points must be linked to basic ideas about the rule of law, legal certainty, the separation of powers, and good governance. How exactly the implications of each of these differ is not essential. Rather, a strong candidate should demonstrate evidence of further reasoning, consider a number of perspectives, and show depth and clarity of thought. It would be helpful if they comment on whether or not the US or UK model is better, and whether or not the US model ought to be applied to countries with very different histories.

Q16: In France, if a person sees somebody drowning, they have a legal obligation to help them. Should this be the case in the UK?

This is about 'Good Samaritan Laws'. The duty to rescue, however, is necessarily a limited one in practice. Candidates should consider this when analysing the actual legal effect of such laws.

Ideas about liberty and an understanding that it is fundamentally more restrictive to force someone to do something as opposed to preventing them from doing certain things (the basic premise of most law) are fundamental to this question.

It must be acknowledged that such laws are morally attractive to prevent repugnant events such as healthy adults ignoring a two-year-old drowning in a paddling pool.

In balancing the two, the role of the law in society and the influence of morality on law must be considered. The practical limits of such a law must be analysed too: it would be unreasonable to expect a man who cannot swim to try to save a drowning person. However, as the rescuer's ability to rescue decreases and the danger involved in rescuing increases, the line to draw becomes blurred and a sensible legislature would generally give the benefit of the doubt to the rescuer, the one whose liberty is being restricted.

Ultimately, a nuanced, thoughtful response which weighs the two competing considerations is necessary. To be successful, links must be made to real-world implications, rather than just theoretical, philosophical considerations.

Q17: Is it fair to impose a height restriction on those wanting to become firefighters?

This is a general question posed within a specific scenario. Ideas about <u>non-discrimination and EU law</u> are relevant. However, it must be highlighted that functional job requirements do not constitute discrimination. Moving on from this, an intelligent candidate ought to question whether or not a height requirement is a genuine job requirement as technology may be used to overcome this. Strong candidates may be aware that public bodies are required to act 'reasonably' (which they must define).

Though their entire response need not be legally-related, this question really tests a legal style of reasoning. This means that they must be able to weigh up and consider a number of factors and be aware of the context of the supposed 'discrimination'.

Q18: Your neighbour noticed your roof had become damaged while you were away, and fixed it, are you obligated to pay him for his work?

This question links to ideas about contract: a good contract is one which predicates upon mutual consent. One cannot make a contract unilaterally -- is this assumption valid? Is it necessary? However, though some traction may be given to such a line of query, it should be accepted that the basic premise of contracts is one of agreement between free agents, who should be at liberty to make decisions and negotiate according to their individual requirements.

With regards to this question, there is a <u>minor assumption</u> that must be challenged: did you ask your neighbour to perform this service and if so, was any payment expected by either party when the agreement was made?

However, given the fact that this question has arisen, it is likely that there was no agreement, or, at most, a casual request for a favour which may have been understood. In untangling these two possibilities, it must be acknowledged that this is not a business context, and that the intention to create legal relations is improbable given that such arrangements are made informally and between (presumably) amicable neighbours who may even regard one another as friends.

Ultimately, though, one may feel it appropriate to make some sort of contribution towards the cost of painting the fence, it must be acknowledged that this is not a business relationship. It would not be fair for the neighbour to do something unilaterally and expect payment had you not expressed a wish for him specifically to paint your fence. Even if I had simply wanted someone to paint the fence and casually mentioned this to my neighbour, it would be a pleasant surprise if my neighbour did this for free. It would not be appropriate, however, for my neighbour to demand payment unless previously stipulated, or else it would be unfair to the householder who may have been able to get a cheaper price or a more skilled painter if that was what he preferred.

The best answers should make some reference to the demands of <u>actual commercial transactions</u> and draw out appropriate principles that are necessary for the proper functioning of a capitalist society.

Q19: Why should we care about the rule of law?

This is a general question which invites the candidate to talk about a range of issues. A sound definition is required for the question to be answered successfully.

Strong candidates should be aware of the different conceptions of the rule of law. It goes beyond 'the law of rules' (that laws must be enacted by the appropriate authority), but is about a culture of fairness and fair-mindedness. The debate centres on to what extent values like human rights or democratic values can be 'read in' to legislation.

This should be linked to other constitutional values like the <u>separation of powers and parliamentary sovereignty</u> and how these sometimes-competing demands need to be balanced against each other, and must be considered with reference to the values of British liberal democracy.

Strong candidates would have a wealth of examples, e.g. the Belmarsh case.

LANGUAGE INTERVIEWS

If you are applying for the French, German, Spanish, or Italian version of the course and are invited to Oxford for an interview, you should expect to be given a short oral language test as part of the interview process. Such a test is important and you must show the necessary linguistic competence. However, it is important to emphasise that the decision as to whether to offer a place on the four-year course is made first and foremost by reference to your potential as a law student, not by your performance in the oral language test.

The language test will be quite relaxed, normally with just yourself and a native speaker alone in a room. The **interview will likely be recorded**. You do not necessarily need to have a great deal of knowledge of the foreign legal system, but you should be able to articulate what it is specifically that interests you about that legal system and why you want to spend an extra year of your degree studying it. Real passion for the language, culture, and country will get you a long way too, of course!

If you are applying for the four-year Law with European Law course (to spend the year abroad in the Netherlands), you will not have this additional language interview as the course is entirely in English.

Q20: What is the difference between Course I and Course II (Law with Legal Studies in Europe) at Oxford?

Course II incorporates all the elements of course I – you will study all of the same topics in years 1, 2 and will have the same choice of options open to you when you return from your year abroad in your 4th year. The difference between the two courses lies in the additional element of the study of the foreign legal system.

In your <u>first year</u>, you will take weekly language classes (French, Italian, Spanish, German, or conversational Dutch). These classes will be around 2 hours per week. They are not obligatory but act as a really good way of allowing you to get to know the other students who you will be going abroad with in your 3rd year. They also help to keep up your language skills.

In your <u>second year</u>, you will take weekly introductory classes to your foreign legal system in the language of that legal system. These will be around 2 hours per week and there will rarely be additional work set. These are obligatory and provide a good basis on which you will build when you begin your studies on your year abroad.

In your <u>third year,</u> you will study abroad at one of the selected universities. You will have exams in your 3rd year but these marks will not count towards your final degree grade, instead, you must simply pass this year. You will likely be taking topics which first-year law students in that jurisdiction take, but your workload will likely be much lighter than the average law student. This year is an Erasmus year and you will be supported by grants from the Erasmus program. Furthermore, there are several Oxford-based grants which are available for students on Course II during their year abroad. You will be given the opportunity to completely immerse yourself in the local culture and custom, perfect your language, and get a real insight into how the law works in that country. You will also have much more spare time than you will have been used to in Oxford, given the significantly lighter workload. This means you'll have more time for travel and recreation. This is a fantastic year.

In your <u>fourth year,</u> you will be back in Oxford and your course of study will be exactly the same as that of someone on course I. You will not be examined on the foreign legal system in your finals.

GENERAL LAW QUESTIONS

Q21: What is the rule of law?

The solution to this question depends on whether or not you have heard of the rule of law. If you have, talk the interviewer through what you know, but don't leave it at that. Interviewers often want you to adopt an analytical approach to answering questions, so repeating knowledge you have about the rule of law without going any further (such as without discussing what you think of it) isn't a good answer.

If you haven't heard of the rule of law before, this does not put you at a disadvantage at all. Simply split the term up in your head and try to understand what it means. This is a good opportunity to show the interviewer your critical thinking skills by 'thinking out loud'. Going through your thought process shows the interviewer you are giving the question real reflection. The interviewer may tell you a bit about the rule of law as you consider what it means, and you can ask them questions, but don't ask them 'What is the rule of law?', since this shows a lack of analytical thinking.

Good answer (if you have not heard of the rule of law): I have not heard of the rule of law before, but I imagine it means a set of rules which can be applied to the law, almost like a higher-order law. For example, if the rule of law said laws cannot discriminate against people, you couldn't have a law that said something like 'blonde people aren't allowed to travel abroad'. Other beneficial characteristics of the law which the rule of law might cover are: clarity – because people cannot obey the law if they don't know what it covers, representation – because the name of the offence should reflect the conduct it covers, and consistency – because the law should be applied to everyone at all times, for it to be fair.

At this point you could offer an opinion on the rule of law, saying something like 'I think it is a good idea, because otherwise discriminatory and unfair laws could be enacted. However, it is important to have the right rules of law for it to be effective.'

Bad answer (if you have not heard of the rule of law): I don't know what the rule of law means. I haven't heard of it. *This is a bad answer because the interviewee has not attempted to understand the term 'rule of law'.*

Q22: Why should we care about the rule of law?

This question gives you a good opportunity to discuss the pros and cons of the rule of law. It is important to always give a balanced answer: never outline one side of the argument without analysing the points you have made and giving arguments contrary to. It is also important to offer more than one point in your answer. The interviewer will often challenge points you have made with a counter example, but this doesn't mean you are wrong, they simply want you to explain your answer with regard to their argument. Don't abandon your point and agree with them instantly, but equally don't stick to your point even if you realise you had the wrong idea. It's okay to say 'that makes me rethink my answer' and offer an alternative.

Good answer: a good answer would use the principles you discussed in relation to the rule of law, as noted above, and apply them to its importance. Such as: 'the rule of law is important because it governs the way laws are implemented. If we did not have a rule of law, laws that are unclear, unrepresentative and inconsistent could be enacted. This means a lot of people would not understand which conduct consists of an offence. Not only would this lead to more law breaking, but it could potentially lead to civil unrest because society would perceive these laws as unfair.

You could argue that Parliament is democratically elected so they should be able to enact any laws they like. However, I disagree with this, because the rule of law potentially stops corruption - since all laws have to abide by a certain standard. If an elected Parliament is trying to break this standard, then they should be prevented from doing so. The rule of law must consist of the correct standards in order to be effective though.

Bad answer: the rule of law is important because otherwise the government could do whatever they want and have no consequences. *This is a bad answer because the interviewee has not given any other reasons for the rule of law's importance or suggested why it could be dangerous.*

Q23: Is it fair to impose a height restriction on those wanting to become fire-fighters?

This question involves giving two sides of an argument and explaining which one you prefer. Weak answers will only explore one side of an argument, or only give one point for either side. You should include a range of reasons in your answer, including both practical and theoretical explanations. Picking apart the question is also a key skill which can be demonstrated here, for example, defining the word 'fair' is important in analysing answers.

Good answer: on one hand, you could argue it is discriminatory to impose height restrictions on those wanting to become fire-fighters. You are preventing people from having the career due to a factor which is outside of their control. If we define fair as giving equal opportunities to everyone, this is clearly not fair.

On the other hand, you could argue that it is fair to impose these restrictions. If we assume 'height restrictions' here encompass a minimum height requirement, you could argue that shorter fire-fighters may not be able to complete the job to the same standard as taller ones. For example, if a person was stuck at a height, a shorter fire-fighter may not be able to reach this. Therefore, you could argue that allowing shorter people to become fire-fighters is not fair to the public, since it potentially endangers them. However, instances such as these are unlikely to occur, especially because a taller fire-fighter could just help in this situation (though this could endanger the people they were trying to help).

I disagree with this argument, because I think it is a very slippery slope. Next somebody could say that women shouldn't be allowed to be fire-fighters, because they are typically less strong than men. Most people would agree that is this is unfair. Moreover, you could argue there should be a maximum height requirement to, because taller fire-fighters would find it harder to get through small spaces if needed. If we massively restrict the height requirements of fire-fighters, we will have far fewer of them, and this could endanger the public too. Additionally, from a practical standpoint, where would this restriction be drawn? If it was 170cm, then is there really a significant difference between people who are 169cm and people who are 171cm tall?

Bad answer: it would be fair because short fire fighters can't do their job as well as tall ones. *This is a bad answer because the interviewee has not given both sides of the argument, or thought of any counter-arguments to their own point.*

Q24: Your neighbour noticed your roof had become damaged while you were away, and fixed it, are you obligated to pay him for his work?

This question involves outlining both sides of an argument, before coming to a conclusion. Typically, with these types of questions, interviewers will give you more examples which push your argument to its limits. Don't be afraid to draw the line and admit when your argument no longer makes sense, but don't immediately abandon your point with no further explanation.

Good answer: on one hand, I should not have to pay the neighbour because I did not ask him to fix the roof. In fact, I could go further and argue he has interfered with my property without my consent, perhaps he has even trespassed on it!

On the other hand, perhaps my neighbour thought I wanted him to fix my roof. I am not sure if this would make a difference to the outcome, but it is a consideration. If he thought I wanted him to fix my roof and had reasonable belief for thinking so, I suppose you could argue that I should pay him for fixing it. Moreover, if my collapsing roof was a danger to the public or to my neighbour himself, you could argue that I had a duty to fix the roof, so a duty to pay him back for fixing it.

Despite this, if my neighbour fixed the roof with an expensive and unnecessary material, so I could have fixed the roof myself for much cheaper, I suppose there is an argument against me paying him back.

However, taking this wider, if I did not pay my neighbour back this means he would be less likely to help again. Perhaps not imposing a duty on me to pay him back actually discourages acts of public service, so for policy reasons such a duty should be implemented.

Bad answer:

No because I did not ask him to do it. *This is a bad answer because the interviewee has only given one reason and not justified it very far. They should also aim to give two sides to the argument in every question.*

Q25: What does it mean to 'take' another's car?

This question involves defining key terms: such as 'take'. It is okay if you do not know the dictionary (or legal) definition of the word 'take', you are not expected to know it at all. Just go through your thought process and give examples for everything you say, and the interviewer may challenge your definition to push it to its limits. This does not mean your definition is bad, if anything it means it is good – they are interested in what you have to say in defending your answer. Don't worry about changing your mind, but also don't do this instantly and with no further explanation. If you do change your mind, it is a good idea to offer an alternative answer. Also, avoid giving 'circular' definitions, such as using the word 'take' in your definition of 'take'.

Good answer: I think taking another's car means using it without their permission, or in a way they did not consent to. For example, if my friend lent me their car and said I wasn't allowed to drive it on the motorway, and I did, then I think this would be taking the car as they did not consent to the way I used it. This also covers the typical examples like breaking into a car on the street and driving it away too.

The interviewer may say: what if your car was unlocked on the road and it was raining, so I got into it to avoid the rain and didn't touch anything, then got out again when it stopped raining?

In this case, you could say something like: well, I think that would be taking by my definition. I had not consented to you using my car as shelter from the rain. I suppose you could say you had reasonable belief that I would consent, maybe if you thought that anyone would let someone shelter in their car in the event of rain, but if I was a stranger I think that is quite a weak argument to make.

Bad answer: taking another's car means taking it away from them when they haven't told you that you can. *This is a bad answer because the interviewee's definition of take is circular, and they haven't given any examples that apply to their definition.*

Q26: If traffic wardens had the legal right to execute people caught parking in restricted areas, and as a result no one did, would this be considered a fair and effective law?

This question requires splitting up: you need to consider, in turn, if the penalty is effective, and if the penalty is just. Defining each of these terms would also be helpful here, as a standard to measure your answers against. You should consider the wider implications for this law, and any practical considerations that need to be made.

Good answer: I think this penalty would not be just, but it would be effective. Considering the former, it would not be just because the punishment of the crime does not represent the nature of the wrongdoing, or the severity of the conduct. It is important for laws and punishments to be proportionate to the offence, and this is definitely not. Parking on double yellow is a very low-level crime, and the death penalty is often associated with the most severe crimes such as murder or terrorism. Aside from representation, there is another issue of justness here. If the penalty of parking on double yellow is death, what is the penalty for murder? If this is also death, you are arguably putting murderers on par with people who commit parking offences, which is not fair at all.

However, the penalty would be effective because, as it says in the question, 'nobody did it'. One of the primary aims of law is to prevent people from breaking it, so this is fulfilled. Though the penalty acts as a deterrent, it does not allow offenders to better themselves and positively contribute to society, which is arguably another aim of law.

Bad answer: no because you are killing people for parking on double yellow lines, which doesn't make sense. *This is a bad answer because the interviewee has not justified their point further than 'which doesn't make sense'. They have also not split up the question into 'just' and 'effective'.*

Q27: If we lived without malice and ill intent, would there be any need to have the law?

This question is quite tricky because it involves you having to explore the aims of the law itself and see if they remain valid even if everyone was an angel. Better answers will give an in-depth and thoughtful analysis of the question and the aims of the law themselves. Weaker answers will give a one-sided and simplistic approach to answering the question and fall into the trap of saying 'no' and leaving it at that.

Good answer: well, I think you have to explore what the purpose of the law is and see if it is still needed if the world was full of good people to answer this question. The aims of law are potentially: to 1) maximise the freedom of individuals, 2) maintain order in society, 3) satisfy the basic needs of people and 4) to protect individual rights. If everyone was an angel, then you wouldn't need 4) because nobody's rights would be endangered. Further, not having the law at all could give everyone maximum freedom as outlined in 1), so it is not required for that either. However, I think laws could still be needed to satisfy purpose 2), because, even if everyone was good, there would still need to be basic rules so society can function beneficially and productively. This applies to 3) too, since laws often govern things like benefits which some people need. I suppose you argue that these things could be covered by conventions, things that everyone just does as a matter of common practise, but putting them into law would arguably make them clearer and therefore easier to follow.

Bad answer: No because everyone would be really good so they wouldn't need to be told to not kill anyone. *This is a bad answer because the interviewee has not justified their point and not given both sides of the argument.*

Q28: Do the girl scouts have a political agenda? Can any organisation be truly 'apolitical'?

This question is quite odd, and the answers to it can cover a very wide range of things. If you know about the girl scouts' affiliation with Trump, you could discuss that. If not, you could explore the topic and suggest some hypotheticals which would/would not mean they have a political agenda. You are not expected to know any prior information for the interview, so don't worry if something like this comes up and it feels like the question is hinting at a piece of information you do not know. The interviewer just wants to see your thought process, and I do think this is quite a hard question, so just give it a go and reason any points you make.

Good answer: I think this question is very dependent on what the girl scouts do. If the girl scouts put all of their profits back into the organisation, I don't think they do have a political agenda, unless perhaps they are funded by a political party. If the girl scouts fund a political party themselves, or a politically controversial organisation, you could argue they do have a political agenda. For example, if the girl scouts donated to an anti-abortion church organisation, you could argue that they do have a political agenda because they financially support one. Likewise, if they themselves are funded by such a company, this suggests a similar thing. However, I don't think they do have an agenda as such. Other companies could donate to political organisations too, and I think it is the buyer's prerogative to decide whether or not to buy from them.

Bad answer: I don't know. *This is a bad answer because the interviewee has not attempted to understand the question or work through their thought process out loud. The interviewee should also give examples to illustrate any points they make.*

Q29: Why do you want to study law?

There is no right answer to this question, it is very subjective and should be completely personal to you, rather than just repeating somebody else's answer! However, there are tips to make your answer stronger. For example, try and link your answer to your personal statement- this gives a sense of continuity. However, do not just repeat what you said in your statement and give no further reasons or explanation — this will just make the interviewer think you're not that bothered about studying law! Also, try and avoid cliches like 'I am passionate about law'- you may well be passionate about a certain area of law or a certain aim involved with law, but specify this — nobody is passionate about the boring bits of law like administration.

Good answer: I chose to apply for law because I am interested in learning more about the interdependence between philosophy, law and politics within our constitutional infrastructure. Appreciating the subtleties of the relationship between these entities will enable me to develop a broad knowledge of the law as a whole and how it works in practise. Once I have this knowledge, I want to use it to drive positive change in the context of human rights law, a cause I am deeply passionate about. When I was doing work experience at Latham and Watkins, I met a lawyer who was working on making FGM illegal across Africa. I would really love to use my knowledge of the law and apply it to causes such as these, representing vulnerable people. I am also interested in learning about why the law is the way it is, and how it can be reformed to enhance its aims of protecting individual rights and maximising liberty for all.

Bad answer: I want to study law because I am passionate about it and I want to be a lawyer when I'm older. I think that law is really interesting. *This is a bad answer because the interviewee is very general about law, and has not specified a specific area they are interested in. They have also not given any specific reasons as to why they want to study law.*

Q30: If someone unintentionally commits a crime, are they guilty?

This question involves an exploration of intention- whether or not someone meant to do something. You are not expected to have any prior knowledge of the law, but you may have an idea of intention and recklessness from your reading – don't worry if not, though. Weaker answers will give one side of the argument, and not justify their points. Stronger answers will explore both sides of the argument and consider wider 'policy reasons' in deciding which one they prefer.

Good answer: on one hand, you could say the person is not guilty as they do not have the intention to commit the crime. They did not set out to do it, as it says in the question, so they didn't commit the crime on purpose and therefore should not be guilty of it.

On the other hand, there is a difference between intention and recklessness. If I climbed up onto neighbour's roof and accidentally kicked the tiles off it, even if I did not intend to commit criminal damage, I still did. Most people would consider damaging the tiles reasonably likely to result from climbing up the roof, and I arguably should have thought of this before I did so. Therefore, I was being reckless so still committed the crime. However, if I was not such a reasonable person, for example I was 10, then this should be measured against my own sense of what is reasonably likely and what isn't, to avoid people being held to a standard they cannot reach for one reason or another. If most 10-year-olds would not foresee criminal damage being caused in this instance, and I didn't, then I would not be guilty of the crime as I did not have the intention and I wasn't reckless.

Bad answer: yes they are guilty because they still committed the crime. *This is a bad answer because the interviewee has not justified their point very far, and has not considered that the person may not be guilty in some instances.*

Q31: When should the state be allowed to violate your privacy?

This question involves a debate between freedom and protection, which is an important balance to strike in every area of the law. Stronger answers will give two sides to the argument and outline specific examples where the state has the right to violate privacy, and where it does not. Weaker answers will give short and unjustified points. If you don't know any specific examples of where the state can violate privacy, just think of hypotheticals where you think it would be justified.

Good answer: the state has the right to violate privacy in cases where the priority of protection outweighs the priority of freedom. For example, I don't think the state should have the right to read people's messages in most instances, to maximise their individual liberty. However, I think when reading messages are in the best interests of the public or the individual themselves (such as when an individual goes missing or in the case of a potential terrorist attack) then it is justified. It is important to strike this balance right. If there is too much unjustified state violation of privacy, then liberty is compromised, and this could lead to civil unrest. If there is too little, then individuals are potentially unprotected.

Bad answer: the state has the right to violate privacy because it is in the interests of the public that they do so. *This is a bad answer because the individual has not given any examples or other arguments to illustrate their point.*

Q32: Should anyone have the right to invade our privacy?

This question looks at an evaluative side to the previous one, which asks for when the state should have the right to violate our privacy. As noted above, the key to these questions is the debate between maximising protection and individual liberty: the autonomy v welfare debate. Stronger answers will give two sides of the argument and give examples for each of them. Weaker answers will give unjustified and one-sided points.

Good answer: the state should have the right to violate our privacy, but only in limited circumstances. Although giving the state unlimited power to violate privacy would arguably maximise protection of citizens, it compromises individual liberty and leaves the state vulnerable to corruption. Moreover, there are concerns of hacking and data protection if the state violates privacy more than it needs to. Despite this, giving the state no power to violate privacy, though upholding individual liberty, doesn't protect citizens. Therefore, there needs to be a balance respecting both principles. For example, if a person has been killed then suspects' internet history should be able to be looked at – because protection is the priority in this case. But in ordinary circumstances, things like messages and emails shouldn't be read because liberty should be the priority here.

Bad answer: the state should not have the right to violate privacy because they could potentially exploit this. *This is a good point but needs to be expanded upon. Also, giving the other side of the argument is a good idea in this case. The autonomy v welfare debate is central to this question, so any responses must address both of these principles and judge the law against them and the relationship between them. Giving situations which justify state violation of privacy and situations where it is not justified is a good idea in these sorts of question.*

Q33: Do you think that the state should be more free to operate as it chooses than the media is?

This question requires the interviewee to give a balanced argument and coming to a justified conclusion. It is similar to the ones above since, again, it balances protection and individual liberty. In law, this is called the autonomy vs welfare debate, but you are not expected to know this. The question is essentially asking you to consider real-world examples and put them into theoretical questions and weigh up different opinions on the issue before deciding which one you agree with. In law, it is really important to always give two sides of the argument. Stronger answers will also undermine arguments contrary to their point, so their conclusion appears more justified.

Good answer: On one hand, media regulation by the state would decrease the spread of 'fake news' which we have seen increase in recent years, especially with conspiracy theories surrounding the COVID vaccine and the origin of the disease. Moreover, media regulation by the state could control extremism recruitment done online and damaging posts on social media such as those promoting self-harm. Although this would undermine freedom of speech and, potentially, individual liberty, it would protect people from harmful things in the media.

On the other hand, media regulation by the state could be used to silence political opposition, any political controversies the executive wants to hide and cover up government scandal. The danger of handing more control to the state over media is that it leaves media control open to exploitation and autocracy. Therefore, a balance needs to be struck between liberty and protection. Perhaps having an independent body which can review media regulation by the state would be a way of achieving this.

Bad answer: the media should be increasingly controlled by the state because otherwise they could spread fake news. *This is a bad answer as there is only one reason for the person's point, and no counter arguments are given.*

Q34: What is the role of honesty in law?

This question suggests a knowledge of the law is needed to answer it, but it is really important to remember that no prior knowledge of the law is needed for an interview. Some people may have some knowledge, but it in no way gives them an advantage- all the interviewer wants to see is you going through your thought process out loud and give a wide range of arguments and counter-arguments to support your point: deliberation is key. This is quite a difficult question simply because it is so vague, but you can actually talk about a wide range of things, so don't worry if you would answer it differently to the sample answers below.

Good answer: honesty fits into law in a wide range of instances. For one, at a judgement level, a person could receive a lesser sentence if they are honest about any crimes they have committed. Also, if a person honestly believes something to be the case and this belief is reasonable, this sometimes means they do not commit the crime. For example, in rape, if you honestly believed someone was consenting to sex and you had justification to think this (i.e. the belief is reasonable) then it is not rape, even if the person did not consent. This can be quite problematic, because the idea of a reasonable and an honest belief are both very subjective ideas so they can be interpreted in multiple ways. Equally, defining reasonable and honest belief narrowly and giving little judicial discretion also means a person may be held to a standard they cannot reach: what may be reasonable for them may but be found as reasonable by the court.

Bad answer: honesty fits into law because if you reasonably believe something to be the case then sometimes it means a crime has not been committed. *This is a bad answer because, although the point is good, there are no examples or wider remarks about how having such a provision could be good or bad.*

Q35: Should the law protect people from themselves?

This question is very philosophical, so it requires a good deal of deliberation of multiple arguments and lots of points and examples given. It is a way for the interviewer to see how you think in terms of what the law is and what it should be like: rather than just the substantive aspects of it and what the law actually says. The most important thing is to give a balanced argument. Interviewers may argue with some of your points, so listen to their contention and try to reconcile it with your point or perhaps explain why you don't agree with it (respectfully). If you find yourself abandoning your point, don't be afraid to do this, but equally don't do it immediately: the interviewer wants you to try to rationalise their points. Every argument can be pushed to its limits, and this is what they're trying to demonstrate.

Good answer: you could argue that the law already does exist to protect us from ourselves, to an extent. For example, people can be detained for their own safety under the mental health act and, if someone attempts to harm or kill themselves, hospitals are under a duty to look after them until it is safe for them to go home. Another example is the law on euthanasia, which remains illegal here. I don't think the law should exist to protect us from ourselves further than these very limited examples, because otherwise it violates individual freedom. The debate key to this question is the autonomy v welfare debate, and having the law exist to protect us from ourselves means the balance shifts to welfare, infringing on autonomy. Despite this, I do agree with detention under the mental health act since an individual is not in the right state of mind to make decisions regarding harming themselves if they are in a bad place. The law on euthanasia is far blurrier, and I think it infringes on autonomy because the majority of the people who want to partake in it have chronic and long-term health conditions and have given the idea a great deal of thought.

Bad answer: the law should not exist to protect us from ourselves because we know what we want to do and should be allowed to do it. *This is a bad answer because it gives no examples of where legal intervention is justified, and no counter arguments too. Also, they do not address the idea that we should be allowed to do what we like as long as we don't infringe on other people's rights, which is important to their point.*

Q36: Can a law ever be truly just if it restricts our freedom to do something?

This question is a bit similar to the one above, since the autonomy vs welfare debate is key to it. If you haven't heard of this before, don't worry, but it can be a very useful thing to know in the interview for wider, more philosophical points considering the law. Autonomy an idea of individual liberty, everyone should be able to do what they like. Welfare is a paternalistic idea, that the law should protect people and make sure their rights are upheld. Balancing these two principles is essentially one of the main things that the law aims to do, so it is a good evaluative tool to use when analysing whether or not the law is effective.

Good answer: on one hand, you could say if a law limits our freedom, then it is unjust with regard to autonomy. If we cannot do what we like because the law has placed constraints on it, then the principle of autonomy is not being upheld, and is potentially even violated, so if autonomy is the standard of justness then it is an unjust law. On the other hand, I think that in limited exceptions the law is just even if it restricts our freedom to do something. The law aims to uphold autonomy, but it also aims to uphold the welfare principle: so, in some cases one of these will need to be curtailed to respect the other. For example, the law restricts our freedom to infringe upon another's rights, like by murdering or stealing from them, which is just since it upholds the other person's welfare. Also, if we are attempting to harm ourselves then the law can intervene, to uphold our own welfare. There are arguments that the law goes to far towards the welfare principle in cases such as abortion and euthanasia, so there is definitely scope for reform and reconsideration in these.

Bad answer: the law is unjust if it restricts our autonomy because it violates individual liberty, and this should be upheld. *This is a bad answer as it doesn't consider any instances were violating autonomy may be justified or offer any further explanation of their point. You shouldn't really give one-sentence answers to these sorts of questions in the interview, but don't be afraid to take some time to think about your answer before saying it.*

Q37: Should laws ever govern what we can and cannot say?

This question involves a consideration of what the law aims to uphold and some limited examples of where freedom of speech can be limited. Avoid giving unbalanced and heavily political answers, interviewers want to see you can step away from politics and view the law from a more philosophical perspective. Of course, some political comment is good and brings your answer into the real world, but too much runs the risk of actually offending one of your interviewer's or making it look like you should be in a PPE interview instead.

Good answer: on one hand, the law should not restrict our freedom of speech. Freedom of speech is integral to individual liberty, one of the principles the law seeks to uphold. We should be able to say what we like, otherwise it is a slippery slope into a state where our non-criminal actions and more and more of what we say is restricted by the law. That is, it becomes more controlling.

On the other hand, the law should restrict our freedom of speech in some cases. For examples, it is illegal to issue death threats to people, and to defame people online. Moreover, hate speech is also illegal. The law should restrict freedom of speech in these limited instances because it arguably violates other people's rights – such as the right not to be discriminated against in the case of hate speech. The slippery slope argument is valid, but it should just promote consideration of restricting freedom of speech, rather than not doing it at all. Some countries such as France go further than us, and criminalise holocaust denial, so there is arguably need for reform and greater consideration in this area.

Bad answer: the law should not restrict our freedom of speech because otherwise it is telling us what to say, which is unjustified. *This is a bad answer because it gives no examples of where the law should not restrict our freedom of speech, and no arguments or examples of where it should.*

Q38: How would you place a value on life? Would you shoot a baby to save another person, to save a thousand people?

This question involves an interesting philosophical principle: do the means justify the ends? If you have studied RS or philosophy at GCSE or A-Level then feel free to use some of the arguments you learnt in these subjects here, and in any other question for that matter. Try not to get bogged down in the subject matter though. If not, do not worry, just consider arguments for and against the question and come to a balanced conclusion.

Good answer: this question involves a discussion of whether the means justify the ends. I would argue they do not, in this case. From a utilitarian, teleological perspective, you should shoot the baby to save x number of people, provided x is greater than 1. This is because the greatest overall happiness should be promoted, and the means justify the ends. However, from a Kantian, deontological perspective, this is not the case because the action matters more than the outcome, so the means do not justify the ends.

I would agree with the latter of these perspectives, because where is the line drawn, and what factors should be considered? In this case, the baby (and everyone else) would die if no action was taken. But what if you were on a runaway train and the track you're on has two people on it, but you can change the track to another lane, which will hit a baby? In this case, important judgements need to be considered. Would it make a difference if the track you're headed onto has 100 people on it instead of two people on it? What if these people all had three months to live, but the baby had years and years? Essentially, examples like the baby in the shopping centre can be pushed further and further to their limits and involve judgements of the worth of one life over the worth of another. I do not think we are qualified to make such judgements, so I don't agree with shooting the baby in any case.

Bad answer: yes because otherwise the baby and everyone else will die. *This is a bad answer as, although the point is good, there is no further justification for it. The individual should also consider the other side of the argument and push it a bit further to other examples.*

Q39: Do you think that euthanasia should be legal?

This question involves a consideration of euthanasia and assisted suicide. While it would be beneficial to know a bit of the current law on this, it is not essential. That said, it is helpful for interviews if you keep up with the news about things such as euthanasia, as they often come up. The current law largely prohibits euthanasia and assisted suicide in the UK. Doctors are allowed to give pain relief medication for the purpose of said pain relief, even if such medication has the consequence of shortening a person's life, but this is the only instance in which euthanasia is legal. People do travel to Dignitas to die, but if they travel with a family member to help them, then that family member can (in principle) be prosecuted, though there is a large amount of discretion in this area. If you didn't know any of this in the interview (and you don't have to), just say something like 'I'm not sure about the current law on this, but…' and you will be fine.

Good answer: I think people should have the right to die, but in very limited cases. On one hand, there are arguments for having the right to die in lots of cases. If there is a right to life, perhaps there should be a right to end that life. If a person has a very bad quality of life, they should be allowed to end it. The law promotes individual autonomy, and the right to die is arguably a necessary provision of this.

On the other hand, the law has a duty to protect people's welfare. A person may not be in their right mind when they decide to die, and as a society maybe cases of euthanasia are actually indicative of our failings to protect the vulnerable: maybe increasing funding to areas which support such people is a better option than allowing people to die. Moreover, allowing people to die means there is less funding going towards terminal illnesses, simply because there are fewer people living with those illnesses.

Despite this, I think euthanasia should be allowed in very limited cases and with provisions such as required counselling and approval for people who want to go through it. This prevents people from making rash decisions.

Bad answer: people should not have the right to die because life is sacred and given by God, so we are not allowed to take it away. *This is a bad answer because it only considers one argument (sanctity of life) and does not consider things such as if an individual is non-religious etc. Aim to give a balanced argument in all of your answers.*

Q40: Should overweight people have to pay extra on planes if they need to take two seats?

This question involves giving a balanced argument to what is quite a current debate. Try and give examples for both sides of your argument, and examples which show the limits of your points. A nuanced answer is key to questions like this, so try and draw distinctions between different situations and apply them to your argument.

Good answer: overweight people should not have to pay extra on planes if they need to take two seats. While some people are overweight because of an unhealthy lifestyle, some people are overweight because of a chronic condition or even a disability. While there are arguments for why airlines should be able to charge them for two seats- because they are taking up the same amount of seats as two people so should be charged as such, and because in some cases being overweight is a choice, I don't agree with these. What 'weight limit' would be imposed if overweight people were charged for two seats? What if they took up 1 and a quarter seats? Could the same be extended to disabled people who take up 2 seats? While you could argue being disabled is not a choice, nor is being overweight in cases of a thyroid condition, mental health conditions, economic status and things like that, and there is often a multitude of factors which contribute to someone being overweight so there is no way of effectively judging them, and to do so is quite disrespectful.

Bad answer: fat people should have to pay extra on planes because the airline is losing money by letting them on if they take up two seats. *This is a bad answer because it does not consider any arguments to the contrary. Also, they should offer alternative scenarios where this economic argument would not work, as well as scenarios which would work along these lines.*

Q41: Do you think it is legally justifiable to charge for access to a toilet in a closed environment like an aeroplane?

This question involves giving two sides of an argument, even though it appears to be relatively simple. Try and give both sides of the debate anyway and give examples to illustrate each of your points. A nuanced approach is key to this question, so try and reflect this as much as possible in your response.

Good answer: airlines should not be allowed to charge people for using the toilet on a plane. Although there are economic reasons why it would be beneficial for the airline to do this, they have a duty of care to their passengers and I think this includes giving them easy access to toilet facilities. For example, should a mother be forced to pay to use the toilet when she has to change her baby's nappy? Should a disabled person who cannot wait to use the toilet be forced to pay for it on an aeroplane? I think that enabling airlines to charge for use of toilet facilities impacts the most vulnerable people in society, and it is even potentially discriminatory in that respect. People should have a right of access to a toilet at all times. Despite this, at some train stations you have to pay to use the toilet, so I suppose implementing a similar policy on aircraft is not a far extension. However, I disagree with the policy in train stations and think toilet fares should be abolished nation-wide.

Bad answer: yes, because people choose to go on the aeroplane so they know ahead of time whether or not they have to pay to use the toilet. If people can afford a plane ticket, they are unlikely to not be able to afford a small fee for using the toilet. *This is a bad answer, though these are potentially good points, because the interviewee has only given one side of the argument and given no examples to justify their point.*

Q42: Should a jury of peers be selected based on the IQ of the defendant?

This question involves considering the justice system and potential reforms that could be made to it. Try and always give a wide range of views and examples on controversial questions like these, even if the question seems to only have one answer, attempt to understand the other side of the argument and say something along the lines of 'some people would argue that... but I disagree because...'. This gives your opinion, but shows you understand the other side too.

Good answer: on one hand, imposing a minimum IQ for jurors in a trial could be a good thing. It means jurors are potentially more intelligent, so more capable of making a reasoned and informed decision. Though it could be construed as offence, when serious offences and people's lives are on the line, it is important for the justice system to be as fair and as effective as possible, and a minimum IQ could go some way towards that.

On the other hand, I disagree with imposing a minimum IQ for jurors. Firstly, what would this IQ be? What about the people who are only just below it? Intelligence is not binary and cannot be defined by a simple IQ test, and there is evidence to suggest IQ tests are not actually very reliable anyway. Imposing such a restriction is potentially discriminatory, and the point of a jury is to give a cross-section of society, and this is inhibited if you are only allowing the 'clever' people in society to be a part of it. Deciding a person's guilt does not have much to do with intelligence, you simply listen to the evidence and both sides of the case and give an informed judgement.

Bad answer: yes it would be a good idea but it is unfair for the people who wouldn't be allowed to be jurors. *This is a good point and a somewhat balanced argument, but the person has not justified why the idea would be good. There are also no examples given here.*

Q43: What would a country without law be like?

This question is quite difficult and requires a high level of deliberation regarding a hypothetical situation. Try and give a range of different points with justification and examples for each one. For questions like these, you can also give a non-straightforward answer, as you can see below. This would take your answer to another level.

Good answer: I don't think it is possible to live in a country with no laws, or at least no rules. Even if we abandoned the law completely and people could do whatever they like, I think a body of custom would build up and essentially do the same thing as the law, but without judicial interpretation and official punishments. For example, even if there was no law governing trespassing, I don't think people would do it all the time just for reasons of custom and convention. In early civilisations, religion acted as a kind of 'law' for some people, and you weren't allowed to do things like use God's name in vain, so I think custom would act in a similar way to this. On the other hand, the only punishment for breaking these conventions would be being an outcast from society, instead of prison or fines etc, so I do think there would be more 'criminal' behaviour simply because there are fewer consequences. However, I do not think a society without laws would be total chaos because of the strength of societal convention and the fear of becoming an 'outcast' or having people take punishment into their own hands.

Bad answer: It would be dangerous to live in a country without laws because people would just do what they like with no consequences for their actions. *This is a bad answer because the interviewee only gives one point and does not give examples to illustrate it.*

Q44: In France, you are legally obligated to help a person you see in distress, for instance, if they are drowning in a river. Why do you think we don't have a law like this, should we?

This question involves a discussion of the pros and cons of omissions liability. All of the information you need to know about omissions liability is in the question, so don't worry if you don't know anything about its technicalities. It is important to consider policy reasons in these types of question: these are reasons which are essentially practicalities and consider how the law would actually work, rather than its hypothetical nature. It is a good idea to take a step back and look at the wider part of the law when you answer questions like these, especially when considering reform.

Good answer: on one hand, this should be the case in the UK. The law aims to protect people and imposing this legal obligation would lead to more people being protected and lives would be saved- this is clearly a good thing, so the obligation should be enacted. On the other hand, I don't think this should be the case in the UK. I don't know how the obligation operates in France, but there are too many questions and variables which would need defining for the law to work here. For example, would I have to save the drowning person if I myself could not swim? What if I was deathly afraid of the water? How far out would I have to swim before my 'obligation' was discharged? Would 100 people on a beach have to swim out to see if someone was drowning there and, if they did not, would all 100 people be prosecuted? These standards would have to be defined and, even if they were, there are always borderline cases in which the law is unknown. This raises issues of legal certainty because some people would not know whether or not they have discharged their obligation, or whether it applies to them in the first place. Also, there is a point about autonomy. There are issues surrounding whether or not the law can infringe upon individual liberty by forcing you to do something, rather than just inhibiting you from doing it as in most cases of criminal law. Forcing people to save people while drowning sets a precedent that the law can force people to do other things, which could be dangerous in practice.

Bad answer: yes because more lives would be saved. *This is a bad answer because the person does not give any examples or counter arguments to their point.*

Q45: Should the law be absolute, or black and white, or should it be more flexible?

This question requires a detailed consideration of the law and how it can be reformed. Strong answers consider two sides of the coin, rather than one, and give detailed and justified points. Weaker answers tend to have a lack of examples, and a largely one-sided argument. Signposting in interview answers is always a good idea and gives your answer a lot of structure, which interviewers love.

Good answer: on one hand, the law should be black and white. Firstly, this means everyone is clear on what the law is and whether or not their conduct is against it. Secondly, this makes the law easier to follow, as it is clearer. Thirdly, it means everyone is held to the same standard, which arguably means the law is fairer.

On the other hand, I think the law should look at individual cases to an extent. There are always going to be subjective questions in determining whether someone has broken the law. For example, theft requires dishonestly appropriating the property of another- so analysing whether or not someone's conduct matches this is not always going to be a black or white yes or no. Also, the point I made about everyone being held to the same standard can be undermined. Some individuals have different levels of capacity to others, so their judgement in law should reflect this. The criminal age of responsibility is 10, and an 11-year-old should not be held to the same standard as a 50-year-old- there needs to be some level of discretion, or the most vulnerable people in society (like the young and the disabled) can be impacted.

Bad answer: the law should be black and white because it makes it easier for judges to decide whether or not someone is guilty. *This is a bad answer because there is a lack of a balanced argument and there are no examples given to illustrate the person's point.*

Q46: Should the law be based on morality?

This question involves a consideration of what the law is based on and what it should be based on. As always, giving a balanced argument is key here. Try and step away from the hypothetical and think about how this would affect the real world too. After all, the law impacts everyone, it is not a purely hypothetical being.

Good answer: on one hand, the law should be based on morality. This is because it might be easier for people to understand the rationale behind the law if it is inherently moral, and therefore they may be more inclined to follow it. Also, society could be united by the law if it is grounded on a set of morals that are common to everyone, which could increase the overall happiness and productivity of civilisation.

On the other hand, I think this is very utopian and unlikely to happen in practice. If the law was based on morality, what morality would it be based on? There is never going to be an entire set of morals everyone agrees on, and why should the law impose a set of morals on someone that doesn't necessarily agree with them? If the law was based on morals, there could be civil unrest for those who don't agree with its basis. For example, some people may think it is okay (or it shouldn't be governed by law) to cheat on someone, but others may think it should be. There is no way of keeping everyone 100% happy. Also, if the law was based on morals, are there any areas which it wouldn't govern? It may be considered immoral to lie, but most people wouldn't want this governed by the law in all instances. Where would the line be drawn between moral laws and morals?

Bad answer: the law should not be based on morality as everyone disagrees on what is moral. *This is a bad answer because the interviewee only gives one point, and only one side of the argument. They do not consider why it could be beneficial having a law based on morality.*

Q47: Let's say that overnight, the Supreme Court took ownership of all judicial functions previously allocated to the House of Lords – what changes?

Although it may seem like it, this question does not require any prior knowledge of the law. It would be helpful to know that the House of Lords is linked to the Houses of Parliament, who enact law, but this can be known through reading the news etc. The question is getting at something called the separation of powers, which is the idea that the legislature (House of Commons), the judiciary (courts) and the executive (government) should be separate to prevent tyranny and to increase efficiency in proceedings. The House of Lords used to be the apex court in England and Wales (the highest court), which is what the question is addressing. This is not needed, but it is helpful to know things like this to seem really knowledgeable and well-read in the interview.

Good answer: I think this will increase public support of the House of Lords and the Supreme Court. Because the House of Lords is linked to the House of Commons, and the Lords are not elected, some people think it is unfair and illegitimate that they decided high-up cases in law. Although the judges in the Supreme Court are also not elected, they are impartial and are not linked to politics, which is not the case for the Lords. Also, the Supreme Court could scrutinise legislation of the House of Commons if it was challenged by a case, which might be hard for the House of Lords to do since it is linked to the House of Commons. It will therefore increase efficiency of proceedings also.

Bad answer: I don't know what the judicial functions of the House of Lords were, so I don't know what impact giving them to the Supreme Court would have. *This is a bad answer because the person does not attempt to rationalise the question and think it through, they just automatically get put off by the fact they don't know much about the topic and leave it at that.*

Q48: Should the legislature and executive be kept separate?

The question, like the one above, is getting at something called the separation of powers, which is the idea that the legislature (House of Commons), the judiciary (courts) and the executive (government) should be separate to prevent tyranny and to increase efficiency in proceedings. The executive executes laws, the legislature amends and enforces them and the judiciary interprets laws, developing a common law precedent. You are not expected to know this, but it would be helpful to in this question. If a question you weren't familiar with the material of came up, just go through your thought process and give reasons and examples for everything you say. The interviewer wants to see you react to unfamiliar material and think on your feet.

Good answer: on one hand, the politicians and the judges should not be kept separate because judges are not elected and politicians are, so having elected people oversee everything could increase the legitimacy of the judicial system as the public sees it. Despite this, I think it would be more beneficial to keep politicians and judges separate. If politicians enacted laws and enforced them, they have too much control and could violate people's freedom or become corrupt very easily. Having an impartial set of judges, even though they're not elected, means Parliament's laws are scrutinised, so the branches of government impose checks on each other. Also, having them separate could increase efficiency of proceedings. Moreover, politicians are elected but they belong to parties who can pressure them to act in a certain way through the use of party whips. Just because they are elected, doesn't make politicians automatically legitimate.

Bad answer: no because judges aren't elected so their actions should be overseen by politicians. *This is a bad answer because it is quite crude and doesn't offer a very nuanced approach to the question.*

Q49: Do you think that judges should be elected?

This question involves a consideration of potential reforms to the justice system. Although it can be hard to think of points for both sides of the argument for questions like this, it is very important to try and do so. Unbalanced arguments can be seen as overly simplistic and not very thought out. The separation of powers, as discussed above, is also relevant here. This is the idea that there are three branches of government (the legislature, the executive and the judiciary) and these should be kept separate to prevent tyranny and increase efficiency.

Good answer: on one hand, it would not be wrong for judges to be elected. If judges are deciding on whether people are guilty of a crime, and sentencing those people, they should be elected by the public as their job directly impacts them. Politicians are elected for similar reasons. Also, it may increase people's faith in the justice system if judges were elected, which would decrease activism and civil unrest surrounding it. On the other hand, judges should not be elected. People arguably don't know enough about the justice system to elect judges who will be effective, though this could be combatted by issuing information about the justice system. However, if judges were elected, they could end up being a party system like in Parliament, which brings politics into law and violates judicial impartiality. It may also be confusing for people to vote for politicians and judges separately. Judges are supposed to scrutinise acts of Parliament which, if elected in a way which brings politics into law, cannot really be done effectively.

Bad answer: no because judges impact people so people should have a say in who is a judge. *This is a bad answer because the interviewee has only given one side of the argument and has not justified their point very well.*

Q50: Which legal barriers prevent daily wars?

This question is quite political, but also involves international law. Try and think out loud, because it is quite difficult, so just let the interviewer know what your thought process is as you go through it. If you don't know anything, just have an educated guess and consider that it must be something to do with law, because you're in a law interview. The interviewer is looking for a range of ideas in this question, and to see how you react to subject material you are potentially unfamiliar. Moreover, they are looking for your ability to make connections between law and other areas (such as politics, like in this question).

Good answer: there are a variety of things that stop countries from invading each other on a daily basis. Firstly, there are treaties which encourage countries not to do this. Secondly, if a country did invade another country without justification, other nations could place trade sanctions on it. The perpetrating country could therefore suffer economic sanctions. Thirdly, if a country did invade another country without justification, other countries would be hesitant to collaborate with them, and their own citizens could perceive the government as illegitimate, causing potential civil unrest or even an uprising. There are also international laws which could be broken by unjustified invasion of a country, and resolutions as implemented by the UN. There is also the threat of another country taking military action against the perpetrator too.

Bad answer: I don't know, I guess countries can invade each other on a daily basis and just choose not to. *This is a bad answer because the interviewee does not analyse why countries choose not to invade each other (usually) and doesn't explain their thought process, even if they don't know much about the subject matter of the question.*

Q51: A simple case, a cyclist is hit by a car, only they were cycling in a car lane rather than the adjacent cycle lane – who is liable? Does your answer change if the cyclist had taken no measures to be visible at night?

This question requires putting the law into real-world examples, such as the one given. Try and give multiple and justified points which back up the conclusion you come to. Then consider the second example, and try to rationalise that with your conclusion, or perhaps tweak it so the ideas are reconciled. In this question, the interviewer is looking for your ability to structure answers and treat two ideas differently.

Good answer: on one hand, in the first instance, the cyclist is liable because he was not cycling in the designated lane. On the other hand, the motorist could be liable because cyclists are allowed to cycle on roads – it is not illegal – and the motorist is under a duty to drive carefully. During the day, he should have been able to clearly see and avoid the cyclist. He has therefore not done his duty of carefully driving, so I would say the motorist is liable in this case.

However, in the second case, I think the cyclist is liable. Though the motorist is under a duty to drive carefully, he could easily have been doing this and not seen the cyclist. Many cyclists wear hi-vis jackets and have lights to make themselves visible to drivers and, if the cyclist was not doing this and was driving in a car lane, an accident was foreseeable. Therefore, in the second case I think the cyclist should be liable, though it depends on whether the motorist could be construed as driving carefully.

Bad answer: in both cases the cyclist is liable because he was driving in the car lane instead of in the cycle lane. *This is a bad answer as it has not separated the examples given in the question and analysed each one individually, they have bundled them together and treated them as one.*

Q52: Which of the House of Lords and House of Commons has more power? What are the main differences between them?

While law interviews do not require any prior knowledge of the law, it would be very helpful to know some for this question. It is important to read the news and have a general knowledge of politics for law interviews, but nothing in loads of depth. In short: there are two chambers of Parliament: the House of Commons and the House of Lords. The House of Commons debates and enacts legislation, and it is elected. The House of Lords is not elected, and it scrutinises and proposes small amendments on House of Commons legislation in some areas. The members of the House of Lords largely used to be hereditary, so they inherited their membership. This was reformed in 1999, and now there are fewer hereditary peers and people tend to become members by being recommended by the Prime Minister (these are called life peers). You don't *need* to know any of this, but it is helpful for this question and any others about the House of Lords.

https://www.youtube.com/watch?v=xgMRiA9dZQs&t=238s – this video is good at explaining it, but don't just watch it and believe everything they say: the Lords aren't all bad! The House of Commons is overburdened, so the Lords provide important scrutiny of legislation.

Good answer: there are a few differences between the House of Commons and the House of Lords. The House of Commons is elected, but the House of Lords is not. Also, the House of Commons enacts law, but the House of Lords scrutinises and advises on it. I think the House of Commons has more power because they are perceived as legitimate by the public, because members of it are elected, and they have more discretion in debating and implementing legislation. The House of Lords used to have more power when it was the apex court in England and Wales, but its role is mainly scrutiny of legislation now, which is still important as the Commons is over-burdened and perhaps doesn't have as much time as is required to do this. You could argue the House of Lords has more power though, because the House of Commons' politicians often have their votes encouraged by party whips, so politicians perhaps don't have as much freedom to vote and express opinions on laws as the Lords do. As the Lords don't belong to parties, they can properly debate without having to toe the party line.

Bad answer: the House of Commons is elected and the House of Lords isn't. The House of Commons has more power because it makes law. *This is a bad answer as the individual hasn't explored the other side of the argument.*

Q53: Why do people who do some particular jobs get exemptions from jury duty.

You don't have to know which professions are exempt from Jury duty for this question, you can just give some examples of some you would think would be exempt and why you think that. Lawyers used to be exempt from jury duty, but this was lifted in 2004. It is quite a tricky question, but just go through your thought process out loud and try to give a reasoned answer. The interviewer here is looking for your ability to think on your feet and how you respond to unfamiliar subject matter. Moreover, this question gives potential for the link between law and the real world to be explored, so you could consider both theoretical and practical reasons why exemptions may be provided.

Good answer: I am not sure which professions are exempt from jury duty, but I think there is an argument against allowing lawyers, prison officers and MPs to be part of a jury. This is because there is a risk that such people will be awarded a special status by the rest of the jury, and they could influence the decision a great deal, since the profession includes a knowledge of the law. Jurors are supposed to be treated equally and are supposed to be an impartial body, so giving one person's opinion more weight than everyone else's on account of their profession is not effective. However, I think juries should be as wide a cross section of society as possible, so I disagree with barring any profession from jury duty.

Bad answer: I don't know which professions are exempt from jury duty so I can't answer that. *This is a bad answer because the interviewee has not attempted to give examples of certain professions which may be exempt and why. If you don't know something, just have a guess and tell the interviewer you're not 100% on the subject.*

Q54: When you become prime minister, what laws will you change?

This question involves a discussion of reform of laws. You can really talk about anything, it is a great opportunity to express your personal interest in a particular area of law. Stronger answers are therefore on any subject matter, just make sure your points are reasoned and give examples. Weaker answers will be blunt and overly simplistic. Explain the current law, then offer a criticism of it before proposing a change to that law you would make to improve it.

Good answer: if I was prime minister, I would change the law on abortion. Over the pandemic, at home abortions have been allowed to keep people safe from catching and spreading COVID-19. With this introduction, there has been a decreased wait time on appointments, and there have been no deaths or serious health impacts as a result of these at home abortions.

I think that the law should enable them to occur all the time, rather than just in emergency circumstances, as it stands now. This is because such a provision removes concerns of the pills taking effect while travelling home from the clinic, and it enables people to access abortions if they are unable to get to hospitals easily for whatever reason. Also, a lot of people are hesitant to get abortions due to the clinical environment in which they happen, and they may feel safer having an abortion in their own home. Moreover, having more readily accessible abortions will almost certainly decrease the number of 'back street' abortions, which are incredibly dangerous.

I would also change the law on assisted suicide. As it stands, people who help their loved ones travel to overseas clinics such as Dignitas to die can be prosecuted in principle. This has not happened for decades, so I do not see the point in leaving the law open to such a risk as it will cause many people anxiety. I actually think criminalising helping disabled people to die is even discriminatory and contradictory, because people who are not as physically disabled can just go by themselves, so the law only effects society's most vulnerable and their families.

Bad answer: if I was prime minister, I would make abortion pills legal as it gives people better access to medical care. *This is a bad answer as the individual has not explained what the current law is in any detail, or given proper justification for their opinion.*

Q55: Two people die as a result of their parachute failing due to a manufacturing flaw, would their deaths constitute murder or manslaughter?

This question involves a discussion of the differences between murder and manslaughter. For this, some previous knowledge is required, but not a lot. The difference between murder and manslaughter is the mindset of the defendant. In murder, the person must either intend the death of the victim or intend to cause them GBH (grievous bodily harm). They can also be reckless to the victim's death, if the death is a virtual certainty of the defendant's action. There are different types of manslaughter, but the standard is lower than that of murder: it tends to involve being reckless as to some harm caused to the victim, or breaching a duty to them etc. The interviewer here is looking for your ability to compare offences, and specifically to acknowledge the similarities in their conduct (i.e. death of a victim) and the differences in the intentions behind said offences. Treating the offences separately and critically comparing them will take your answer to a higher level.

Good answer: although the manufacturer has caused two people to die, I think this is manslaughter rather than murder as it was not a deliberate defect: the manufacturer did not intend for the two people to be injured or die. However, they had a duty of care towards the people, which arguably involved providing them with safe equipment. This was evidently breached, so I think they would be liable for manslaughter. Potentially, if the manufacturer was being reckless, the death of the victims could be construed as murder, but I think in this case it would be manslaughter because there doesn't appear to be any malicious conduct.

Bad answer: the manufacturer would be liable for murder as they indirectly killed two people. *This is a bad answer because the person has not considered if this killing could be manslaughter and has not treated the two crimes separately.*

Q56: If a person is convicted of a murder which did not take place, and upon release kills the original victim, can they be sentenced again?

This question considers the principles which underpin our legal system. The idea of double jeopardy is one of these, it holds a person cannot be trialled for the same crime twice. This is the principle which must be reconciled the example given here. The interviewer here is looking for your ability to pick up on potential issues with the law, and understand the principles which underpin it.

Good answer: on one hand, the convict could not be sentenced again. The principle of double jeopardy (holding that a person cannot be trialled for the same crime twice) applies here, and the convict has already been trialled for the murder of the victim once and has been punished for it. Potentially, the person served punishment enough as their initial prison sentence was for a crime they did not commit.

On the other hand, I think there should be some sort of loophole or way the convict could be trialled again for the crime. Although this would violate the principle of double jeopardy, not trialling the defendant again would violate a principle of justice which equally underpins the law – these principles must be balanced. The defendant has committed a crime and this should not go unrecognised, and he has clearly not been through 'punishment enough' as some people would argue, because he has done the very crime he was wrongfully convicted in the first place.

Bad answer: the convict can be sentenced again because he has committed a crime, which requires a sentence. *This is a bad answer because the interviewee has not picked up on the concept of double jeopardy. Even if you don't have knowledge of this, think about why the question is being asked if it seems overly simple. The interviewee here could have picked up on the issue with being sentenced twice for the same crime, even if they did not know the technical term for it.*

Q57: What does it mean when something is "beyond reasonable doubt"

This question involves analysing the actual content of the law. No previous knowledge of law is required for this question, because everything you need to know is given to you. With definition questions like these, avoid giving a circular answer, and try to ensure your answer is as reasoned as possible. The interviewer here is looking for your ability to come up with comprehensive definitions. They may give you examples of instances and ask you to see if they fit with your definition, so don't be afraid to amend it if these are inconsistent with your idea of 'beyond reasonable doubt'. When giving examples, the interviewer will push your conclusion to its logical limits. Don't be afraid to acknowledge when something is inconsistent with your answer, but equally don't abandon it instantly. If you do change your answer, make sure to give justification for doing so.

Good answer: I think 'beyond reasonable doubt' is a standard which cases have to be proved to. It requires there to be little to no uncertainty surrounding the decision, and any uncertainty is unreasonable, or irrational. The issue with such a definition is that the idea of reasonableness is very subjective. What is reasonable for me may not be reasonable for another person, so imposing such a standard in criminal cases means there will inevitably be different opinions on it. This potentially violates the principle of legal certainty, because people may be unsure of whether their conduct meets this standard. Moreover, the idea of predictability in law is not upheld by such a standard either. On the other hand, the subjective nature of the standard allows for discretion in borderline cases and for such cases to be assessed individually.

Bad answer: I think 'beyond reasonable doubt' means you have to prove a criminal case so there is no reasonable doubt of the decision. *This is a bad answer because it is circular: the interviewee has used the phrase reasonable doubt to define the phrase reasonable doubt.*

Q58: What are the legal implications of gay marriage?

This question requires you to consider the legal ramifications for a real-world issue. It would be relevant to discuss the position of gay marriage from religious perspectives here, as well as civil partnerships, which used to be the equivalent of marriage for same-sex couples. This question demonstrates the importance of keeping up with the news, because anything you know about gay marriage could be applied here, provided you make it relevant to the question. Stronger answers will consider a range of implications and justify each one. Weaker answers will give little to no justification for their points.

Good answer: there are multiple legal implications of gay marriage. Firstly, churches can currently refuse to marry same-sex couples. A legal implication of this could be that such a provision must be legally reconciled with discrimination rights which they potentially infringe upon. Secondly, civil partnership used to be the 'equivalent' of marriage for same-sex couples. Perhaps some couples in a civil partnership want to change this to marriage, so whether or not this can happen without dissolving the civil partnership must be clarified and, if not, a new provision must be added to the grounds of dissolving civil partnerships to account for this circumstance. Thirdly, any legal marriage documents should be amended to have inclusive pronouns such as they/them, instead of just having he/him and she/her, so they apply to all couples, rather than just heterosexual ones.

Bad answer: the legal implications of gay marriage are that churches can't refuse to marry gay people as this would be discrimination. *This is a bad answer as it is quite blunt, a better way of approaching this point (which is untrue: churches can refuse to marry gay people) would be to discuss potential implications of churches refusing to marry same-sex couples and how the law would have to deal with this.*

Q59: What data should our government be able to find out about us? Should foreign citizens be treated any differently?

This question involves a consideration of data privacy. With questions that ask 'to what extent' is important to give a balanced answer and justify whatever conclusion you come to. Stronger answers will consider a range of extents (high, medium and low) and decide which one they agree with. Weaker answers will only consider the extent they conclude with and won't justify their answer very well.

Good answer: there are arguments that data should be available to the government to a high extent. It would help with criminal investigations, as people's messages and internet history would be more readily available. For example, if someone is a suspected terrorist, their card purchases and social media activity could be analysed easily. This would also help with missing person's cases. Moreover, data being available to the government would mean they could prevent radicalisation and even paedophile rings on the internet, protecting people and upholding the welfare principle.

Despite this, there are also arguments that the government should not have data available to them. If there was a data leak, this could easily get into the wrong hands and end up subverting the welfare principle it tries to uphold. Also, it gives the government too much power: if they became corrupt or started using data for something the public didn't agree with, this could lead to civil unrest or mass riots. Therefore, I think data should be available in some circumstances, but not all. Considering foreign citizens, I think their country should monitor their data- unless they are potentially going to have an impact on British society, then the British government shouldn't have access to their data.

Bad answer: data should not be available to our government as they could go corrupt. *This is a bad answer as the interviewee has only considered one argument and hasn't justified their point very much.*

Q60: What is the significance of differences between American and British Law?

This question involves a comparison of US and British Law. Some knowledge of the law is required for this question, but not much. Since the differences need to be 'fundamental', try to take a step back and look at the bigger picture: there is no point talking about the gun laws in America as that isn't really a 'fundamental' difference. The biggest differences are probably that the US has a codified constitution, but the UK doesn't. Also, the US has a federal government system so each state can make its own laws to an extent, but, again, the UK doesn't. When analysing the implications of these differences, consider the relationship between the countries.

Good answer: there are two fundamental differences between the US and British Law. Firstly, the US has a codified constitution, but the UK constitution is uncodified. Secondly, the US has a federal government system, but the UK does not. The implications of these differences come to light when considering the relationship between the UK and the US. In treaties, the UK will have to clarify their position on constitutional issues as our constitution is unclear (since it is uncodified). If a new convention was formed, the UK's flexible constitution could adopt this easily, but the US would have to go through a special process of amendment to implement it into their law. Also, trade agreements between the countries depend on the state in America, as the states may have different regulations, whereas the UK (or at least England) has universal regulations on trade. These provisions will make trade agreements more complex.

Bad answer: in the US you can have a gun, but in the UK you can't. in the US, some states are trying to ban abortion, but the UK is not. *This is a bad answer because the interviewee has got bogged down in individual laws, rather than taking a step back and looking at the bigger picture.*

Q61: How would you advise a client who is refusing to attend court despite multiple summons?

This question involves a consideration of law in the real world. Stronger answers will give a lot of justification for the point, whereas weaker answers will be more simplistic. The answer is quite an easy one so, to reach a higher standard of response, try and have a very structured approach to the question here. The interviewer is assessing your knowledge of law in practical contexts, and of course in a legal career (though it is worth noting that you don't have to want to be a lawyer in order to do a law degree). Signposting is a really good idea for interview responses (using first, second and third or a, b, c and things like that) because it makes your answer far easier to understand and splits up your points so the interviewer can appreciate how reasoned your answer is. Clarity is very important in your answers, and signposting helps you achieve that.

Good answer: I would advise my client to go to court. There are three reasons I would do this. Firstly, not going to court is a crime in itself, so if my client doesn't go to court it will only add to his multiple charges. Secondly, I would tell my client he can't run away forever, at some point he will be forced to go to court, so it is better if he goes of his own accord. Thirdly, I would tell my client that not going to court will reflect badly on him in the proceedings. If he pleads not guilty to the charges, he will seem more guilty if he is not forthcoming with the judicial system. If he pleads guilty, he is less likely to get a lenient punishment.

Bad answer: I would tell him to go to court. *This is a bad answer because there is no justification for the interviewee's point, and no structure to his answer.*

Q62: A General orders a soldier to kill his squad mate. Would this be murder?

This question involves getting into depth surrounding the law on murder, and what defences apply to it. In law, there is a defence of necessity to murder, as well as others such as loss of control and diminished responsibility. It might be worth having a read up on these since they come up very often at interview. For example, the interviewer may give you some legislation outlining the requirements of loss of control, then give you examples and ask you to see if they fit with the requirements. Stronger answers to this question will consider arguments for and against this action being murder, whereas weaker answers will be one-sided. Using examples to illustrate your point and its limits would be a good idea in questions like these. The interviewer is looking for your ability to separate the conduct (like killing here) and mental (like intention or recklessness) aspects of an offence here, and analyse them according to a situation.

Good answer: on one hand, this could be construed as murder. The soldier has killed his squad mate and did intend to- the issue is whether or not the General ordering him to do it awards the soldier with any defence to murder. If the General said 'kill your squad mate or I will kill you', or pointed a gun at the soldier, then I think this would be a defence to murder because the soldier was fearing for his own life and was coerced into killing his squad mate. However, this is not the case here. The soldier may have been under some unseen pressure or fear from the General's order, but I don't think this justifies him killing someone.

Bad answer: this would be murder because the soldier killed his squad mate. *This is a bad answer because it is circular and unjustified. The interviewee also hasn't considered any circumstances where a defence would apply here.*

Q63: A doctor is asked by the wife of their patient to end the patient's suffering by killing them. Do you think this would be murder?

This question involves a consideration of the law on euthanasia and assisted suicide. Moreover, it involves patient consent and whether or not a family member can make a decision on behalf of the patient. Stronger answers will consider both of these issues in turn, giving a reasoned approach to their conclusions and analysing circumstances where their answer would be different. Weaker answers will treat the two issues as one and give a less considered approach to the question.

Good answer: firstly, I don't think the patient's family member should be able to dictate the patient's death in this instance. This raises issues of the patient being coerced or forced into dying, or even not consulted at all. Moreover, if the family member is set to inherit money from the patient's death, issues of intention must be addressed. Of course, if the patient was in a coma or unresponsive, family members would have to make decisions for them. In this case, though, I think more than one family member would have to make the decision to avoid corruption and ill-thought-out judgements.

Secondly, I don't think this situation would be murder, but it depends on the interpretation of it. If the patient was not in a lot of pain, then giving the patient pain medication to kill them would be murder, because the intention to end their life is there. However, if the doctor gave the patient pain medication to ease their severe pain (as the situation is here) then this would not be murder, because the doctor's primary intention would be to ease the pain, but this has the secondary effect of shortening the patient's lifespan. Such passive euthanasia is legal in the UK, and the doctrine of the double-effect is essentially what governs it.

Bad answer: it would be murder because the patient isn't asking to die, and the doctor can't just kill them. *This is a bad answer because the individual has not treated the two issues separately. There is also little justification of their point.*

Q64: Which law is broken most frequently?

This question involves considering law in the real world. Stronger responses will give lots of justification for their point, whereas weaker ones will not. The interviewer is looking for your ability to think on your feet, but also to explore the reasons of why someone may break the law and how these reasons can be mitigated. To take your answer to another level, discuss practical ways you could stop the law being broken, rather than just the hypothetical reasons of why it is.

Good answer: I think that driving laws such as going through a red light or parking on double yellow lines are broken most frequently. People may be confused on laws such as eating while driving (which is illegal), so may break the law unknowingly. Also, some people may not 'see the point' in these laws, or think they are lesser than other laws like theft or assault, so choose to break them knowingly. This illustrates the importance of having justified laws, but also communicating this justification to the public so they understand the rationale behind the law and are more likely to follow it as a consequence. This could be achieved by advertising statistics on car accidents considering parking on double yellow lines or eating behind the wheel: if people understand why the law is in place they are more likely to follow it.

Bad answer: I think the law on underage drinking is broken most frequently because a lot of parents and teenagers don't see the point in it. *This is a bad answer because the person has only considered one reason for why the law is broken so frequently and has not proposed a reform to the law to prevent it from being broken. It is important to consider the wider aspect of your answer when responding to the question. Moreover, they should give more reasons as to why the law is broken in their answer.*

Q65: When people are tried by their peers, why bother with a judge?

This question involves considering the state of the judicial system in the UK. No knowledge of the law is required for this question, just think out loud and give a reasoned approach to whatever you say. Try and step back and look at the bigger picture: what would happen if there weren't judges? This will help you figure out reasons for why judges are required in judicial proceedings.

Good answer: judges are required for court cases for a few reasons. Firstly, not every case has a jury, only criminal cases in the Crown court do. This means for lesser offences, judges are required to make decisions on cases. Secondly, judges are required to oversee proceedings and handle questions and challenges from lawyers. Thirdly, judges are required to direct the jury on what certain concepts in the law mean and if they apply in the current case. For example, the phrase beyond reasonable doubt, or on the balance of probability may require direction. Whether things should be construed narrowly, widely or in the ordinary sense of the word is also required to be directed by the judge. The lawyers can't do this as they're biased. Fourthly, judges sentence criminals so they are required for this aspect of the judicial process too.

Bad answer: I don't know what the point of having a judge is when decisions are made by the jury. *This is a bad answer because the interviewee has not attempted to respond to the question, had an educated guess at the answer or even gone through their thought process out loud. Always try and think of an answer, even if you take 30 seconds or so to think before you say something. It is also okay to tell the interviewer 'I am going to have a think for a second' if it feels awkward for you to just be silent.*

Q66: You take shelter from a thunderstorm in an unlocked car – have you committed the offence of allowing yourself to be carried in a conveyance without the owner's consent?

This question considers the offence of theft, and in which context it applies. Stronger answers will consider two sides of the argument and give examples which illustrate the logical limit of their conclusions. Weaker answers will be more blunt and less justified. You don't need any previous knowledge of the law for this question, since it is given to you. The standard you need to apply the example to is 'the offence of allowing yourself to be carried in a conveyance without the owner's consent'. The key to this question is the definition of 'carried', and possibly consent too.

Good answer: on one hand, this could be construed as the offence of allowing yourself to be carried in a conveyance without the owner's consent. I have not asked the owner if I can shelter in their car, so there is no consent given. If 'carried' includes remaining stationary in the car, then this is equally satisfied. On the other hand, this example could be interpreted as not fulfilling the offence. I did not ask the owner for their consent, but what if they would have consented? Whether or not this counts as consent for the offence is debatable. Also, 'carried' implies the vehicle is moving, which it does not in this instance. If I drove their car to buy an umbrella then returned it to the parking place, I would be carried in it, but whether staying still in the car as in this case counts as carried is again debatable. I don't think it would in this instance though.

Bad answer: I am not guilty of the offence because I haven't been carried in the car. *This is a bad answer because the person has not considered the issues of consent and the definition of carried separately and has not properly justified their point.*

Q67: How would you separate the words: Mislead, Deceive, and Lie?

This question involves giving your own definitions of key legal terms and pointing out the differences between them. Stronger answers will be more nuanced in this question and possibly highlight both similarities and differences of the terms. Weaker answers will be more blunt and potentially circular (i.e. using the term to define the term). The interviewer is looking for your ability to critically compare key legal concepts and come up with comprehensive definitions for them. You do not need to know the technical or legal definitions of these terms, just try and define them in their normal sense. However, avoid giving definitions that overlap to a high extent, because the interviewer says in the question that the concepts are not the same.

Good answer: I think lying is actively concealing the truth from someone by directly telling them false things. Deceiving is more indirect than this, I think it entails concealing the truth from someone, like lying, but telling them things from which they derive false information. I think misleading is the most indirect of the three, but again entails concealing the truth from someone. In this case, this is done by withholding the truth or avoiding discussing it. The differences between misleading and deceiving are few, and I think the terms overlap in some instances.

Bad answer: lying is when you tell someone untrue things. Deceiving is when you make a person believe things that are false, and misleading is when you cause them to be misled. *This is a bad answer because the person's definitions are unjustified (and circular in the case of deceiving). They have also not directly compared the terms. Since the interviewer said in the question that the concepts are similar, pointing out the similarities of these terms would make this answer a lot better.*

Q68: Why are manslaughter and murder treated differently, what separates them?

This question involves a direct comparison of two offences. You don't need prior knowledge of the law to answer this, but it would be useful to know the differences in mens rea (guilty mind) of them. The mens rea of murder is intent to kill or cause GBH (grievous bodily harm), or foresight of virtual certainty that such harm/death will ensue from the defendant's conduct. The mens rea of manslaughter depends on the specific offence, but it is generally lower than this (or the same where a defence is used). Another thing that is relevant here is the mandatory life sentence for murder. If you are convicted of murder, you have to be sentenced to life in prison, but most people don't actually serve this long: they just have a minimum term. The life sentence means that they are monitored for the rest of their life, even when they get out of prison.

Good answer: there are a few differences between murder and manslaughter. Firstly, murder is perceived by society as much more serious than manslaughter. If someone is convicted of murder, they are more likely to be a social outcast and struggle to rehabilitate than if they were convicted of manslaughter. Secondly, murder has a higher level of mens rea than manslaughter, which reflects its harsher labelling. Thirdly, murder has a mandatory life sentence, whereas manslaughter does not. This also reflects the offence's severity, and why there are specific defences to murder – we should be cautious to subject people to this sort of sentence. Even though a murderer may not serve life in prison, they will spend the rest of their life monitored and are much more likely to go to prison again for a less serious crime.

Bad answer: murder is killing with intent and manslaughter is killing without intent. *This is a bad answer because a) it's wrong and b) they have not defined what this 'intent' means. They have only given one point and, even if it was wrong, this would be okay if they had properly reasoned and justified it, which they have not.*

Q69: Should stalking remain legal?

This question involves a proposed reform to the law and weighing up the pros and cons of it. Stronger answers will consider both of these, whereas weaker responses will be more one-sided. Try and consider examples to justify your points where possible.

Good answer: on one hand, stalking should not be illegal. Telling someone where they can and cannot go arguably violates the principle of autonomy which the law seeks to uphold. Moreover, telling someone what they can and cannot say, and how they can and cannot interact with another person potentially does the same thing. Also, a person can get a restraining order against someone if they are being stalked, and breaching this order is illegal, so perhaps there is not a need to make stalking itself against the law.

Despite this, I think stalking should be made illegal. While it potentially infringes on autonomy, not making it illegal infringes on the principle of welfare. Likewise, freedom of speech is only a right when it does not violate someone else's right, and I think people have a right not to be harassed. While restraining orders go some way to stopping stalking, there are cases which will slip through the cracks, so we need a stronger law in this area. The mental health impacts which stalking can have on someone are severe, so this should be reflected in its legal treatment. For example, a person could be stalked for years and end up with an anxiety disorder or PTSD: this is a level of harm that must be addressed by the law directly.

Bad answer: stalking should be made illegal because it can cause people harm. *While this is a good point, the interviewee here has not justified it very well or given examples which illustrate it. Also, they have not considered the other side of the argument – not making stalking illegal.*

Q70: How do civil cases differ from criminal ones?

Some knowledge of the law is evidently required for this question, but if you didn't have any in the interview, just go through your thought process out loud. The question is asking for a direct comparison of two areas of law. Stronger responses will be structured and clear, explaining each difference individually. They may touch on some similarities also. Weaker answers will give fewer differences and use more vague and complex language. Law is really about explaining hard concepts in easy terms, and you can demonstrate your ability to do that in this question: this is essentially what the interviewer is looking for. The interviewer here is also looking for an ability to consider the different types of law and how each one can be broken. Not every case is an offence of assault, or rape etc- this is what they are trying to get you to appreciate here.

Good answer: there are a few differences between civil and criminal cases. Firstly, the state prosecutes in criminal cases (via the CPS), whereas private individuals prosecute in civil cases. Secondly, criminal law relates to offences which negatively affect society as a whole and can result in prison sentences. Civil law relates to duties and rights which have been breached, and results in compensation being awarded (not prison). Fourthly, I think criminal law seeks to punish, but civil law seeks to redress. Criminal law has the ultimate aim of maintaining stability in society, but civil law deals with disputes between organisations and individuals.

Bad answer: I don't know the difference between criminal and civil law. Criminal law deals with things like rape, assault and theft, but civil law doesn't. *This is a bad answer because the interviewee has given a weak attempt at understanding the question: the question is holistic and needs looking at as a whole, rather than just discussing examples (although these could be useful to demonstrate a holistic point). The person has also not justified their answer or given it any structure.*

Q71: What would you say are the advantages and disadvantages of juries?

This question involves deliberating an aspect of the judicial system. No legal knowledge is required to give a good answer to this question, all you need to do is think of wider implications of the jury service and how they relate to the principles the law seeks to uphold (such as legal certainty, fair labelling and autonomy). Try and give a balanced argument i.e. a similar number of pros and cons. Also, try and justify your answer and give examples which illustrate it. Stronger responses will consider pros and cons within the judicial system itself, then zoom out and consider the wider ramifications of these.

Good answer: considering pros first, juries ensure citizen participation in the criminal law system. Judges are not elected so juries increase the perceived legitimacy of the justice system and the position of judges. This also may lead to more people following the law as they respect it. Moreover, juries ensure the impartiality of judges. Although judges do direct and guide juries in their decisions, the final say always comes down to them. This reduces the bias of the judge in deciding if someone is guilty.

Considering cons, you could argue that juries lack the expertise to decide on whether someone is guilty. Judges have years of experience in the field, so arguably should make the decision, instead of leaving it to 'ordinary' citizens. Moreover, there are arguments that juries are not representative of the population. A sample as small as 12 people, even though it is randomly selected, is never going to represent the different religions, ethnic groups and sexualities etc that are present within the UK population. Also, if the defendant was a member of a minority group, there is a risk of unconscious bias.

Bad answer: the pros of juries are that they prevent judges from making biased decisions. Juries also increase involvement in decisions and, because there are 12 people, mean there is greater deliberation of the decision and is being left to more people rather than just one judge. *This answer, though it contains good points, is bad since it does not outline any cons of juries. The interviewee should also work on structuring their answer and signposting (i.e. firstly, secondly).*

Q72: To what extent can you know how much you do not know?

This question is very broad, and very philosophical. You can discuss almost anything in your answers, just make sure every point you make is justified and structured. The interviewer is assessing your ability to address unfamiliar material and make connections between the law and philosophy. A lot of a Law degree considers the black and white letter of the law (i.e. what it actually says), but some of it considers why the law is the way it is and how it can be improved. The philosophical analysis that is required for such a deliberation of the law is what is being assessed here.

Good answer: I think you only know some things you didn't know before once you know them. That is, by the time you know what you don't know, you already know it! For example, I didn't know how vaccines work until I studied them in Biology, but I only became aware of my ignorance once I was no longer ignorant – because I learnt about them. Some things, however, you can know you don't know by considering whether or not you do know them. For example, I know that I don't know how to fix a toilet, simply by asking myself if I can. However, I don't think you can ever know the extent of what you don't know. I suppose how much you don't know is one of the things that you don't know. There are some experiences I will never have, so my ignorance surrounding them will never be illustrated. I can hardly think of all possible things of the world and realise I don't know them.

Bad answer: you know what you don't know by asking yourself if you do know it. *This is a bad answer because the interviewee has given no examples, which would be very helpful to clarify things in a confusing question like this. Their answer is also too short and not well-justified.*

Q73: What would you say differentiates solicitors from barristers?

This question does require a knowledge of the law or, at least, the careers that accompany it. If you don't know what the difference between a barrister and a solicitor is, have a read up on it, and read the sample 'good' answer below for some basic points. I would still recommend you read up on the difference between them though. Here is a link explaining them in some more depth:

https://www.brightknowledge.org/law/what-is-the-difference-between-a-barrister-and-solicitor

While you don't have to want to be a lawyer to do a law degree, the majority of people do and the interviewer in this question will be looking for your commitment to and interest in the course, through assessing your knowledge on a career the course leads to. The interviewer is also looking for your knowledge of how law interacts with the 'real world', taking it out of the hypothetical one.

Good answer: there are a few differences between barristers and solicitors. Firstly, barristers represent people in court, whereas solicitors mainly advise on necessary courses of legal action depending on their area of expertise. Solicitors work directly with clients, whereas barristers receive information on their client's case and work off that. Secondly, barristers tend to be self-employed and a member of Chambers or are sometimes employed by companies or solicitor firms to advise clients. Barristers provide specialist legal advice in a select area, but solicitors are more all-round, and can advise on a range of issues.

Bad answer: barristers wear wigs and gowns in courts and examine witnesses, but solicitors work a desk job and do advocacy work. *While this is true, this answer is a bit simple and doesn't go into much depth considering the differences of the work of barristers or solicitors, and the relationship between the two jobs. A consideration of the similarities of the professions would also be good, rather than just the differences.*

Q74: If you were made Queen's Counsel tomorrow, what do you think your responsibilities would be? What would you have to do to be made a Queen's Counsel?

This question does require some knowledge of the law considering what a Queen's Counsel is, but not so much considering how one becomes a member of it. With the latter, just think of the senior nature of the Queen's Counsel and what sort of qualities someone might look for in a member's application. Tell the interviewer you're not sure, but you think these things are involved in people becoming a Queen's Counsel. This shows the interviewer your thought process, and that you can think on your feet when faced with unfamiliar and unknown material- this is essentially what they're looking for here.

Good answer: A Queen's counsel is a senior barrister appointed by the monarch. Queen's Counsels take on fewer cases than regular barristers, and charge more, because these often require very in depth and specialist knowledge of the law. Queen's Counsels tend to represent each side in important legal cases, such as at the Supreme Court, because their arguments used in the judgements often set a common law precedent for lower courts to follow. I'm not sure how to become a Queen's Counsel but, given the rank's seniority, I imagine it requires a high level of knowledge of the law, perhaps a lot of experience and public speaking skills. Communication with both clients and colleagues may also be beneficial to the application process, as well as integrity of character.

Bad answer: A Queen's Counsel is like a really important barrister. I don't know how you become one though. *This is a bad answer because, although the person doesn't know how to become a Queen's Counsel, they have not attempted to figure it out. Just going through any thoughts they have would be enough, it doesn't have to be a completely comprehensive answer: the interviewer just wants to see you give it a go.*

Q75: If a parent slaps their child, are they abusing them? Does your answer change if they bruised the child?

This question involves an analysis of current law. The call to ban smacking altogether is a controversial debate at present, so it coming up in an interview question illustrates why it is so important to keep up with the news, especially surrounding legal issues. Stronger answers will treat the two examples separately, because this gives the response a great structure. Weaker answers will give unjustified points, and treat the two examples as one, or with little distinction between them.

Good answer: In the first case, I don't think slapping a child is abuse in some situations. If the child is behaving badly enough that a slap is reasonable punishment, then I don't think this is abuse. Though it is controversial, it remains legal to slap your child in this situation and some people think it is a way of teaching discipline. However, the key lies in the definition of a 'reasonable punishment'. If the child in this case had not done their chores, I don't think a slap would be reasonable punishment for this. If the child had threatened their sibling or bullied another child at school, then this could be more readily construed as a 'reasonable punishment' for their actions.

Considering the second case, I think this would be abuse. While slapping as a reasonable punishment remains legal, I don't think it is legal if such slapping amounts to actual bodily harm. The key becomes whether a bruise satisfies this requirement, but I think a bruise on a small child is worse than a bruise on an adult, so these circumstantial aspects must be considered. Moreover, if a slap causes a bruise, the punishment of slapping is less likely to be reasonable, so more likely to be disproportionate ie abuse and illegal.

Bad answer: this is abuse because the parent has assaulted the child. *This is a bad response because the interviewee has treated the two examples as one, instead of dividing them up. Their point is also not very justified, and they could give some examples to help illustrate it.*

Q76: What prevents European nations from combining into a United States of Europe?

This question considers a comparison of two types of government system. Stronger responses will give a wide range of points and discuss both practical and hypothetical reasons: a zoomed-in and a zoomed-out perspective. Weaker answers will be less justified and give fewer points. The interviewer here is looking for an ability to appreciate the relationship between law and politics, and the differences between constitutions and government systems on an international scale, rather than just within the UK. Constitutional law is interlinked with history, politics and even philosophy so appreciating such relationships will take your answer to a higher level.

Good answer: from a practical perspective, Europe is arguably too big to be a United States system. There are many political and cultural differences between countries, let alone between individuals, and grouping all of these into a federal government system would potentially not represent them enough. Moreover, when the US was created, a strong centrality was required to unite the country and its citizens after the British invasion. Europe, on the other hand, has always been fragmented and its constitutional inter-country relations evolved, so they did not need to be clarified as in the case of the United States. A United States of Europe would also be hard to govern simply because of the distance and separation of the countries, whereas the United States of America is all one landmass. Arguably, membership of international organisations like the EU (though not for Britain) gives some of the benefits of a federal government system, so it is not needed in Europe.

Bad answer: there is no United States of Europe because it is not a federal government system. *This is a bad answer because it is circular, and it doesn't give any proper reasons considering why Europe is does not have a United States system.*

Q77: What impact did 9/11 have on western law?

No legal knowledge is required to answer this question, you just have to think of the wider implications that 9/11 may have had on law. Stronger answers will consider a range of ideas including ones very closely linked with the event but also broader ramifications which follow it. Weaker answers will think of fewer points and give little justification for them. If you do know about the legal consequences of 9/11, definitely say them, but make sure you justify each of them to make your response look original, rather than just repeating things you already know.

Good answer: I am not sure of what specific legal changes were made to Western law after 9/11, but I imagine a tightening of laws surrounding airport security is one of them. Also, I think there could have been new data collection laws introduced which authorise the government accessing suspected terrorists' messages and internet histories. Moreover, I think there would be more deradicalization laws implemented and perhaps data collection provisions in respect to these, for example stronger laws surrounding radicalisation on social media platforms and chatrooms. From a wider perspective, I think 9/11 encouraged governments to share data with each other in order to prevent such an event happening again, so maybe laws allowing that were implemented. From a labelling point of view, perhaps the standard required to convict someone as a terrorist was lowered, or the offence was given harsher punishments, to deter people from becoming an extremist and to accurately represent public opinion of terrorists at the time.

Bad answer: I don't know what the consequences were, but I think they would tighten airport security. *This is a bad answer because the interviewee has only made one point and not justified it very well. The response must be more reasoned than this.*

Q78: Who can change the law, or make a new law?

This question considers the British constitution and government. There are three branches of government in the UK: the executive (who executes law), the legislature (who passes law) and the judiciary (who interprets law). This question is essentially asking for a comparison of these three branches, and an examination of their roles. Stronger answers will consider the subjectivity of the terms in the question, and the overlapping nature of the three branches of government. Weaker answers will not be so nuanced and treat the roles of the branches of government as more discrete variables.

Good answer: while the executive executes laws, Parliament is able to amend and 'change' these laws before they are enacted. Within this, the House of Commons can make more changes than the House of Lords, who are not allowed to impose wrecking amendments to most legislation. Moreover, the public also have some weight in proposing changes to laws. Things like protests or petitions can put pressure on Parliament to amend problematic or out-of-place legislation. Courts too can set a common law precedent regarding the definition of certain concepts in the law. Though this is not a 'change' as such, it could be considered an amendment in some instances, especially when the precedent is a deviation from a previous approach to the law. Ultimately, Parliament has the most power to write and change laws, but other political and legal bodies can influence its decisions. *To improve even more, this answer could treat 'write' and 'change' separately and discuss the differences of the terms.*

Bad answer: Parliament has the power to write and change laws. The public can also influence them to change laws. *This is a bad response because the interviewee has not considered many points or many examples to illustrate the ideas they give. How could the public influence parliament to change laws? Discussing petitions or protests here would be good.*

Q79: If you could change any 3 laws, which ones would they be and what would you change about them?

This question is incredibly subjective, you can essentially discuss anything. It is a good question to demonstrate your particular interests of the law which you have a lot of background knowledge in. The interviewer will see your passion for the subjects you discuss. If you do this, which is something they look for. Just try and make your answers as reasoned and structed as possible, so the interviewer can follow what you're saying easily.

Good answer: I would change the law on abortion, the law on assisted suicide and the law on voting. Firstly, I would make at-home abortions legal. Over the pandemic, 'abortion pills' have been made accessible so people can have abortions at home without risk of catching or spreading COVID-19. There have been no deaths from such abortions and the waiting time for appointments has decreased. Moreover, this provision removes worries such as the pills taking effect on the way home from the clinic, concerns about being far away from a clinic or unable to take time off work to get to an appointment and even things like fears of being in a hospital. This will also decrease dangerous 'back-street' abortions which are what happens when proper medical abortions aren't accessible.

Secondly, I would make it legal to accompany a disabled person to Dignitas so they can die. Though this is currently illegal, nobody has been prosecuted for it in years, so the rationale behind the law is unclear, as is its effectiveness. Judicial discretion applies in the situation where it happens, but I think people have the right to know how their case will be treated, rather than having an elusive and subjective notion deciding their liability.

Thirdly, I would lower the age of voting to 16. I think if you can pay tax, get married and join the army at 16, you should be allowed to have a say in who runs the country. Though there are arguments that 16 year olds don't know enough about politics to vote, a) this could be solved by compulsory politics lessons in school and b) this introduces a slippery slope into the electoral system: what about 50 year olds who don't know anything about politics? If we base the ability to vote on knowledge of politics, where is this 'knowledge' standard made? Also, conflating age with knowledge is arguably too blunt.

Bad answer: I would change the law on abortion, assisted suicide and voting. *This is a bad answer because the interviewee has not said how they would change the law and why they would change the law, or even said what the law currently is in these areas.*

Q80: Which law do you think is broken the most often in the UK?

This question involves considering law in the real world. Stronger responses will give lots of justification for their point, whereas weaker ones will not.

Good answer: I think that driving laws such as going through a red light or parking on double yellow lines are broken every day by most people. People may be confused on laws such as eating while driving (which is illegal), so may break the law unknowingly. Also, some people may not 'see the point' in these laws, or think they are lesser than other laws like theft or assault, so choose to break them knowingly. Moreover, a lot of people drive every day, so there is a lot of opportunity to break driving laws for whatever reason. This illustrates the importance of having justified laws, but also communicating this justification to the public so they understand the rationale behind the law and are more likely to follow it as a consequence.

Bad answer: I think the law littering is broken every day by most people because there aren't enough bins in public areas. *This is a bad answer because the interviewee has not really justified their point or proposed a reform that would make the law easier to follow.*

Q81: Do you think a mandatory uniform contravenes the rights of school children?

This question is a more discursive question designed to test your argumentative skills and see your legal thought process. It would be advisable to clearly state your position at the start and outline your arguments and evidence for your position. It is likely that your interviewer will play the devil's advocate so do not be put off if they press you on certain points.

You should demonstrate your logical thought process and ability to think on your feet, as these are qualities which the interviewer will be looking for. It is usually unlikely that you will be able to prepare and predict the topic of the question that will come out in the interview so you should focus on developing skills like being able to argue for and against your position as well as presenting a clear and compelling argument.

A **good applicant** would clearly state their position and the brief arguments for their position. They should also, if they can, provide some real-life examples as evidence in support. They could also present counter- arguments to their position and how they would resolve these in favour of their position. A very good applicant would consider the different nuances in the argument and weave this into their answer. This does require to think very quickly on your feet so it would be advisable to get some practice thinking in this way and identifying the nuances quickly.

A **sample** answer is as follows: If we assume that wearing school uniforms are mandatory this could be a contravention of human rights as they violate an individual's freedom of expression. Freedom of expression is a fundamental human right which we have been given which cannot be taken away from us in a democratic society. By making school uniforms mandatory, we are not enabling children to express themselves in a way they please. In 2017, the Swedish School Inspectorate said that school uniforms were a human right violation and use of them must be voluntary.

Some may argue that school uniforms do not breach this freedom as having school uniforms does not prevent people from wearing cultural or religious symbols like the hijab or cross. This preserves the identity of the wearer. School uniforms are also thought to be useful for uniformity and ensuring that they do not distract the children during school. However, these arguments are not mutually exclusive with making school uniforms mandatory. These benefits can still arise if school uniforms are made voluntary.

A **poor applicant** might give short, non-committal answer by not assuming a clear position or changing their position the moment they are pressed on it. While it is encouraged to engage in discussion, you should not get too passionate and start see the arguments as the interviewer's personal beliefs. If you have debated before, you should not start discrediting the interviewer or adopt an aggressive manner at any point. The whole point of the exercise is to see how you argue and attempt to formulate arguments and how they will stand against resistance. They are looking for law students who think carefully and argue logically.

Q82: A man points a gun at you and says "If you don't shoot your friend or I'll kill you both". If you shoot your friend are you guilty of murder? Would you be guilty if, instead, the man had said "If you don't shoot your friend, I'll shoot you"? How about if he had said "If you don't shoot your friend, I will"?

This question has a more legal element and would likely require you to be familiar with the definition of murder and how to apply it to the facts. You are not required to know any law to answer this question, but it might be useful to understand the concepts to be able to apply them effectively in an interview. It is not advisable to cite law terms or any technical cases as this will not win you favour with the interviewer since the law faculty explicitly states that you do not need any legal knowledge. They would be more impressed if you were able to apply the underlying reasoning behind these concepts and explain how they would work in alternative situations such as this one.

The interviewer is not looking for someone who can give the answer but is looking to assess your train of thought and whether it is logical. It does not really matter whether you arrive at the "right" answer in the end if you can demonstrate that you are able to think inquisitively and logically when formulating your answer. You should ask questions, pose alternative scenarios and fully explain why you reached a certain answer.

A **sample** answer is as follows: It is important to first define what 'murder' might mean and then to consider each scenario in turn. [the interviewer might interrupt to give you a definition they want you to use or you can try to create one in layman terms]. I will assume that the definition of murder is an intentional, through an act or refusal to act, killing of another person. If I had shot in all three scenarios, under this definition I have intentionally killed my friend therefore would be guilty of murder.

However, I might try to argue that I would have a defence as I was threatened by someone else to kill my friend. Even though I shot my friend intending to kill them, I could argue that it was against my will to do so. If I had not shot, this person would have killed both of us. If I think about this in utilitarian terms, it would have been better for me to shoot my friend so that at least one of us would have lived. It could also be that my friend would have, out of care for me, pleaded for me to shoot them so that I could live.

In the second scenario, I shot my friend to save myself. Here the pressure to shoot my friend could be arguably amplified as the threat was directed at myself and I might be able to argue self-defence.

In the third scenario, I shot my friend to prevent the other person from killing them. I could argue that they might have encouraged me to kill them instead of dying at the hand of the killer. This was, similarly, against my will and I was forced to do it. However, this is harder to justify than the previous two scenarios. In the first, I killed my friend to ensure that at least one of us lived. In the second, I killed them to save myself. The third one seems a bit illogical as I kill them to ensure that they is not shot by the killer. They would die in both instances so it is harder to see the defence that might be available to me in this scenario.

A **poor applicant** might have a long, unstructured answer with assertions not backed up by logic. They might be visibly flustered and confused, leading to contradictory or inconsistent positions. The content of the answer matters less than how you attempt to solve it and go through the different alternatives and reasons you reached that conclusion.

Q83: Do we have an innate moral code, or are we taught it?

This question is a discursive question designed to get the applicant to argue and defend a position. It is likely that your interviewer will play the devil's advocate so do not be put off if they press you on certain points.

You should demonstrate your logical thought process and ability to think on your feet, as these are qualities which the interviewer will be looking for. It is usually unlikely that you will be able to prepare and predict the topic of the question that will come out in the interview so you should focus on developing skills like being able to argue for and against your position as well as presenting a clear and compelling argument.

A **good applicant** would clearly state their position and the brief arguments for their position. They should also, if they can, provide some real-life examples as evidence in support. They could also present counter- arguments to their position and how they would resolve these in their favour. A very good applicant would consider the different nuances in the argument and weave this into their answer. This does require to think very quickly on your feet so it would be advisable to get some practice thinking in this way and identifying the nuances quickly.

A **sample** answer is as follows: I think babies are born with an innate moral code and it is not learned but further developed as they grow older. Their moral code is shaped by society, their upbringing and other factors but is not created by them. Philosophers and psychologists have long believed that babies are "blank slates" and it is their upbringing and society that form their moral code. However, I believe that it is more convincing to argue that babies are endowed with a moral code form birth. A team of researchers at Yale have been studying the behaviour of babies for decades. When shown an example of good behaviour and then an example of bad behaviour, babies tend to prefer the example of good behaviour.

A **poor applicant** might give an unbalanced argument or not defend their position well. For example, they might try and adopt a 'middle' position by trying to argue that babies are born with a moral code, but they are also learnt. This is not advisable as it shows that you are unable to argue for a certain position. While you must acknowledge that there are arguments against the ones you made, you should always adopt a clear position.

Q84: What compels us to obey the law?

This question is more philosophical and relates to jurisprudence (theory of law). It is a hard question with no 'right' answer. You can impress and differentiate yourself by clearly stating your position and presenting arguments in favour of your position. You should also think about why you disagree with the arguments against your position and include these.

A **good applicant** would have done some research into common topics such as this one and be able to formulate nuanced arguments. They should clearly state their position on the question at the start and put forward their arguments in a clear manner with pertinent examples illustrating their point. The Stanford Encyclopaedia of Philosophy and Cambridge HE+ pages are good websites to start with. There are many ways to answer this question and it is a rather personal answer so do not take the sample as the only answer.

A **sample** answer is as follows: A moral obligation to obey the law should be differentiated from the moral requirement to obey the law. If it is a requirement and we decide to just follow, it does not mean we are obliged but we do so because we fear the consequences of not following. A moral obligation could be that we feel compelled to obey the law because we believe in the innate good of that law.

The interviewer is likely to interject and ask you more questions about how you defined the parameters in this answer, they might take issue with how you defined certain issues. This question opens up the applicant to some interesting line of questioning and you should just try your best to follow the guidance of the interviewer once you have given your initial position.

A **poor applicant** might give a short answer with no space for further engagement or proper explanation or make assertions without developed arguments. They might go off-tangent or give an irrelevant answer. They might show holes in their arguments or contradict themself while becoming hopelessly confused. This is not an easy topic or question, so it is best to prepare a strategy and approach with caution to avoid becoming confused.

Q85: What is the relevance of Roman Law to your course?

This question is a good opportunity to show the interviewer that you have done detailed research on the Oxbridge Law degrees. You can demonstrate that you understand the reason why Roman law is a mandatory first year module and differentiate yourself from other candidates. It helps show to the interviewer your genuine interest in the Oxbridge law degree. However, do make sure to answer the question at hand and not "why is Roman law studied at Oxford/Cambridge" which would elicit a different response. The question here is specifically asking about the relevance of Roman law to the modern study of law.

This does require a little bit of research and the Cambridge law faculty website is the best place to start for this (https://www.ba.law.cam.ac.uk/studying-law-cambridge/first-year-focus). There is a very short video by Ms Amy Goymour which I recommend you watch to understand the nature of the subject and the reasons behind its compulsory status.

A **good applicant** would have watched that video but also provide some original insight into the answer and not just paraphrased the video. It would also be good to include a brief example as it shows the logical pattern of your thoughts.

A **sample** answer is as follows: Roman law is relevant to the modern study of law because it provided solutions to many complex factual problems which also arise today. There are also many examples of traces of Roman law in English law. For example, prescription by long use was a concept which originated from the Roman system. We can see how our modern study and system of law has built on these ancient solutions and this gives us a better and deeper understanding of our modern laws.

A **more detailed** answer could also include an example: One example would be where A owns a chariot, but this was stolen by thief who then sold it to an innocent party B. A finds the chariot and wants it back but B alleges that it is his since he purchased it in good faith and paid money for it. The Romans position on this issue influenced and is very similar to the English position which is that the law generally allows the original owner to retrieve their item except in certain exceptional circumstances.

A **poor applicant** might go off tangent and start talking about why Roman law is a mandatory subject at Oxbridge without really addressing the focus of the question which is the relevance. They might also try and dispute this question and say that Roman law is not relevant which is again, not what the question is asking for. The question did not ask you to debate or discuss the relevance but rather wants you to address how learning Roman law can be useful when learning the modern systems of law.

Q86: What would you say was the most ignored law?

This question is designed to see whether an applicant can put forward a law and explain logically why they think it is broken most frequently. The laws you propose must be backed up a good reason and you must explain how you reached this conclusion. It is likely that your interviewer will play the devil's advocate so do not be put off if they press you on certain points.

You should demonstrate your logical thought process and ability to think on your feet, as these are qualities which the interviewer will be looking for. It is usually unlikely that you will be able to prepare and predict the topic of the question that will come out in the interview so you should focus on developing skills like being able to argue for and against your position as well as presenting a clear and compelling position.

A good applicant would clearly state the law they think is broken most frequently and the brief reasons for their position. They should also, if they can, provide some real-life examples as evidence in support. They could also present counter- arguments that might arise to their proposal and how they would resolve these in favour of their position.

A **sample** answer is as follows: I think that littering is a law broken most frequently. We are all guilty of having littered at least once in our life and if this was multiplied by even 90% of the population this would be the law that was broken most frequently. While laws like underage drinking and speeding might also be other laws broken frequently, there are sections of the population such as people of drinking age and people without cars whom the offence would not apply to. Littering applies to a wider range of people.

A **poor applicant** might not be able to explain why they decided a certain law was most frequently broken or not go into enough detail. They might say something generic like "I think speeding is a law broken the most because many people speed" and fail to explain why. Whilst speeding is a perfectly acceptable answer to this question, it is important to be able to explain your reasons. You could say that speeding is frequent because a lot of people on the earth own a car and be able to contrast it to another similar offence like jaywalking and why speeding is more frequently broken.

It is important that the interviewer is able to see your thought process or where you derived your ideas from, so they are able to engage with you in conversation and further develop their impression of you.

Q87: *Do you think that the state should pass laws governing what we can eat? What laws would you introduce to combat obesity?*

This question is designed to see whether an applicant can formulate convincing and practical laws. The laws you propose must be backed up with good reasons and you must be able to explain why you decided to propose such laws. It is likely that your interviewer will play the devil's advocate so do not be put off if they press you on certain points.

You should demonstrate your logical thought process and ability to think on your feet, as these are qualities which the interviewer will be looking for. It is usually unlikely that you will be able to prepare and predict the topic of the question that will come out in the interview so you should focus on developing skills like being able to argue for and against your position as well as presenting a clear and compelling argument.

A **good applicant** would clearly state their proposed law and the brief reasons for their position. They should also, if they can, provide some real-life examples as evidence in support. They could also present counter- arguments that might arise to their proposal and how they would resolve these in favour of their position.

A **sample** answer is as follows: I would introduce a law to regulate advertising, food and presentation. Research has shown that individual food choices are associated with cultural and socio-economic circumstances and can be manipulated through advertising and presentation. As food choice is one of the main factors contributing to obesity, law can help curb obesity if it can redirect consumers to eat more healthy food. This might be in requiring certain food categorised "unhealthy" to have plain packaging or limit their ability to advertise in certain spaces.

A **poor applicant** might not explain why they decided to introduce a certain law or not go into enough detail. They might say something generic like "I would introduce a law requiring more people to exercise" with no actionable steps or clear reasons. It is important that the interviewer can see your thought process or where you derived your ideas from so that they are able to engage with you in conversation and further develop their impression of you.

Q88: What does law have to do with the environment?

This question is an opinion-based question designed to see whether an applicant can formulate convincing arguments in favour of a certain position. It is likely that your interviewer will play the devil's advocate so do not be put off if they press you on certain points.

You should demonstrate your logical thought process and ability to think on your feet, as these are qualities which the interviewer will be looking for. It is usually unlikely that you will be able to prepare and predict the topic of the question that will come out in the interview so you should focus on developing skills like being able to argue for and against your position as well as presenting a clear and compelling argument.

A **good applicant** would clearly state their opinion/position and the brief arguments for their position. They should also, if they can, provide some real-life examples as evidence in support. They could also present counter-arguments to their position and how they would resolve these in favour of their position.

A **sample** answer is as follows: I think there are several reasons why we bother with environmental protection. The main reason is for human health and all the other reasons can be linked to this. The state of the environment largely impacts our current and future quality of life. It is in our bests interests that we help maintain a healthy and functional ecosystem. As the climate change is quickly becoming a problem for our generation, it is imperative that we take serious steps to protect the environment if we want to live comfortable lives in the future and for future generations.

We also bother with environmental protection to protect the earth we live on. We currently are currently not able to live on any other planet. This is imperative to ensure that we do not go extinct as a race. We also bother because we might want to preserve the natural beauty of the earth for us to continue enjoying.

At this point it is likely that the interviewer will interject and ask you more questions about what you said.

A **poor applicant** might give an unbalanced argument or not defend their position well. For example, they might misinterpret the question and argue for or against environmental protection without addressing the part of the question that asks for your opinion on the issue. The question specifically asks why we bother – you must tell the interviewer why you think people bother with it not just generic arguments for and against environmental protection.

Q89: What is a country?

This question is a rather open-ended question designed to see how you define a term. This seemingly easy question is rather complex! It is an important skill for a law student as you would often have to define vague terms in your essays concisely and succinctly. You can impress the interviewer by giving both the surface-level and alternative definitions (with examples). This shows that you can go beyond the surface definition and demonstrate depth in your thinking and answer.

Don't worry too much if you do not know the 'right' answer or have the 'right' arguments/content which would have required a lot of research. It is better and advisable to focus on the way you **structure** and **approach** it. The interviewer is also likely to be able to help you out or guide you if you are stuck.

A **good applicant** would first give a layman definition before delving into the deeper meaning or alternative definitions/grey areas to this term. A good applicant will be able to see that there are many layers to this word and be able to concisely explain this to the interviewer.

A **sample** answer is as follows: There is no universally agreed definition to 'country' and the definition varies depending on various factors. For political reasons, there are examples of countries which do not recognise other 'countries' as such. For example, Taiwan claims to be a country, but China does not recognise it as such and sees Taiwan as another part of China. As a result, other countries who do not want to maintain good relationships with China might choose to also not recognise Taiwan as a country.

A common definition of country is one with a population, a defined territory, a government and capacity to enter in relations with other states. But there are many people who oppose to this definition and prefer the definition that if enough countries recognise you as a country, you are one despite not having control over territory or your population. Another common way may be that if a place is a member of the UN, it's a country. But this definition is problematic as Vatican City is considered a country but is not a member of the UN.

A **poor applicant** might give a long and simplistic answer. It is not how much or how quickly you speak in an interview but the quality of your answer that is important. You should, as much as possible, give a concise answer that addresses the question.

Q90: Define a miracle.

This question is a rather open-ended philosophical question designed to see how you define a term. This is an important skill for a law student as you would often have to define vague terms in your essays concisely and succinctly. You can impress the interviewer by giving both the surface-level and alternative definitions (with examples). This shows that you can go beyond the surface definition and demonstrate depth in your thinking and answer.

Don't worry too much if you do not know the 'right' answer or have the 'right' arguments/content which would have required a lot of research. It is better and advisable to focus on the way you **structure** and **approach** it. The interviewer is also likely to be able to help you out or guide you if you are stuck.

A **good applicant** would first give a layman definition before delving into the deeper meaning or alternative definitions to this term. A good applicant will be able to see that there are many layers to this word and be able to concisely explain this to the interviewer.

A **sample** answer is as follows: A miracle can be defined as an extraordinary event that defies natural or scientific laws. This is the most common definition and a simple example of a miracle is when the dead come back to life. Another definition would be a miracle as an interruption of the order or course of nature. This is a rather vague definition as we are unable to ascertain from this definition what is meant by the order or course of nature. Thomas Aquinas narrowed this definition by defining it as an event that exceeds the productive power of nature, where nature is construed broadly enough to include ourselves and other creatures like ourselves.

A miracle could also be defined more negatively as a violation of the laws of nature. David Hume famously adopted this definition which raised the bar higher for something to qualify as a miracle. However, I prefer the Aquinas definition to Hume's because bringing the concept of natural laws into the definition is problematic.

At this point, it is likely that the interviewer will ask you another question about this and you will engage in a discussion surrounding this.

A **poor applicant** might give a very long and irrelevant answer. It is not how much or how quickly you speak in an interview but the quality of your answer that is important. You should, as much as possible, give a concise answer that addresses the question.

PPE & HSPS

A law applicant may be asked a question relating to politics or wider philosophical issue. Despite being focused on law the questions you're asked may come from a wide range of areas, however, you will not be expected to demonstrate specific detailed knowledge in an area not studied previously, you will simply be expected to apply your own point of view and understanding to the topics. We've included practice questions from these subjects which we think will be valuable to you.

HSPS & PPE interviews generally consist of a large question with many smaller sub-questions to guide the answer from the start to a conclusion. The main question may seem difficult, impossible, or random at first, but take a breath and start discussing with your interviewer different ideas you have for breaking down the question into manageable pieces. Don't panic.

The questions are designed to be difficult to give you the chance to show your full intellectual potential. They will help guide you to the right idea if you provide ideas for them to guide. This is your chance to show your creativity, analytical skills, intellectual flexibility, problem-solving skills and your go-getter attitude. Don't waste it on nervousness or a fear of messing up or looking stupid.

The interviewer wants to see what you know and what you are capable of, not what you don't know – "positive interview".

When answering a question, you should be responsive to the interviewer and take on board their prompts and suggestions. If you are making an argument that is clearly wrong, then concede your mistake and try to revise your viewpoint – it is ok to say 'I didn't think of that' when taking on board a different viewpoint. Do not stubbornly carry on arguing a point that they are saying is wrong. **Making mistakes is not a bad thing** – if you can show that you have addressed a mistake and attempted to revise your argument upon the realisation of more information, you are showing a skill crucial to getting through essays and supervisions at an Oxbridge university.

Due to the amount of subjects available under the HSPS and PPE courses, **there are no set patterns to the questions you can get asked**. Most questions, however, will focus on a topic for which it is possible for any individual to have an opinion without previous knowledge of the area. This is to test the way you think about a topic and to test whether you are able to apply your own experiences and knowledge to an unknown subject area. These skills are important when studying HSPS/PPE as the courses are essay-based and rely strongly upon the ability to construct an argument based on the information provided. Many questions are related to society today and may require the individual to be familiar with current affairs and big events in the news.

A sociologist may be asked sociology questions or questions from a related subject, such as politics. An archaeologist will likely be asked questions on archaeology, history, and anthropology. Given the very broad nature of the course, candidates are required to have a general interest in all aspects of the course, but which subject will be the main focus of any interview should be clear beforehand.

The questions will usually take one of a few possible forms based on highlighting skills necessary to 'think like a social scientist.' **Five main questions types** are:

- Why do we need... (borders, welfare state, international institutions, museums etc.)?
- Compare X to Y... (normally based on your essay or personal statement, so something you are familiar with)
- Distinguish between... (state and nation, race and ethnicity, liberalism and libertarianism etc.)
- What do you think about... (the current British school system, nature vs. nurture debate etc.)?
- Why is there... (gender inequality in the workplace, poverty etc.)? How would you solve it?

Questions also have recurring themes that appear because they are important for social sciences: legitimacy and role of government, human rights, poverty, feminism, international institutions, the purpose of education and different educational systems, voting systems, inequality and social classes.

WORKED QUESTIONS

Below are a few examples of how to start breaking down an interview question, complete with model answers.

Q1: Can a violent protest ever be justified?

[Extremely clear-headed] **Applicant**: Well, I know that the law states that violence against other people or property is not acceptable, and yet I also know that violent protests still occur and this makes me wonder why. There must be a reason that people feel the need to turn to violence. This might be because of their personality or it may be something deeper such as the feeling of having no choice. If a point is important and the protest is for a serious reason, such as fighting for human rights, and all other forms of protest have been avoided, then maybe the only way to be heard is through violence. However, I don't think a violent protest can ever be justified. For example, take the 2011 UK Riots – violence didn't solve anything – it is a way of being seen and heard, but a horrific one. I don't think being heard for doing something that is wrong is the right way to be recognised.

This shows that **the question can be broken down into smaller-parts**, which can be dealt with in turn. At this point, the interviewer can give feedback if this seems like a good start and help make any necessary modifications. In this particular case, the applicant might be asked to expand on the reasons a person might resort to violence in protests and to give an example if possible. They may also be asked to provide a suggestion as to a better way to be heard than a violent protest. The details are unimportant, but the general idea of breaking down the question into manageable parts is important. The interviewer is not looking for an expert, but someone who can problem-solve in the face of new ideas.

A **poor applicant** may take a number of approaches unlikely to impress the interviewer. The first and most obvious of these is to simply answer 'yes' or 'no' with little justification or reference to an alternative point of view and with no attempt made to move forward. The applicants who have done this only make it worse for themselves by resisting prodding as the interviewer attempts to pull an answer from them, saying "fine, but I'm not going to be able to expand because I don't know anything about this", or equally unenthusiastic and uncooperative responses.

Another approach which is unhelpful in the interview is the '**brain dump**', where instead of engaging with the question, the applicant attempts to impress or distract with an assortment of related facts or events: In this case, reeling off the law on violence or a list of historical riots and their outcomes. Having gotten off to this start isn't as impressive as a more reasoned response, but the interview can be salvaged by taking feedback from the interviewer.

Many of these facts could start a productive discussion which leads to the answer if the applicant listens and takes hints and suggestions from the interviewer.

Q2: How do you know the moon isn't made out of cheese?

[Extremely clear-headed] **Applicant**: What I am first going to think about is what needs to be considered when deciding whether or not something is true. This raises questions like "Is it patently absurd?", "Is it backed up by evidence?", and "What types of evidence do we require?". Next, I consider whether it is reasonably possible that this statement fits with other associated and established pieces of knowledge, e.g. the formation of the planets, stars, and satellites. If the claim is at odds with established knowledge, then I may be more inclined to believe it untrue. However, this does not necessarily prove anything. For example, in this case, what is meant by cheese? If we are talking poetically, or aesthetically then it may be considered reasonable to make the above claim.

Moreover, whose reality are we talking about, and indeed does the result vary depending on this? I mean, is it really possible to 'know' anything, or are we just making educated guesses based on a set of assumptions married with some data – and does this count as 'real'? Essentially, when I first looked at the statement I thought it was completely absurd and previously proven otherwise. However, after consideration of perspective, definition, reality, and knowledge, I am now not so convinced.

Just like the previous example questions, this is a step by step answer. The applicant has broken down their thoughts and provided the interviewer with a stream of their own workings of their mind. This allows the interviewer to understand how the individual is breaking down the question and gives an opportunity for the interviewer to intervene with further questions if required.

A **poor applicant** may state something like "Well because it obviously isn't" – without any further justification. The point of a question like this is to consider the many different ways in which we experience reality and develop our understanding therein. If the applicant fails to address more than the superficial, then they are unlikely to show an understanding for the point of the question.

Q3: Despite knowing the health implications of smoking, why does it remain legal in the UK?

Good Applicant: I'd like to think about what other areas are considered by the **legislators of the UK** when they allocate legal status to things, as it can't just be health implications. With regards to smoking, there are a number of vested parties including tobacco companies and smokers themselves. Tobacco companies rely on smoking being legal in the UK for their income. If smoking were made illegal, then these companies would lose 100% of their UK revenue, which in turn, may impact the economy as a whole (these sales are far from insubstantial). Secondly, when thinking about smokers who are 20% of the UK's adult population (equating to around 10 million people), they represent a large fraction of the potential electorate.

Therefore, banning smoking would have significant implications for political intervention due to unpopularity, loss of freedom, etc.

As another point, smokers may claim that they have an addiction which is difficult to stop. They may also argue that smoking was legal when they first started to smoke. Thus, the government may face a legal battle if they were to suddenly make the product illegal. This may make a total ban on smoking impractical and a breach of an individual's right to choose. However, banning smoker on a more gradual basis may be feasible and is happening today; for example, it is now against the law to smoke in cars, in the workplace, and in public areas. Maybe **phasing out smoking** is more realistic, and is therefore what is being attempted in the UK. This would imply that it is not the case that legislators are unaware or uncaring of the health implications of smoking, but that they are attempting to reduce smoking in a less disruptive manner.

A **poor applicant** might fail to address the reasons why smoking has not been made illegal. It is not simply a case of saying "smoking is bad, therefore the government should ban it". The question of whether it should be banned impacts many people and showing an understanding of different perspectives and potential arguments is important for answering this question sufficiently.

Q4: If all countries have nuclear weapons, would there still be wars?

A **Good Applicant**: We all have learnt how dangerous nuclear weapons can be when **Hiroshima and Nagasaki** were destroyed at the end of World War 2. The threat to the environment, human lives, and even future generations is known, and the risk is too high. Nuclear weapons should not be used at all. On the other hand, it is true that there was no direct war between the USA and USSR during the Cold War and both had nuclear weapons. It seems possible that countries with nuclear weapons do not engage in war with one another as the high risk of a catastrophe deters them from using nuclear weapons, and hence the proliferation of nuclear weapons may prevent wars.

This shows that the candidate understands the question and is able to draw on some examples from A-level History. A **better candidate** would then engage in a discussion with the interviewer about the moral aspect of the topic or may choose to draw on a broader range of examples and realise that although proliferation of nuclear weapons may deter another world war, it could lead to more frequent small-scale wars. Examples of wars in Iraq, Vietnam, Afghanistan, and Korea during the Cold War demonstrate that there were, in fact, "real wars", and the USSR and USA backed smaller countries in war. So, the proliferation of nuclear weapons may have led to small-scale wars, yet prevented another world war. Making a moral case against any use of nuclear weapons, for instance, referring to the experience from Hiroshima and Nagasaki shows sensitivity about the topic.

A **poor applicant** may make a moral argument against the use of nuclear weapons before providing any insightful analysis and attempting an answer to the question. Another approach which is unhelpful is focusing too much on providing a yes/no answer to the question, and hence missing the point that the proliferation of nuclear weapons is a gradual process with various political, moral, and economic difficulties, and it is not plausible that all countries could get nuclear weapons overnight. The question is very broad and raises many interesting arguments for discussion, but 'brain dump' is not helpful here.

Q5: When we make contact with an extra-terrestrial civilisation, what should we tell them is humanity's greatest achievement?

[Extremely clear-headed] Applicant: The concept of humanity's greatest achievement is very subjective. It can either be measured in terms of effort needed to accomplish it, or in terms of impact. In the first case, humanity's greatest achievement could be the pyramids, since they required a tremendous amount of work with little technology, and are still standing today after thousands of years. In terms of impact, humanity's greatest achievement could be the discovery of penicillin for example. I think that it makes more sense to focus on a ground-breaking achievement from the past, rather than the most recent accomplishments of humanity.

If I were to tell an extra-terrestrial civilisation about penicillin, however, I would also have to provide an explanation on humanity's problems which it solved. Finally, I would have to take into account the aim of my message: am I trying to impress, intimidate, or simply inform?

A good applicant will understand the true aim of the question: creating an abstract situation in which he is encouraged to problematise the subjective concept of 'greatest achievement' and make an argument.

A poor applicant could misinterpret the question, and focus on the extra-terrestrial civilisation, talking about space technology and means of communication. Alternatively, he could choose an accomplishment and fail to justify his answer, or provide a lot of facts on the subject without problematising the concept of 'greatest achievement'.

Q6: In a democracy, can the majority impose its will on the minority?

[Extremely clear-headed] Applicant: First, I am going to think from the practical point of view: if by 'minority' we mean 'the ruling elites', does the majority have the actual ability to impose its will? The population only gets to make decisions on rare occasions: elections and referenda. Most of the time, decisions are made by a small group of people: the government. In 2002-2003, there were mass protests against the war in Iraq, but this did not stop Tony Blair from sending troops. It seems that once a government is in power, there is little that the majority of the population can do before the next elections. Secondly, we could think about the question from a normative point of view: should the majority be able to make most decisions in a democratic system? There is a difference between democracy and populism, where power is held by the masses. The latter could be problematic. If by minority we understand things such as small ethnic or religious groups, in a populist system they would have no say and could end up being oppressed. In a democratic system, minorities are protected by laws. However, we can see that the system is sometimes flawed. For example, in the US, there are only two major political parties: people with different agendas than Republicans or Democrats are pushed away from power.

This question can be answered in a number of ways, but a good candidate will show his capacity to deconstruct it, and think for a moment before replying. He will support his points with examples.

A poor applicant will rush into an answer without thinking and might end up getting confused between the different aspects of the question. He will either make generalisations without giving examples, or focus exclusively on a single real-life case, giving a lot of facts but without any argument or acknowledgment of a different point of view.

Q7: Why is there social inequality in the world? How would you resolve this issue?

[Extremely clear-headed] Applicant: I do not think that there is a single reason for social inequality in the world. Of course, it is not normal that 1% of the population controls almost 50% of its wealth. Greed and self-centeredness seem to be inherent flaws of humanity. However, I also think that there are other underlying factors behind social inequality. I cannot imagine a society in which everybody would have the same proportion of wealth and the same professional opportunities. People live in different places, speak different languages, and simply have different talents and skills. Thus, I do not think that social inequality can ever be fully resolved. Experiments such as communism in the USSR have attempted to artificially suppress inequality. This has not only entailed terrible crimes such as the extermination of entire groups in the society, but has also proved economically unsustainable in the long-term, with the Soviet economy eventually collapsing. Nevertheless, perhaps some form of **efficient taxation and governments granting more funds** to international organisations and NGOs could help reduce inequality.

A good applicant can have a different opinion on the subject, but will take into account other points of view, and will identify the difficulties associated with resolving such a complex problem, supporting his argument with solid A-level type factual knowledge.

A poor applicant could focus on only one of the two questions. He might give a 'trendy' answer such as "It's all because of the rich" or "Humans are bad so there is nothing you can do", without giving any real explanation or evidence, and refuse to engage fully with the questions.

Q8: To what extent is taxing the rich likely to lead to greater equality in society?

[Extremely clear-headed] Applicant: There is a big disproportion in terms of wealth between a small group of the 'rich' and the 'poor' majority. Therefore, it would seem logical to find a way of redistributing that wealth. As we can see, altruism does not suffice, since the problem persists despite a few notable examples of rich people giving big proportions of their fortune to charity, for instance, Bill Gates. Taxation does seem like a good solution. However, it needs to be designed efficiently. For instance, we must make sure that such a tax does not affect the economy negatively, for example, by dissuading the wealthy from opening new businesses and sources of income. Secondly, there have been cases where large funds were not used efficiently, but rather usurped by local warlords and criminal organisations, for instance in Somalia in the 1990s. It might be necessary to establish an international body of experts to design and monitor the implementation of projects funded by this tax.

A good applicant will be able to **identify both the positive and the negative sides of such a policy**. Regardless of whether he has any knowledge on the subject, he will provide a well-structured, logical answer.

A poor applicant might be intimidated by the question and refuse to answer by saying something like "I don't know anything about taxes". Alternatively, he might provide an answer which focuses only on one side of the coin, making it very vulnerable to counterarguments.

Q9: Is alcohol addiction always a result of the social environment, peer pressure, and negative role models?

[Extremely clear-headed] **Applicant:** Alcohol addiction is more widespread in certain social environments or countries: for instance, it is a much bigger problem in Russia than in the UK. I don't think that it would be appropriate to argue that nationality or ethnicity inherently determines the likelihood of alcohol addiction.

This is why explanations such as **peer pressure and negative role models** are very useful. Indeed, peer pressure can become integrated into culture. For example, drinking alcohol in large quantities on a teenage trip abroad or on an American Spring Break has become almost a ritual. In some cultures, drinking vast amounts of alcohol can be considered as a mark of virility, or politeness, which is conducive to alcohol addiction. However, we should not generalise. It is possible for someone to develop an alcohol addiction in an environment where drinking is frowned upon or rare, just as it is possible to remain abstinent while being surrounded by alcoholics. If an individual's parents and friends do not drink, and yet he becomes an alcohol addict citing a musician with questionable habits as his role model, it seems reasonable to assume that other factors, perhaps psychological, were at play. Thus, while the social environment is a very potent explanation for alcohol addiction, ignoring the possibility of other factors could have negative consequences, such as failing to properly address the issue.

A good applicant will **note the use of the word 'always'**, and attempt to come up with a counter-example.

A poor candidate might fall into the trap of agreeing with the statement without thinking of other points of view. He could refuse to reply stating his lack of knowledge on the topic, or give anecdotal evidence from his experience or environment without constructing an argument.

Q10: Imagine you are a historian a hundred years in the future, looking back on today. What aspects of society would you focus on?

[Extremely clear-headed] **Applicant:** I do not think that any aspect of history should be discarded as unimportant. However, I am most interested by politics and geopolitics. It is basically impossible to predict the future, and very hard to fully understand the present and its implications. A hundred years from now, we will have a much better understanding of some of today's unanswered questions. For instance, how successful are international organisations in fostering cooperation and preventing conflict? After all, the UN and the EU are relatively recent constructs, and did not fully exploit their potential until the end of the Cold War.

Determining whether international institutions have any real influence or whether they are just tools in the hands of self-centered states is one of the big debates in the study of international relations. Secondly, it would be interesting to see whether in the **age of mass information** and communication, humanity is able to learn from its previous mistakes. Parties of the extreme right are currently gaining a lot of votes in Europe, due among others to economic hardship. Will European countries suffer a fate similar to the Weimar Republic?

A good candidate will demonstrate a certain degree of knowledge on the current topic of his choice, and will be able to identify the way in which it might be perceived by a historian.

A poor candidate might avoid the question by saying something like "I think that humanity will destroy itself within a hundred years so there will be no historians left". He could also lose track of his argument by trying to impress the interviewer with his factual knowledge on a current topic, or attempt to make unjustified predictions of future developments.

Q11: Tell me about some political texts that you have read.

[Extremely clear-headed] **Applicant:** I have looked at some political theory texts, such as Plato's Republic. In this text, the author is describing a perfect political system, an ideal city led by a philosopher-king. He also talks about other flawed political systems, such as tyranny or democracy. I think that this text is very interesting and useful for understanding political systems from the past, and has also inspired other, more recent authors. However, it is important to note that Plato writes from the perspective of Ancient Greece, and many of his concepts are outdated. I think that the term 'political text' could also apply to other types of documents, for example, party programmes, but even literary fiction. I recently read Bulgakov's Master and Margarita, a novel with fantasy themes such as the devil and witchcraft, written in the Soviet Union. Its focus on religion and the occult was also a hidden critique of the atheistic Soviet society. Similar things could be said about the Animal Farm or 1984.

A **good candidate** will try to go beyond simply giving factual knowledge on a text studied in class. He will try to come up with a critical approach towards the text showing a certain degree of independent thought, or problematize the term 'political texts'.

A poor candidate might panic if he has not studied texts of political theory in school, instead of making the best of it by trying to come up with different types of political texts. Alternatively, he might opt for dumping a lot of factual information on a text, instead of showing his understanding of it or demonstrating a critical perspective.

Q12: What are the main reasons for persistent unemployment in the UK?

Extremely clear-headed] Applicant: I think that people are often tempted to look for simple explanations behind complicated issues. This is why extreme political parties are so successful: they provide the population with easily identifiable scapegoats such as 'the current government', 'immigrants', or 'the EU', and blame them for every economic and social problem. In reality, issues such as unemployment have many reasons. One of them could be the discrepancy between supply and demand: what type of jobs people are prepared for at schools and universities, and what type of jobs are offered on the market. For instance, in Scandinavian countries, when an unemployed individual cannot find work for a certain period of time, he is offered courses which allow him to perform a different type of work, where there is more demand.

Another reason could indeed be **globalisation**, with the **international economic crisis**, and many companies moving abroad to reduce costs. However, this does not justify oversimplifying the issue by blaming solely external factors such as foreigners or international organisations. Instead, efforts should be made to better adapt the national system to the realities of the globalised world.

A good candidate will try to provide a balanced and well-argued answer, regardless of his political or moral stance. He will stay away from generalisations and normative statements based on little or no evidence.

A poor applicant might refuse to engage with a question on which he has little previous knowledge. Alternatively, he may make sweeping generalisations or provide an exhaustive list of factors without really explaining any of them.

Q13: Should prisoners have the right to vote?

[Extremely clear-headed] Applicant: I think that in a democracy, voting is one of the **citizen's basic rights**. The question is: should prisoners still be considered as citizens? It could be said that when they break the social contract of norms governing the society, their rights are also revoked. However, if a prisoner is deprived of all his rights, his eventual reintegration into society will be even harder. In my opinion, the right to vote should be granted to those prisoners who have not committed the gravest of crimes, such as murder or rape.

Moreover, in some countries, the issue of 'political prisoners' is still prominent, for instance, in China or Ukraine. If someone is imprisoned for disagreeing with the regime and has no right to vote for a different party or candidate, then there is little chance of change and the system moves one step further towards authoritarianism.

A poor applicant could focus too much on providing a yes/no answer based on personal beliefs or anecdotal evidence, without trying to engage with alternative perspectives on the question.

Q14: Is there such a thing as national identity in the world of globalisation?

[Extremely clear-headed] Applicant: In my opinion, while borders are becoming more and more permeable and people can communicate and travel from one part of the world to the other, national identity is not necessarily losing its potency. According to the Marxist theory, national identity was supposed to disappear, giving way to an international movement of workers. This was not really accomplished, and the communist countries which survived the longest such as the Soviet and Chinese systems, were those which mixed communism with nationalism. While from our 'Western' perspective it might seem that national identity is dying, this might be related to the fact that we live in relatively peaceful times: there has been no war on the current territory of the EU for decades.

However, in times of conflict, national identity becomes very powerful. We can see this on current examples such as Ukraine and Russia, but also in post 9/11 USA. I think that in times of external threat, people tend to unite under a symbol which differentiates them from the 'other'. Since the nation state remains the main actor in international relations, most conflicts are likely to oppose one nation against another, thus reinforcing the sense of national identity.

A **good candidate** can argue either way, but should be able to acknowledge both sides of the coin. He should be able to support his ideas with some factual A-level type knowledge.

A poor applicant might fail to engage properly with the question, instead of trying to impress the interviewer by dumping facts. Alternatively, he could make broad generalisations without supporting his argument with any real evidence.

PPE INTERVIEW QUESTIONS

Q15: Do you believe that the market should be completely free, or should government intervene?

This is an economics question which seeks for you to discuss the problem of market failure in macroeconomics. The interviewer will be looking for the candidate to demonstrate knowledge of the ways in which the market can fail, and governments can intervene to solve this. With this type of question, it is impossible to talk about every possible way in which the government should intervene, and so a stronger candidate will try to stick to one or two examples, and go into significant detail on this.

Bad answer: The government should not intervene because the market allocates resources much more efficiently than governments will ever be able to.

This is a bad answer because, whilst the candidate is right to discuss the allocative efficient which markets may have over the government, they assume that allocative efficiency in markets is <u>always</u> higher, and in doing so, they do not consider cases when there is market failure. It is unlikely that a candidate will perform well by claiming that there is never any way a government needs to intervene, even if they are in favour of less governmental intervention more generally. They should instead opt to explain cases of market failure and how the government can fix this.

Good answer: Yes, there are cases when the government should intervene in the market. This should happen when there is market failure, as is the case with public goods and merit or demerit goods. For example, public goods are goods which are non-rivalrous and non-excludible. This means that there is no profit to be gained by providing the good, and thus the market is not incentivised to provide it. This occurs in street lighting, which local governments fund, to make up for the failure of markets to provide it. If the government did not intervene in this case no street lighting will be provided. Merit goods can also benefit from government intervention because, in the case of merit goods, the market fails to provide the good at the level which is socially desirable. These goods, such as education, have positive externalities. The government should therefore subsidise merit goods to increase the production and consumption of the merit good to the socially desirable level. Therefore, there are some cases when the government should intervene in the market.

This is a good answer because the candidate focuses on a few cases of market failure, and explains why the government should intervene in these cases. The candidate demonstrates good understanding of market failure, and gives a very good answer, especially, of why public goods need to be provided by the government.

Q16: Was the financial crisis of 2008 a failure of regulation?

This is an economics question which expects the candidate to have an awareness of current affairs, and of economics in the real world. The interviewer will be looking for the candidate to apply core economic ideas to this real life situation, and to show a strong ability for critical analysis. These kind of questions are very common, and so candidates should prepare themselves by researching some of the largest events in current affairs and the economic impact these will have, prior to the interview.

Bad answer: Yes, it was a failure of regulation because if the government told banks to stop lending to those who couldn't pay it back, there wouldn't have been a crash.

This is a bad answer because, whilst it shows that the candidate is broadly aware of the reason for the financial crisis, they clearly do not show a deep understanding of it. They also do not explain how regulation could have helped the situation. In general, this answer is far too brief, which will give the interviewer the impression that the candidate cannot think of anything to say.

Good answer: Yes, it was a failure of regulation. This is because the financial crisis happened when banks lent out large high-risk loans for mortgages in America to people who would be unable to pay them. This led to a housing market bubble which then crashed when people found themselves unable to pay back the loans with interest, and therefore had to default on the loans. This meant that many financial institutions failed in America. As a consequence, banks around the world, including in the UK, found themselves in crisis, as there became a shortage in funds to cover day to day costs, causing a liquidity crisis. There are two ways in which financial regulation may have helped.

Firstly, if the markets had been more regulated in America, then American banks would not have been able to lend out such high risk loans, which were very likely to be defaulted on. Secondly, If the financial market in the UK had been more regulated, UK banks may not have been so reliant on American banks for their own stability, and thus, they would have been more resistant to the spread of the financial crisis from America. Therefore, the financial crisis of 2008 was a failure of regulation.

This is a good answer because the candidate demonstrates an in depth knowledge of the financial crisis, and its causes. They discuss how regulation may have prevented the crisis, and therefore persuasively argue that the financial crisis was a from a failure of regulation.

Q17: Let's say that the value of the Yen and the Dollar exchange places overnight, what do you think the impacts of this would be on the global market?

This is an economics question which expects the candidate to have a good grasp of the way that currencies work. This is a very hard question, so make it is important to take a few minutes to think about it, and not to become too stuck on the question. Work through the question bit by bit to make it more manageable.

Bad answer: The Japanese Yen in America would eventually become equivalent to what the US Dollar is currently, as the currency adapts itself to the economy. The same thing will happen the other way round, with the US Dollar in Japan becoming equivalent to how what the Japanese Yen currently is. The two will therefore swap value.

This is a bad answer because, whilst it shows that the candidate shows an awareness of the fact that currencies reflect the economy they belong to, and therefore should in the long run settle down to the usual rate that the relative countries would expect their currency to be at, the candidate shows no understanding of the short run consequences. It is not enough to say that the two will simply swap value, which may well happen in the long term, but after a very tumultuous short term in which the respective countries will see huge changes in their balance of trade. Furthermore, the explanation which the candidate does give is confusing.

Good answer: If the values of the US Dollar and Japanese Yen were swapped overnight, there would be a huge swing in the economy of both America and Japan, as well as of other countries. In America, the US Dollar would very suddenly be worth considerably less. This would mean that there would be a surge to buy the US Dollar, as it becomes a comparatively more price-competitive option on the global financial market. This will cause it to suddenly increase in price. In contrast, Japan will have the opposite effect, where people will rush to sell their Yens, due to them being worth a lot of money. This will lead to a devaluation of the Yen. In the process, in America, as US Dollars are so cheap, there will be a huge increase in demand for US goods from foreign markets, leading to an increase in exports from America. This means that there will be a sudden trade surplus. The opposite will happen in Japan, where Japanese goods will become comparatively expensive, and foreign goods comparatively cheaper, and so there will be an increase in imports for Japan. This means there will be a sudden trade deficit. In the long term, the currencies will therefore return to normal. However, not without economic chaos which will result in the short term from such sudden and drastic changes. As well as this, so many other currencies linked to US Dollars, and so many countries' reserves are held in US dollars, as the currency usually considered the strongest in the world. Therefore, these countries would lose a lot of money overnight as the US Dollar suddenly became worth less. This would cause these countries to suffer from further economic problems, including the potential to enter a recession as a result.

This is a good answer because the candidate demonstrates an awareness of exchange rates, the trade balance, and the ways in which foreign markets interact. They also do well to bring in how it would affect other countries than America and Japan.

Q18: Do you think that property tycoons should pay more attention to how you win in monopoly? Why?

This is an economics question which is the type of unusual and unexpected interview question that is typical of an Oxbridge interview. The interviewer will be looking for the candidate to demonstrate that they can think creatively, and to apply some of the tactics they would use in monopoly in real life. The question also requires for the candidate to have an awareness of the problems economists face with applying economic principles to reality.

Bad answer: In monopoly I buy the properties which are most likely to be landed on. In real life, you should also produce goods and services which are most likely to be demanded by consumers.

This is a bad answer because the candidate fails to discuss the difficulties involved in applying monopoly tactics to real life. They also do not give that creative a discussion of their monopoly tactics, and only discuss demand and supply in a very simplistic way.

Good answer: In monopoly, the best way to win is to buy up properties which are most likely to be landed on, of the same colour, and then develop these as quickly as possible. In real life, there obviously doesn't exist the same colour scheme which incentivises buying one colour property in monopoly, but we can compare this to buying similar businesses in real life, which would give a company greater market share. Therefore, this it is a good tactic to purchase more businesses in the same market in order to increase your market share as much as possible, so that you have more power over price setting in order to profit maximise. As well as this, you should, just as in monopoly, develop the business as quickly as possible in order to become more efficient, as happens with business expansion, and therefore to be more able to cover costs and profit maximise. This happens because the marginal cost per additional unit produced is often diminishing, and, thus, the business will make marginally increasing amounts of profit through expansion, until they reach economies of scale. However, such expansion is not always possible in real life, due to limited resources, other competitors who may make it significantly harder to expand than is the case in monopoly, and market regulations which prevent monopolisation and strong concentration of markets.

This is a good answer because the candidate considers creatively the ways in which monopoly tactics can be applied to microeconomics. They demonstrate a good knowledge of core business principles. They also go on to show an awareness of the difficulties that businesses face in expanding, and trying to increase market share.

Q19: What makes diamonds so much more valuable than raw steel?

This is an economics question which looks for the candidate to assess their knowledge of how goods end up having their particular level of demand, and why demand doesn't always match usefulness of the good. It also invites the candidate to discuss how supply affects price of goods.

Bad answer: Diamonds are expensive because there are less diamonds and so there is small level of supply. This means that the place on a demand/supply diagram at which the two lines cross is at a very high price. Because there are so few, there are a small amount of people who will be willing to pay lots for diamonds. In contrast, there is a large supply of steel, and so the supply curve crosses the demand curve at a significantly lower level. Therefore, steel is cheap.

This is a bad answer because, although the candidate does explain the supply side reasons for the price, they do not discuss any demand side reasons at all. This misses the point of the question, as interviewers will be looking for candidates to explain why there is such demand for diamonds, which have significantly less functionality than steel, which has a large amount of uses.

Good answer: Diamonds are so expensive for two reasons. Firstly, because the supply is very limited of diamonds in comparison to steel, the market price for diamond is very high, as the market allocates the few diamonds to those who are willing and able to pay for them. In contrast, the high quantity of steel that can be supplied means that the market price for steel is significantly lower. However, this does not really explain why demand for diamonds is so high, given the limited function we have for diamond in comparison to steel. This can only be explained by the fact that fashion has caused demand to be higher for diamond than the amount of uses we have for them would suggest. This is an irrational human behaviour which has made the relatively useless good desirable because it acts as a symbol for wealth – the lack of availability of diamond is therefore what makes them fashionable, which drives them to have such high demand.

This is a good answer because the candidate explains both the supply side reasons and the demand side reasons for why diamonds are so expensive and steel is so cheap. The candidate does well in seeing that the lack of supply for diamonds is what may actually drive demand for them.

Q20: Many industries are outsourcing less and less as it is disincentivised by government policy, do you think this is a bad thing?

This is an economics question which allows the candidate to talk about outsourcing, both from the point of view of businesses and of governments. This is a fairly simple question, so you should make sure not to overcomplicate your answer

Bad answer: Outsourcing is a bad thing because outsourced companies only look for their own profits, and therefore do not offer the best service to consumers, which the government can do better.

This is a bad answer because the candidate seems to think that the only type of outsourcing is governmental outsourcing. The candidate is right to explain that outsourcing business tasks from the government to the business introduces a profit motive which was previously not there, and therefore may mean they don't act in the interest of the consumer. However, this candidate does not realise that private companies may outsource business processes to other companies. Therefore, it cannot be the case that in <u>every</u> example of outsourcing, a profit motive is introduced which was not previously there.

Good answer: Outsourcing can be good in some situations, and bad in others. Many private companies outsource business processes to other private companies in quite simple ways which help to create efficiency. This can happen when, for example, a café outsources a painting business to decorate their café. This is quite a simple example of outsourcing and one which is non-controversial. In this case, no new profit motive is introduced where there wasn't one before. However, when the government outsources business processes to private companies, this becomes more controversial. In these cases, I believe that outsourcing is a bad thing. This is because, the government has the responsibility and the electoral motive to act in the interest of the public. When they outsource business processes to private companies, they do so under the argument that they are more efficient due to the fact that they have a profit motive which the government didn't. However, quite often the reason they are more efficient is because they strip the costs of the businesses down in order to increase profit margins. In the process, the consumer or the general public who they are paid to provide for, are likely to lose out on some of the services the government would have provided. Private companies will seek to act for the sake of profit, instead of in the interest of the people they are supplying the good or service to.

This is a good answer because the candidate does not simply talk about government outsourcing, but considers outsourcing more generally. They also provide a clear and persuasive justification for their argument, and consider the argument from the other side.

Q21: Imagine you have just opened up a new airline that flies a unique route (London and Tokyo). How would you determine what price to set tickets at to ensure maximal profit?

This is an economics question which expects the candidate to demonstrate knowledge of microeconomic principles, and specifically with how a company should profit maximise. The interviewer will expect the candidate to demonstrate knowledge of market concentration and monopolisation, as well as being able to work out how costs effect profits.

Bad answer: You should look around to see what other airlines are charging. Then you should charge less than them to undercut those airlines.

This is a bad answer because, whilst the candidate demonstrates some knowledge of competition theory, they do not consider other important factors such as cost of flying and the fact that , as the new airline flies a unique route, there are some ways in which the new airline is a monopoly. Therefore, the airline does not need to undercut other airlines.

Good answer: The first thing which should be considered is the cost involved in flying from London to Tokyo. Tickets must at least cover costs. The second thing to consider is the competition for pricing. If the company is a monopoly, then they will have complete market power to set prices as they please. The new company does fly a unique route, and for this reason it is in some ways a monopoly. However, it does not truly have 100% of the market share due to the fact that there will be some indirect ways to get between London and Tokyo. Nevertheless, the company will be able to charge a very high price as their large amount of market power means they have a lot of freedom to set their own prices.

The next thing to consider is at which specific price they should pick for maximum profit. It usually will be the profit maximising solution to charge the highest price that enough people will be willing and able to pay to completely fill the plane. However, if some are willing to pay such a high price that they make up for some people being priced out of plane tickets, then it may not be profit maximising. This is unlikely is unlikely as it would require for these people to be willing and able to pay a significantly higher amount. Therefore, the price the airline should set is that which is the maximum that enough people are willing and able to pay in order to sell a ticket for every seat.

This is a good answer because the candidate discusses core economic concepts in a good amount of detail. They especially do well in analysing what kind of market share the business has, and therefore what kind of freedom they will have to set their own prices. They do not make the mistake that the bad candidate does in presuming that the company will have to act very competitively.

Q22: Why do you think financiers and financial institutions are so preoccupied with the golden ratio?

This is an economics question which requires the candidate to have some knowledge of banks and investment, as well as how the stock market works specifically. Don't worry if you struggle to get the answer to this in an interview. It is a very difficult question. Start by thinking about what the golden ratio is in maths, and seeing if you can apply this to banks and investment firms.

Bad answer: The golden ratio is considered the mathematically perfect number, and therefore markets stock markets will naturally increase or decrease in proportion to the golden ratio.

This is a bad answer because, whilst the candidate demonstrates that they have some knowledge of the way in which the golden ration comes into the stock market, they do not really explain this in a non-confusing and clear way. Furthermore, they don't really explain what the golden ratio is.

Good answer: The golden ratio is a special number in mathematics, symbolised by the Greek letter phi, which is the ratio between consecutive Fibonacci numbers that the Fibonacci sequence tends towards. This is considered in many ways the mathematically perfect number, as it is a number which occurs frequently in nature. The number also occurs, so the theory holds, in the stock market. For example, when an individual stock market sees an increase in stock price, the amount it increases and then the amount it retrospectively decreases, is propionate to the golden ratio. Therefore, banks and investment firms obsess over this number because it allows them to help predict how much stock prices will rise and fall, and therefore, at which points they should sell stocks, and at which points this should buy stock. This helps them to maximise profit.

This is a good answer because the candidate shows knowledge on a complex theory. The candidate will not be expected to have perfect knowledge of this, but it is good to show knowledge of the ways in which banks and investment firms seek to predict the rise and fall of stock markets. This candidate also does well in explaining the benefit of predicting this.

Q23: How would you go about trying to identify the warning signs of an economic recession - if you could spot it soon enough, can you think of a way to avoid depressions?

This is an economics question which requires the candidate to explain some of their core macroeconomic concepts in order to show how they might predict recessions and depressions. However, the candidate must also show awareness of how economic shocks may unexpectedly happen.

Bad answer: We can predict an economic recession by seeing if GDP is about to slow down. A depression can be avoided by the government investing in the economy to encourage spending, and therefore to encourage growth.

This is a bad answer because the candidate does not really show how an economic recession can be predicted. A recession does happen following a slow down of growth in GDP, which is followed by a decrease in the rate of growth of GDP, but in waiting for the economy to slow down, we are not really predicting a recession, but seeing it happen in real time. The candidate does not acknowledge that it is actually very difficult to predict a recession. As well as this, the candidate fails to fully explain why their solution for preventing a depression would in fact prevent it.

Good answer: A recession occurs when the rate of growth of GDP is negative for two consecutive quarters. A depression occurs when there is a decrease in real GDP over a significant period of time. It is quite difficult to predict a recession as it is hard to know when the upturn of the business cycle will change (ie how long a boom will last). However, there are some warning signs which may show that we are leading towards a recession. These may be things like a decrease in consumer confidence, which leads to decreased expenditure, or an increase in unemployment. However, often, when these things are significant enough to be noticeable, it is too late to avoid a recession. There may be earlier sign that the economy may later suffer a recession, such as the existence of market bubbles, which may crash and cause a recession. However, it is very difficult, again, to see which markets are bubbles, and when they will crash. Once there is a recession, there are some things which the government can do to prevent it being prolonged, and becoming a depression. These include investment to create jobs. This helps to tackle unemployment, and therefore to increase the disposable income available to economic agents. This mean they will increase expenditure, leading to an increase in growth of GDP, thus helping to prevent a depression. This will serve as an injection into the economy, will would also have a multiplier effect, leading to even more economic growth.

This is a good answer because the candidate shows awareness of the causes of recessions and depressions, as well as how to prevent a depression. They also demonstrate a good level of understanding of how difficult it can be to predict an economic recession.

Q24: Do you think that India, which has a substantial space programme, should still be getting aid payments from other countries?

This is an economics question which requires the candidate to discuss the controversial topic of aid, and to critically analyse whether aid should be given to countries who choose to allocate their own resources to things such as international space programmes, which do not help those in poverty. The candidates which perform best will be prepared to pick one side of the argument, rather than remaining on the fence. They must also, however, consider the arguments against their viewpoint

Bad answer: Aid should not go to countries that have international space programmes because they have enough resources to allocate to space programmes, and, therefore, they should allocate these resources instead to helping to fight poverty in the country.

This answer shows potential insofar as they begin to make a compelling argument for why aid should be given to countries that have international space programmes. However, the candidate fails to use much of an economic justification for this, and therefore gives a fairly superficial answer.

Good answer: I can see why we would want to avoid giving aid to countries which have international space programmes, on the grounds that these countries should allocate their resources to higher priority areas, such as tackling poverty. However, the fact that the countries have international space programmes does not mean that they would reallocate these funds towards helping to solve poverty in the country if aid is removed. It is true that it should be the government of India's responsibility to tackle these problems in their country if they are able to. However, this doesn't mean that we shouldn't give aid if they do not opt to do so, as this would mean taking away financial support in the form of aid for those who may not get the support from the government instead. Furthermore, there are reasons beyond helping these people which make aid a good thing to do, such as maintaining good relations with other countries.

Giving aid which is well targeted may help lift these people out of poverty, which means that they have more disposable income, and so can increasing spending, which will lead to economic growth. However, at a certain point, once the country is developed enough, the UK may be able to stop giving aid and instead increase trade with these countries, which has economic benefits for both countries involved. This is, however, most efficient once countries have a large enough level of development that consumers have disposable income to be able to increase spending. Therefore, we should not look towards whether a country has a space programme to see whether we should continue to give aid, but whether the poorest are at a level in which they will be able to survive, and the economy is strong enough to be able to benefit more from trade instead.

This is a good answer because the candidate shows a clear knowledge of the benefit of aid, ad the reasons why aid might be stopped in a country. The candidate evaluates the arguments against their position, and arrives at a nuanced answer.

Q25: How would you judge the extent of the differences between a capitalist and a communist system?

This is a question which could be asked for both economics and politics. It invites the candidate to demonstrate their understanding of the different political and economic systems, as well as to critically analyse the difference between the two. The candidate should seek to utilise real world examples where possible.

Bad answer: Capitalism is an economic system in which goods, property, and businesses are owned privately, whereas communism is an economic system in which they are owned by the state. Therefore, the two are different.

This is a bad answer because the candidate demonstrates a lack of critical analysis about the difference between the two economic systems. It is perfectly fine to argue that they are different, but the candidate fails to engage in the alternate argument. They could also benefit from stating more clearly why the two are different.

Good answer: Capitalism, it is standardly claimed, is an economic system in which goods, property, and businesses are privately owned, and resources are therefore distributed through market mechanisms. Communism is an economic system in which these are owned by the state instead, and so resources are distributed by the government. The main difference between these, therefore, is the fact that, in communism, private property doesn't exist, and so the allocation of resources does not depend upon the free market. However, this picture is complicated by the existence of mixed economies. These exist when some things are owned and distributed by the government, and some by the free market. Most countries which have a mixed economy are considered capitalist countries, on account of the fact that they have private markets. The standard definition is in fact not that suitable for capitalism because it is impossible for nothing to be owned and distributed by the government, if a country has a government. Therefore, there is at least some way in which all capitalist countries allocate resources through the government, unless they are an anarchist country, which is an oxymoron. Therefore, a line must be drawn in order to determine at which point a mixed economy is a capitalist country, and at which point it is communist. This is what causes people to argue that they are not so different. However, I believe that the existence of any private market at all makes a country capitalist, and, therefore, capitalism does maintain a fundamental difference to communism.

This is a good answer because the candidate is able to engage with the arguments on the other side of their argument, because reaching a persuasive conclusion. They also engage critically with the standard definitions of capitalism and communism, in a way which enhances their argument.

Q26: Your friend is running a struggling corner shop, she knows you've done some work on economics and asks for your advice - they have £25 they'd like to spend on developing their sales, what three things would you recommend that they do, with or without that money?

This is an economics question in which the candidate needs to show their knowledge of core microeconomic concepts, as well as their understanding of businesses. With this kind of question, it is important that the candidate does not over think the answer.

Bad answer: The business should spend money on expanding, on marketing, and on innovation to create new and unique products.

This is a bad answer because, whilst the candidate demonstrates awareness on the ways in which businesses can increase their sales, they are overoptimistic with how far the £25 will go. As well as this, the candidate fails to explain why these things will increase sales, or give any kind of discussion on how much each measure will cost them. Furthermore, the answer is far too brief and vague.

Good answer: One thing to consider is that £25 is not that much money, and will only stretch so far. Therefore, businesses should be smart with how they utilise this money. The best way to increase sales would probably be to spend the majority of the money on advertising. Facebook provides a useful and free platform to promote the business. Some of their advertisement may come at no cost, such as by posting about the business in local Facebook pages. They can also use Facebook to target ads at people who will most likely use the goods and services they produce, and who are local to the business. Some money may also be used on making the front of the business, such as the store if it is a shop, appealing for customers. Some cleaning products and a bit of paint can go a long way in encouraging customers to visit their store, without involving a large expenditure. Finally, the business owner can spend time teaching employees how to be approachable, and to cultivate an atmosphere of good customer relations.

This again can help make the business appealing to customers, and encourage local people to see the business in a good light. These collectively will increase the number of customers and therefore increase sales.

This is a good answer because the candidate explains their three recommendations, and explains in detail why these will help increase sales. They also give a vague idea of how much each of their recommendations would cost, which helps to show the interviewer that they know what they're talking about.

Q27: Do you think the separator between a global company and a failed company is innovation, or are there other factors at play?

This is an economics question in which the candidate needs to show their knowledge of core microeconomic concepts, as well as their understanding of businesses. It also requires the candidate to have some knowledge of the difference between international markets and home markets.

Bad answer: Some brands go global because they sell highly desirable goods or services at a good price, whereas others fail because people in different countries do not want to buy their goods or services.

This is a bad answer because the candidate shows a lack of awareness about the reasons some brands are able to go global. They do not explain specifically what it is which may make a product desirable in a global market, and why some brands will fail to appeal them. This answer could also benefit from a discussion of the ways in which exchange rate mays affect which brands go global, and the ways in which marketing of a brand may affect this.

Good answer: Some brands may go global because they have a good understanding of the new markets which they are entering. As demand for a good or service may be affected by the culture of the country they look to trade in, it is important for the brand to have properly researched this, in order to cater their product towards this market. It is also important, for the same reason to cater their advertising and marketing towards the new market they seek to enter. One of the most common reason that a brand may fail to break into a global market is because they fail to understand the cultural differences which affect demand for certain products. As well as this a brand which is based in one country may have an advantage over another, when it comes to breaking into a foreign market, on the grounds that the goods are cheaper to produce in that country, and the exchange rate is favourable to them exporting the good. This means that government policy on trade may affect whether a brand is able to go global.

This is a good answer because the candidate shows an understanding of both the microeconomic and the macroeconomic reasons why a brand may be able to go global. The candidate gives an insightful analysis on the ways in which culture affects demand in a country, and therefore shows that business should cater their goods and marketing towards the markets they wish to enter into.

Q28: What do you think were the main factors driving the American Great Depression - do you think that understanding its causes could teach us valuable lessons?

This is an economics question which invites the candidate to discuss the history of economics, and the kind of real life consequences which economics can have. It is very important that candidates should have an awareness of the cause of the great depression before the interview, as a question on this kind of topic, or related to it, has a high chance of coming up.

Bad answer: The great depression happened in America as a result of the Wall Street crash which led to millions of Americans becoming unemployed. We should avoid this in order to ensure that unemployment doesn't increase as it did them.

This is a bad answer because, whilst everything the candidate explains is true, they fail to really explain what caused the great depression, the reasons for the Wall Street crash, and how this effected markets other than the financial market. Furthermore, they do not explain why this led to unemployment, and they do not go into much detail on what we can learn from it.

Good answer: The great depression happened in America because, following a large expansion in the stock market in the 1920s, there was a sudden crash. This became known as the Wall Street crash. This led to a panic, with investors pulling out of the stock market, leading to many investment businesses going bankrupt. It sent shockwaves through the economy, and drastically reduced consumer and producer confidence, which led to a decrease in expenditure on consumption and investment, and therefore, a decrease in productive output. This mean that there was a drastic decrease in growth. One of the most significant consequences of this was that individuals got laid off, and unemployment reached a record high. As unemployment became so high, people were unable to spend, and the depression therefore continued to worsen. One lesson that can be learnt from this is for the government to regulate the financial sector to help avoid crashes in the stock market, and to temper the damages when these crashes do happen. As well as this, we can learn that, when a crisis begins to unfold, an increase in unemployment can make matters worse, and allow the crisis to dig itself even deeper. The government should therefor act early to save as many jobs as possible, by investing to create new jobs.

This is a good answer because the candidate shows a good awareness of what happened in the great depression. Furthermore, they very effectively apply their knowledge of economics to this event, and come up with some good and detailed recommendations for what can be learnt from this event in history.

Q29: You've been presented with an unknown symbol - how might you go about trying to decipher its meaning?

This is a question which looks at assessing how you reason in logical tasks. This is the kind of question which may throw a candidate in an interview, so it is important to have a few moments to gather your thoughts and think about how you would logically approach the question. It is also worth noting that the question does not just want you to discuss how you decipher symbols, but what you <u>first look for</u> when deciphering symbols. This means that it is unnecessary to give a full explanation of the full process you might go through to decipher a symbol.

Bad answer: I look to see if it looks like anything I am familiar with and then we can assume that the symbol will likely be this.

This is a bad answer because the candidate assumes that a symbol will be alike something you are familiar with. Just because a symbol might look like the letter d, does not mean it represents the letter d. The interviewer will also be unimpressed by the lack of creative thinking from this candidate, and the fact that they do not consider whether the symbol will be seeking to describe words, letters, or concepts.

Good answer: The main thing I first look for when deciphering a symbol is any contextual clue which may lead us in the direction of deciphering the symbol. For example, the date or location might help us. If the date that the symbol was written is from before writing as we know it existed, then it is unlikely to represent individual letters, but may instead represent concepts or words. As well as this, the location can help us to have an idea of what language it may be written in, which can be particularly useful if, for example, it is a symbol is a part of a broader sentence. This is because we can tell that, if it is written in English, single letter words will probably be either I or A, and a similar approach can be applied towards other languages. Another thing we should initially look for, which can be helped with this context, or by looking at other symbols around it, is whether the symbol does in fact seem to represent a letter, word, concept, or any other thing. This will significantly help us to decipher it.

This is a good answer because the candidate gives a very logical approach to how this question can be tackled. They also show that they can think creatively by considering how context will help to decipher a symbol.

Q30: What makes you human?

This is a very broad question which tests the candidate's ability to think about concepts that are often taken for granted. The candidate is not expected to reach a full definition of a human being, but should instead engage in a critical discussion about the difficulty of defining what it is that makes us human.

Bad answer: What makes us human is having an opposable thumb. *Or* What makes us human is the fact that we have a conscience.

These are both bad answers because they do not go into enough detail, as could easily be done by explaining why it is that these things make people human. Furthermore, they do not engage critically with those counterpoints which may be made against their definition of what makes us human. The first answer is bad because, though it is true that humans are unique in having opposable thumbs, it does not follow that this is the specific thing which makes us human. It seems that there is a lot more to being human than this. The second answer is bad because it does not address the fact that some people may argue that other animals have a conscience too.

Good answer: I'm not sure there can be one single thing that makes us human. Instead, I think it is probably a combination of a few things. The main one, I think, is our ability to reason. We seem to be unique as animals in our ability to reason. It is likely that other animals can reason to a degree, but nowhere near as much as humans can. Secondly, another thing that makes us human is the way we interact with other humans, and form societies. Humans are sociable animals, and therefore naturally form these communities. We would not be human if we lived in highly individualistic ways.

This is a good answer because the candidate goes into a lot more detail about some of the things which makes us human. Furthermore, they develop on this, explaining why it is that each of these things makes us human. They also consider arguments against their point, such as when they claim why reasoning makes us human despite the fact that other animals may be able to reason.

Q31: How would you go about assessing the number of people in here?

This is a philosophy question on the concept of personhood and identity. It is the type of question which might throw you so make sure that before you tackle it, you take a moment to sit back, and think about what it is the interviewer is really asking you. This type of question is one which you will not be able to give a definite answer for. Given this, it is important that you explain your thinking out loud, as you try to reach some kind of answer.

For the sake of the mock answers, I will assume that there are three people in the room: two interviewers and the interviewee.

Bad answer: There are three people. There cannot be more than 3 people, as I can only see three. There cannot be less than three, because I can see three. Anyone who thinks overwise is wrong.

This is bad because it fails to consider any other potential approach to the idea of personhood. It assumes that the way we tend to count people is inherently true, without questioning this at all. It also becomes argumentative in a way which can be tempting if faced with a difficult question like this, but is unhelpful in a philosophy interview. You should show that you are willing to be persuaded to consider other potential solutions to this question, rather than immediately shutting yourself off from different ideas.

Good answer: We would usually say that there are three people in this room. However, that assumes that the other people in this room are in fact people. We do not really know this. For example, you may both be philosophical zombies [*i.e. someone who looks and acts like a person, but doesn't really have a conscience or soul*]. I don't know that you have a conscience, so, assuming that being a person is in some ways defined by the existence of a conscience, I don't know whether either of you really are "people". If we think about what defines what it is to be a "person", we will find it hard to prove, in fact, that any of us have the features which make us by definition a person. For example, we might instead claim that a person is an entity that has free will. However, we don't really know that we have free will. We may be controlled by a God or something else to perform the actions we do, and be programmed to think that this is our own freewill. Therefore, we cannot truly know how many people are in this room.

This answer is good because it considers a range of approaches to the question of what it is to be a person. This candidate does not close themselves up to considering different philosophical arguments, as the weaker one does, and instead embraces a philosophical debate. They also demonstrate that they have a basic understanding of core philosophical ideas, such as free will, and the idea of philosophical zombies.

Q32: Do you think you know anything?

This is a philosophy question on epistemology, which is the branch of philosophy concerned with knowledge. It is fairly likely that you will get a question similar to this one, or which touches on some of the ideas you will consider for this question. There are a lot of ways you may consider answering this question. One thing which is important is to know that they will not be expecting you to have an in-depth knowledge of epistemology. They are just looking to see how you go about approaching questions like these.

Bad answer: No, it is not possible to know anything because, even though I think I know something, how do I know that I know it?

This answer is bad because, whilst the candidate begins to consider an interesting point in philosophy, they do not explain what they mean by "how do I know that I know it?". This is a commonly heard expression which has little meaning if you do not go onto explain what you actually mean. This makes their answer superficial.

Good answer: I'm sure we 'know' some things, but the problem comes in trying to prove that we know anything, and in trying to define what knowledge actually is. For example, I know that this is a chair, because I see it, and it looks like a chair. However, how do I know that chair-like things which are perceive are really chairs? Just because I see it, doesn't mean that it is really there, or that it is really a chair. I have no proof that what I perceive is knowledge. We might, instead, consider non-perceptual forms of knowledge, to see if we can 'know' anything. We can use deductive reasoning to argue that 2+2=4. I know that 2+2=4. However, these numbers are purely abstract, and are only assigned by humans. I therefore don't really have any proof that 2+2=4, beyond the fact that I have been taught that this is the case, and other people assume it to be so. However, this cannot be a satisfactory account of what it is to know something. Therefore, whilst I want to say that we do 'know' some things, I think it takes a lot to prove that we do.

This is a good answer because it really considers what the question asks. It is significantly less superficial than the bad answer, and considers different approaches to the problem of knowledge, especially how it can be possible to define knowledge. Although the candidate does not know overly-technical terms, this is not expected of them. They have noticed a difference between knowledge of things which we perceive (a kind of inductive knowledge) and deductive knowledge, which shows that they are thinking deeply about the problem.

Q33: You mentioned that you read [a philosophy book], tell me about it!

This is a broad question. You are likely to be asked a question along these lines, or asking you about a specific work you may have mentioned in your personal statement. The best way to tackle this question is to talk in as much detail as you can about the work. It is worth preparing some thoughts you have on a specific work beforehand, especially if you write about any philosophical texts in your personal statement.

The most important thing is to pick a work which isn't too easy, but also isn't too hard that you can't understand enough to engage in the argumentation. Be honest, and say when you didn't understand parts of the work. The interviewer isn't expecting you to have a perfect understanding of complicated philosophical works yet.

Bad answer: I read *An Introduction to Philosophy*, and I learnt that we cannot really know that we exist, or that we have free will. I enjoyed the book because it gave me a simple overview.

This is a bad answer, firstly, because it is short. The candidate gives some examples of philosophical issues, but does not expand upon them. It's not particularly necessary to say whether you enjoyed the book or not – the interviewer is more looking for you to engage in the particular arguments of the text. Finally, the main problem with this answer is that, whilst it is perfectly fine to read introductory philosophy books, these will not be the most impressive for interviewers. Furthermore, they do not provide philosophical argumentation to engage in.

Good answer: I read Plato's *Republic*, which I think gave a unique perspective on justice and political philosophy. I found particularly interesting his discussion in the first book about whether justice goes against your own interest. I think that this is an issue Plato preoccupies the rest of his work discussing, but I'm not sure if he ever really found a satisfactory answer. I struggled to understand some of the middle parts of the text, but I think he shows that justice is the same in a city and in an individual persona, and just as it is good for a city, so too is it good for a person. However, it seems like he doesn't fully explain why this means that justice doesn't go against your own interest as an individual.

This is a good answer because it shows that the candidate is aware of the arguments within the text, and they try to engage in them. It is an honest answer which does not try to be over-smart, or pretend to understand things that they don't know, and would not be expected to know.

Q34: Do you feel that economists trust models too much?

This is a fairly broad economic question which will ask you to consider the merits of the way we usually approach economics, and to discuss behavioural economics, and the fairly recent academic move by behavioural economists away from relying on models.

Bad answer: No because economic models allow us to measure the economy, and therefore it is good that we have economic models.

This is a bad answer because the question does not ask the candidate to say whether economic models are good, but whether economists can rely too heavily on them. It is easy to argue that there are a huge amount of merit to economic models, and still discuss whether there are some cases in which economists rely too heavily on these models. Instead, this candidate fails to engage properly in the question.

Good answer: Models serve an important role in economics, both for helping us to try to measure the economy, and for predicting what may happen in the future. It helps to guide policy in order to aim towards good economic consequences, such as seeking high employment and economic growth. However, there are situations in which economic models will fail to properly predict what will happen in the economy, and thus, what policy makers should do. This usually happens, either because humans act in unexpected, irrational ways, or because some other thing happens which is unexpected. For example, even our most basic demand/supply models predict that the economy will follow certain rules to set the price and quantity of goods in an economic system.

However, just because there is an increase in supply, which, as the models would posit, means that there should be a decrease in the price of a good, doesn't mean that humans will automatically adhere to the new price. There may be delays in shifting to the price, or they may not change at all, due to consumer habit or other behavioural reasons. As well as this, surprise events may occur for which economists are unable to use models to prepare and plan policy. This happened with the coronavirus pandemic. Economic predictions which followed from models became invalidated by the sudden escalation of the coronavirus situation. Economists, in situations such as these, must be prepared to move away from the models and to adapt to new situations, as well as shifting focus towards examining the behaviour of how humans interact in new economic situations such as this.

This answer is good because it engages with the question. In doing so, the candidate doesn't jump to say that economic models are always either good or bad, but instead gives some examples of when they cannot be relied upon so heavily. This adds nuance to the argument, as well as showing knowledge of current affairs, and how recent events may affect the economy.

Q35: Should you or I care about inequality?

This is an economic question which asks the candidate to think more about the good and bad effects of inequality. Often economics is concerned with things such as profit maximising, and being economically efficient, and in the process, forgets about inequality. This question therefore invites the candidate to discuss this in more detail, and to make the case for or against inequality. The candidate, however, does not need to focus purely on the economic effects of inequality, and can also bring in moral arguments to make their case.

Bad answer: Inequality is bad because it is unfair for some people to have less than others when it is through no fault of their own.

Or

Inequality is good because it is the result of the market deciding where to allocate resources, which benefits the economy overall.

Both of these answers are bad because they do not consider the other side of the argument. This is a very contentious debate which will lead candidates to have a strong conviction in favour of one side of the argument, but a good candidate will still consider the other side, and give reasons for why the other argument is wrong. Furthermore, the first answer fails to consider economic arguments, and the second answer fails to consider moral arguments. Both could be strengthened by exploring equality in a greater depth.

Good answer: I strongly believe that inequality should matter to all of us. This is on two grounds. Firstly, inequality is morally wrong. Inequality means that a huge amount of people are born in situations where they are unable to improve their lives, due to being unable to access the same resources as those who are lucky enough to be born comparatively better off. If people were more equal, then everyone would be on a more equal level when it came to accessing opportunities, such as being able to study at Oxford. It is unfair that some humans are predestined not to have these opportunities due to the situation which they are born into. There is no way we can morally justify this, and those who argue that inequality is fine tend to overlook the moral arguments to make this case. However, there is also an economic argument in favour of reducing inequality. A small amount of inequality may be both economically and morally justifiable, however, at the moment, inequality is so large that many of the millionaires and billionaires hoard a lot of their wealth. Poorer people have a significantly higher marginal propensity to spend, and, therefore it is more economically sensible for this money to be distributed to less well off people. This would lead to an increase in aggregate demand, with a multiplier effect as more money circulates in the economy. This would lead to an increase in real GDP, and therefore economic growth. This therefore makes more economic sense than allowing the market to allocate resources, which turns out in this case to be less efficient. Therefore, inequality should matter to economists.

This is a good answer because the candidate goes into a lot of details to explain why their answer, both on an economic justification, and a deeper, moral one. They demonstrate a good knowledge of the concept of marginal propensity to spend, which is important for this question.

Q36: You're a politician in charge of the country, and you've accumulated a considerable deficit in the national balance of trade - is this an issue?

This is an economics question which asks you to analyse one of the core concepts in macroeconomics. It expects you to have a familiarity with the idea of the balance of trade, and to critically engage with the assumption that it is bad to have a trade deficit.

Bad answer: Trade deficits are bad because it leads to a devaluing of the pound and that makes the economy weak. Also, it means that people become unemployed as jobs go to those who create goods in foreign markets instead.

This is a bad answer because, whilst the candidate shows some awareness of some of the consequences of a trade deficit, they do not discuss why these consequences happen. Furthermore, it is not true that the pound being devalued makes the economy weak. A weak pound may be a sign of a weak economy, but the candidate is confusing cause and effect. It is likely that the economy was weak first, and that this caused a trade deficit, which caused the pound to devalue, rather than the other way round. Thus, the candidate shows a lack of economic understanding.

Good answer: A trade deficit isn't inherently a bad thing. It may be a sign that there is a problem with the economy, and in such a case, we shouldn't view the trade deficit as the problem, but the underlying causes of this. For example, if the economy is suffering from a lack of productivity, there may be a trade deficit as the UK will be unable to provide all the goods and services in home markets to satisfy demand, and thus may import more goods than they export. This causes a trade deficit.

However, it is not the trade deficit which is inherently bad, but the productivity. In fact, a trade deficit can be thought of as good because it naturally fixes itself. For example, when there is a trade deficit, the pound gets devalued as there is less demand for the pound owing to the fact that consumers are not buying goods from the UK. However, when the pound is devalued, it is lower in price compared to other currencies, and therefore, it becomes comparatively cheaper to buy UK goods using pounds. This means that there becomes an increase in demand for the pound. Therefore, the trade deficit should in some way fix itself, and the value of the pound should return to normal. This means the trade deficit doesn't matter as much as some might argue.

This is a good answer because the candidate demonstrates clear knowledge of the ways in which the balance of trade works. They give a clear and detailed explanation of the consequence of a trade deficit, as well as persuasively argument.

Q37. What attracted you to the PPE course?

Good Answer: What excites me most about PPE is the academic breadth of the course, and the opportunity it provides to engage deeply with subjects that are both academically challenging and have real-world applications. I first became interested in studying PPE through my philosophy A level. I was excited to apply the critical thinking skills that I developed during those studies to other real-world examples and became deeply interested in the way that politics and economics interact to influence our current systems. I'd really like to look at these subjects through an academic lens during my time at university. I'm keen to continue to develop these skills during my time at university and see PPE as the perfect course through which to do so.

This answer shows that the candidate has really thought about why they want to study the course and have demonstrated both their academic interest and aptitude. They demonstrate that they have taken a wider interest in their studies at A Level and are keen to challenge themselves further through engaging with the PPE course. They also show that they are excited to tackle the challenging content of the PPE course and will approach it with enthusiasm and dedication. This is the type of candidate that an interviewer will want to have on their course.

Bad Answer: A candidate might suggest that they are applying to the course for the career opportunities it might offer them, or because they have a family member who took PPE.

While there is no "wrong" answer to this question, the answers above demonstrate that the candidate is applying to the course for a reason that wouldn't be attractive to the interviewers. Remember, you want to be showing the interviewer that you are excited to engage with the academic content of the PPE course – this is the type of student that they will be excited to teach.

Q38. Is there an area of politics that you are most interested in?

Good Answer: Yes, I'm particularly interested in how international relations and domestic government policy influence aid decisions. When I read about the cuts to the government's aid budget, I was struck by how much difference a small percentage cut can make to the total amount of aid that the UK government sends overseas. I'm really interested in learning about the mechanisms behind these decisions, and how they are influenced by wider government policies, and hope that I can engage with this through the PPE course.

This candidate is demonstrating that they engage with politics in their everyday life, through reading about government decisions (which also indicates that they try to keep up with current affairs), and that they are interested in pursuing this further through their academic studies. The candidate does not need to show that they are already an expert in this field, just that they have given some thought to what they are particularly interested in when it comes to the subject and that they are keen to learn more through the PPE course. Showing this type of enthusiasm will show the interviewer that you want to engage with their subject and will put in effort during your time on their course.

Bad Answer: A candidate might shrug or say something along the lines of "nothing in particular, just the whole subject".

A bad answer to this question is one that indicates to the interviewer that the candidate has not really taken an interest in the subject. This demonstrates that the candidate isn't really interested in studying the subject or that they haven't really thought about why they are applying. The interviewer isn't expecting the candidate to be an expert in politics already, or to be able to recite in great detail a niche area of the course. They will be expecting, however, that the candidate has taken an interest in the subject and taken the time to look into different areas of the course at least a little before applying.

Q39. What have you seen on the news recently that has interested you?

Good Answer: I've been keeping up to date with the news around the conflict between Palestine and Israel, and the social media movement that has united behind the Palestinian cause. This isn't an issue that I was aware of until recently and, given the extensive history behind the conflict, this really surprised me. I wanted to know more about the history of Israel and didn't want to rely solely on social media for my news so I dug into past news pieces on the region and was really fascinated by what I found. I was particularly interested in the role of the West in the formation of Israel and how that potentially has influenced the governmental reaction to the conflict today.

This answer demonstrates firstly that the candidate has been keeping up with relevant current affairs by watching the news/reading a newspaper regularly. This is a bonus for a PPE candidate. Secondly, the candidate is demonstrating that they are not satisfied by taking the news at face value and have decided to read more widely to fully understand the topic that they are hearing about through the news. This demonstrates an intellectual curiosity which will resonate well with the interviewer.

Bad Answer: I don't really watch the news; I'm too busy studying for my A Levels.

Interviewers will appreciate that you are busy studying and aren't expecting you to be keeping on top of everything that happens around the world all the time. They are, however, expecting you to take an interest in current affairs or at least have some engagement with the news.

Even if you can't think of anything relevant that you've seen on the news (or your mind goes blank – it happens), a strong candidate will find something of interest to say in response to this question. For example, they might try talking about an opinion piece they've read, or a documentary that they've watched recently. They will demonstrate to the interviewer that they are taking a wider interest in their subject, even if they cannot think of a news article or specific event to talk about.

Q40. Why do you think some countries are rich and some countries are poor?

Good Answer: I think it must be rooted in a number of factors. The first that I can think of is how many resources a country has. For example, if a country is rich in a valuable resource such as oil or diamonds then they have the natural capacity to be much richer than a country that doesn't have anything that it can trade. I don't think that this is enough to make a country rich or poor, however. Nigeria has a lot of oil but it isn't rich compared to the US, for example. The second factor that needs to be present is the ability to trade with other countries; it is no good simply having a lot of oil if you can't get anything in return! Therefore, I think you need to have good international relations and a secure trade route in order to be able to participate in the global market. Another factor that I can think of would be good governance and a transparent leadership system so that no money is lost through corruption. If you have all of these factors then you are more likely to be rich, as you have access to natural resources that give you a trading advantage, a secure system in which to trade your good, and a leadership structure that doesn't steal money from the country.

This answer shows that the candidate is thinking critically about the question. They indicate a number of different factors that go into making a country rich or poor, highlighting that they are taking a nuanced approach to the issue and trying to come up with a well-rounded solution rather than seizing on the first thing that comes into their head. They also use examples to back up their points which is very valuable and demonstrates to the interviewer that they have read into the subject which indicates their wider interest in studying PPE.

Bad Answer: It's just to do with how the country grew and how much money they have.

This answer really doesn't answer the question. It's not considering *why* one country might be richer than another. Instead it is simply stating a very vague response "how the country grew" and reiterating the fact that being rich/poor is to do with how much money one has. This isn't providing any sort of academic or critical thinking insight into the issue.

Q41. What makes a nation "successful"?

Good Answer: I imagine that different people would have different criteria for what makes a nation successful, depending on what they value most. From my perspective, there are a couple of factors that are most important in judging the success of a nation. The first factor would be the ability of the government to protect the rights of its citizens. For example, the nation needs to have strong governmental systems in place to protect people against crime, ensure that people have access to work, and that there is accountability in government. The ability to protect these areas means that the government would be safeguarding some of its citizens' most basic human rights and ensuring that they have access to systems that protect them. The second factor would be the nations' ability to make money, whether that is through successful trade with other nations or a strong tax system that gives the government the capacity to collect funds and resources from its citizens. A more successful nation will be able to do both, as that will give it increased capacity to generate income which can then be implemented for the good of the nation.

The candidate could now go on to give a number of other factors that can be used to judge the success of a nation, but through highlighting these two components they had demonstrated a number of things. They have demonstrated that they understand that this is a nuanced question that can be taken from a number of angles by any number of people. They have also demonstrated that they are able to think critically about which factors are most important and they have shown the interviewer that they can back up their points when they are giving them. Overall, this answer shows critical engagement with the question and uses examples and analysis to present a strong case.

Bad Answer: A successful nation is one that makes lots of money and has a lot of international friends.

This answer might have picked up on a couple of key criteria that makes a nation "successful" but is bad because it fails to explain why these are factors. To make this answer better, the candidate should consider backing up these points, for example explaining why having lots of money makes a nation more successful than another nation. Is this because they have managed to create strong institutions that keep its money safe? Is it because they have successfully managed their available resources and created strong trade networks with other nations? This candidate should elaborate more on their response and show the interviewer that they are thinking critically and responding with justified answers.

Q42. Do you think it's important to represent minorities in democracies?

Good Answer: Yes, I do think it's important to represent minorities in democracies. This is because a democratic state is one in which all citizens are represented. As citizens who are part of minorities are still citizens, it is therefore essential to represent them for democracies to truly be democratic.

This answer is short and to the point, directly answering the question that the candidate has been posed. They explain what a democracy is and why representing minorities in democracy is essential to the nature of a democracy. They then make a strong conclusion based on the reasoning they have just set out.

Bad Answer: It might be important to represent minorities in democracy but I don't think it's possible. This is because the party that the majority of citizens wants is the one that is elected, so that minority will never get representation in Parliament, unless they are able to swing more people to support them, and then they are no longer the minority.

This answer contains some good reasoning and provides an answer but unfortunately doesn't answer the question. It just assumes that it is important to represent minorities in democracies without actually explaining why that is the case. It then goes on to answer a different question to the one that the interviewer has posed – this alternative question might be "Do you think it is possible to represent minorities in democracy". It also takes a very British-centric approach to the question, implying that there are no other acceptable examples of democracy across the world.

Q43. How can we achieve minority representation in a democracy?

Good Answer: I think this is a really difficult question and one that no current political system has adequately figured out yet. I think the problem is that a system like proportional representation which represents all of the votes cast – and therefore the votes of minority groups – is quite unstable and ineffective, as there are too many parties all trying to be heard and in the end the largest or most powerful party will probably end up taking control anyway. This was shown through Weimar Germany's attempt at proportional representation. More stable political systems, like the Westminster system, only has one or sometimes two parties ruling so the votes of minorities are not represented within the actual ruling body. Therefore, I think we might need to look outside of the formal political system for representation for minorities. For example, pressure groups and protests are a means through which the voices of minorities can be heard in democratic systems, while maintaining a strong and fairly stable ruling body.

This is a carefully considered and well-rounded answer. It considers why representing minorities in democracies might be a difficult task and then presents a solution to the problem. It directly answers the question and shows that the candidate is critically engaging with the topic.

Bad Answer: The way that Parliament is structured means that we just can't represent minorities in democracy. The ruling party has the political power and that party won't get into power unless they have the support of the majority.

Again, the answer approaches the question from a British perspective, without considering the idea of "democracy" in theory – it is possible to have a proportionally representative democratic system rather than simply the Westminster system that is practiced in the UK. Furthermore, this answer doesn't even try to come up with creative solutions to the problem of representing minorities in democracy. To improve their answer, this candidate would need to suggest what could be a solution to the problem of representing minorities in democracy and then show that this wouldn't work in practice. This would be a way of coming to the same conclusion (that minorities cannot be represented in democracy) but through far more persuasive means).

Q44. Do you think that democracy is the only acceptable form of government?

Good Answer: To answer this question I think we need to decide what constitutes an "acceptable" form of government. I'm going to assume that an acceptable form of government is one that protects its citizens and their rights, and creates an environment in which they can pursue their own lives and desires. This means that any form government which by nature exploits it citizens cannot be an acceptable form of government. However, I don't think that we necessarily have to have a democracy for citizens' rights to be protected and for them to be able to pursue their own desires. I think that in some kind of dictatorship where the dictator protects her citizens, ensures that they have everything they need, and would never interfere in the lives of her citizens would also be an acceptable form of government. In practice, however, I think that this would be very difficult to achieve because people are easily corrupted and anyone with the power of the dictator is likely to act at least a little in their own interests, rather than just protecting their citizens.

Therefore, I do not think that democracy is the only acceptable form of government in theory, but in practice it might be the only plausible form of acceptable government.

This answer is good because the candidate has given a reasoned, justified response to the question and has provided a conclusion that directly addresses what the question is asking them to address. They have thought about the subject in a creative way and one that pushes beyond what one might typically feel comfortable asserting.

Bad Answer: All developed nations have a form of democracy and therefore democracy must be the only acceptable form of government.

This response is bad because it assumes that just because something is currently done, it must be the only way of doing things. It fails to consider an alternative to democracy and therefore fails to address the question. The reason that it gives for democracy being the only acceptable form of government is flimsy and does not show personal academic engagement with the question, which is what the interviewer will be looking for. To improve this answer, the candidate should consider why democracy is practised in developed nations (and in developing nations) and whether this reasoning gives adequate justification for democracy being considered the only acceptable form of government.

Q45. Why do you think some countries go to war?

Good Answer: I think it's very difficult to define exactly why countries go to war but I believe there are a number of factors that contribute to that decision. One factor might be humanitarian. For example, a country might declare war on another country when they believe there has been a significant human rights violation by that country and all other methods of punishment have failed. A country might have already imposed economic and political sanctions against the other nation but this hasn't stopped the perceived abuse of their citizens. This might lead to a country invading another as a last resort. Another reason might be material gain.

A country might invade another country in order to acquire their resources (oil, for example) and this leads to war breaking out between these countries. In this case, the country that is being invaded might declare war as an act of self-defence and hope that, in doing so, they gain support from the international community against their invaders. This also makes me think that another factor might be political alliances. For example, in WWI most of Europe ended up going to war because of the interlinking network of political alliances that had been drawn between all the countries. Country A might declare war on Country B because B has threatened A's political ally, Country C, and their alliance decrees that A must defend C against attack. All these factors might contribute to different extents and it might be very difficult to actually determine which one is the main reason that a country went to war, but I believe that these are some of the factors that might contribute to that decision.

This answer is very extensive but shows a nuanced and critical approach to answering the question. The candidate demonstrates that they are aware that this is a delicate subject matter and that there might not be just one acceptable response, but that they are willing to dive into the content and try to come to their own conclusion on the issue. They consider a number of different factors and even show how some might be interlinked. To make this answer even better, the candidate might try to explain which factor they think might be most important, and why, to show that they are critically assessing each of the options that they have been presented with.

Bad Answer: Countries only go to war to get something out of another country. They might want their money or resources and they go to war to fight them for it.

While this answer might identify one possible reason that a country goes to war, it fails to recognise that this is a nuanced problem. There might be a number of factors that lead to a war starting and it is rarely as simplistic as just wanting something from someone else (otherwise countries would be going to war far more often than they really do!). By saying that countries "only" go to war for this reason, the candidate is closing themselves off to being proven wrong or to considering another perspective which indicates to the interviewer that they don't have an open mind when it comes to academic problems.

Q46. How far do you think governments should interfere in the lives of their citizens?

Good Answer: I think there are some instances in which a government is legitimate in interfering in the lives of its citizens. For example, if someone has committed a crime, the government, or the systems that they enforce, should be able to prosecute the criminal and punish them appropriately. This is in order to protect the lives of the other citizens. Therefore, I think that the government should be able to interfere in the lives of its citizens to the extent that it upholds laws necessary to keep the peace and protect the rights and lives of its other citizens. However, the government should be strictly limited in the extent to which it can interfere without consequence; otherwise the government can get too powerful and use its position to exploit the nation for its own gain. For example, the government should not be able to interfere in the lives of its citizens just because it doesn't like something that they are doing (but that thing doesn't harm anyone else). One instance of this might be in the case of gay marriage. I don't think that the government should be able to stop people getting married just because they don't necessarily approve. Overall, therefore, I think that governments should be able to interfere in the lives of their citizens to the extent that they are acting to protect them and their rights, but they should not be able to interfere where no harm is posed and they simply don't like what the citizens are doing.

This is a good answer because it gives a nuanced, balanced response to the question. It considers critically when it might be the role (or duty) of the government to interfere in people's lives, but highlights that there might be limitations on this interference. It should be noted that there is no "correct" response to this question, but the candidate needs to show that they have a reasoned response and that they can adequately justify their response. It wouldn't have been enough for this candidate to just say "the government can interfere in some cases, like prosecuting criminals, and not in other, like gay marriage" without fully justifying their response.

Bad Answer: A good government never interferes in the lives of its citizens, otherwise that's just paternalism.

This candidate might have a valid answer, but they haven't given any form of justification for their response. If they do truly believe that there is no instance in which it would be acceptable for the government to interfere in the lives of their citizens then that's a perfectly fine response to give. However, just asserting that interference is "paternalism" isn't enough to support this claim. The candidate should give an explanation of what they mean by paternalism and explain why this is a bad thing when exercised by the government.

Q47. What do you think are the key differences between the UK and US forms of government?

Good Answer: The first difference that springs to mind is that in the US they have a President who is elected separately from the other representatives. There is an independence Presidential vote and the President is directly elected. In the UK, on the other hand, the Prime Minister is appointed because they are the leader of the party that has the majority of representatives in the House of Commons, in almost all cases anyway. This means that the power of the leader is separate from the other representatives in the US, while in the UK the power of the Prime Minister is more directly tied to the House of Commons. Also, the UK has the House of Lords which is a body of unelected individuals who have some power over the House of Commons. As far as I'm aware, the US doesn't have an equivalent to the House of Lords, as all of their representatives are elected. Therefore, the two key differences that I'm aware of between the UK and the US styles of government are the fact that the President is independently elected in the USA and has powers separate from the Senate, and the fact that the UK has an unelected body that oversees political decisions.

This answer directly answers the question that has been asked and has identified two key differences between the two systems of government. It is important to stress here that the interviewer isn't expecting the candidate to know everything about the two systems of government and be able to highlight all of the key differences between the two. What is more important is that the candidate is able to draw on the knowledge they do have to give an accurate comparison of the two styles of government. They haven't been thrown by the fact that they do not have a complete understanding of the subject matter, but have used the information they have available to give a comparative response.

Bad Answer: At the moment I think the key differences are that the US has a left-wing political party in power – the Democrats with Joe Biden as President – and the UK has a right-wing political party in power – the Conservatives with Boris Johnson as Prime Minister. This means that the governments will have different focuses, with right-wing governments more typically focused on security and lowering taxes, and with left-wing governments more often focused on social welfare and raising taxes on businesses and the rich.

This answer might appropriately answer a question, but it is not answering this question. The candidate has misinterpreted the question to be asking them to show that they know who is in power in the UK and US currently, and to demonstrate that they can name the difference between some of their key policies. However, the question is actually asking about the different *styles* of government employed in the UK vs the US. When answering a question, make sure to fully understand what the interviewer is asking you to do before you respond. If you don't think that you have fully understood the question, be sure to ask for clarification from the interviewer – they won't mind and it's much better that you give an answer to the question they have actually asked, rather than the one you think they've asked.

Q48. What do you think causes a rise in populism?

A candidate should not be afraid to ask for clarification on any terms in the question that they do not understand. In this case, for example, a candidate should be willing to ask for a definition of populism if they do not understand precisely what that terms means. It is much better to ask for clarification and ensure you are answering the question that has been asked, than guess what it means and end up answering an entirely different question.

Good Answer: I think that there are a number of factors that might cause populism to rise in any given society and it is likely that a combination of any of these factors might be needed to create a strong populist movement. One factor might be disillusionment with the current political status quo. For example, citizens might feel as though the main political parties do not adequately represent their political interests and so look to other actors to be their voices on the political stage. This might be particularly prevalent where members of society are particularly isolated, both socially and politically. Some groups might feel as though things are changing in society too quickly and they are being left behind. For example, in the UK, UKIP voters may have voted that way because they did not like the fact that there were a number of immigrants entering the UK. They may have felt as though their views were not being represented on the political stage and so looked to the more populist group UKIP for support and representation.

This answer is good because it directly answers the question, identifying that it is a nuanced issue. They provide a couple of different factors that might combine to cause a rise in populism and have backed up their points by using a real-life example. This demonstrates that they are paying attention to current affairs and are able to apply their real-world knowledge to a more theoretical question. To improve this answer, the candidate might want to point to unifying factors of those individuals who are feeling disillusioned or isolated. For example, they might need a charismatic leader to unite behind.

Bad Answer: UKIP was a prominent populist party in the UK, although they have recently faded from the political limelight. A Eurosceptic party, they stand for tighter border controls and appeal to rising fears of immigration and unemployment in Britain.

Using an example is a great way of supporting your answer. In this case, however, the candidate doesn't directly answer the question that is being asked. They need to give a more theory-based answer and then support this response by appealing to the UKIP case study. They need to consider a more general response to the question, supported by relevant examples, in order to fully answer it.

Q49. Why do you think political parties might have increasingly similar policies, most of which sit at the centre of the political spectrum?

Good Answer: I'm not entirely sure but let me try to work through this question. The main aim of political parties is to get into power by best representing the views of the population. In order to do this, they need to appeal to a majority of voters. If you think about the political spectrum, I think it's unlikely that everyone will be evenly spaced along it, as most people tend not to have radically right-wing or left-wing views, but tend to fall somewhat towards the centre of the political spectrum. Therefore, I think we can say that the political spectrum will look a little like a Normal Distribution curve. For a political party to gain a majority of the vote, they will want to appeal to the largest number of voters possible. It would make sense for them to do so by aligning their policies somewhat with the centre of the political spectrum, as the majority of people sit here. All parties will have the same idea so they will cluster their policies towards the centre of the spectrum in order to try to gain the majority of votes in the population.

This answer begins by admitting that the candidate is not entirely sure how to answer the question – this is absolutely fine! What is good about this answer is that the candidate then proceeds to reason through the question. They clearly set out their logical process for the interviewer so that they are able to fully understand how the candidate comes to their conclusion. After this reasoning process, the candidate clearly identifies their conclusion and responds directly to the question that the interviewer has posed.

Bad Answer: That can't be right, because in the UK the Conservatives are right-wing and Labour is left-wing. This must mean they have different policies.

This answer doesn't even attempt to address the question. The candidate might be able to come to the conclusion that it wouldn't make sense for political parties to have closely aligned policies because they sit on different sides of the political spectrum. In this case, however, the candidate has drawn on their (seemingly limited) knowledge of UK politics and made an assumption about political alignment in general. To make this a good answer, the candidate would need to try to work through the question logically, setting out why in the general case it might not make sense for political parties to align themselves at the centre.

Q50. Do you think that countries should interfere in the running of other countries when human rights are at risk?

Good Answer: I think there cannot be a black-and-white answer to this question. It depends highly on the case that we're talking about and the type of interference that is involved. For example, I think that interference such as economic or political sanctions can be a powerful force to protect human rights in other countries. If a group of countries, for example through the UN or the EU, all impose sanctions on a country where there are perceived human rights abuses, it might encourage the offending country to change their policies and act to protect the rights of their citizens. However, I do not think interference in the form of war or violence is an acceptable form of interference, unless used as an absolute last resort and done in such a way as to protect the lives of innocent citizens. This is because war itself can threaten human rights and the lives of citizens, rather than simply target the offending government.

This answer deals with a delicate topic in a nuanced manner. The candidate uses examples to justify their response and highlights why interference might be a problem, particularly in cases where we are talking about protecting human rights. Another angle that the answer might take is to consider whether the external country has the right to interfere in the running of another country. Some people might argue that nations should not interfere in the affairs of other nations, as their concern should solely be what happens within their borders. A good answer to this question does not depend entirely on the content of the answer, but on the candidate's ability to justify their response and defend their opinion using examples and reasoning.

Bad Answer: In all cases of human rights abuses I think we should deploy military sanctions against the offending country.

While the candidate might be able to come to this conclusion, this answer is problematic because it asserts a very strong viewpoint without any substantial justification. The candidate would need to explain why they think that deploying military sanctions is the answer to any violation of human rights. The answer would also benefit from the use of examples. Overall, this answer needs significantly more justification and explanation before the candidate can assert such a strong viewpoint.

Philosophy Questions:

Q51. Do you have a particular philosopher whose work particularly interests you?

Good Answer: I'm not too sure about which philosopher I'm particularly interested in, but I'm very keen to study free will and determinism. I think considering whether what we do is done freely, and what impact this has on social and personal responsibility and punishment, is absolutely fascinating. I completed a MOOC recently on Free Will and Responsibility which I thought was so interesting and, while I can't remember specifically any of the philosophers that I was most struck by during the course, I am very keen to understand the topic better and look at it through a more academic lens.

While in this situation a candidate would ideally be able to name a philosopher and why they are interested in their work, this response shows that the candidate is interested in the subject and has engaged more widely in a particular area of philosophy, even if they are unable to remember a philosopher's name in that particular instance.

Bad Answer: I've read quite a lot of Mill's work on Utilitarianism because I had to for school so probably would have to say I'm most interested in him.

While this answer can name a philosopher who they've read, they do not give a compelling answer to this question. Firstly, they are only able to name Mill because they "had to" read his work for school. This suggests to the interviewer that they haven't engaged with the subject more widely which does not show any particular academic interest. Secondly, they don't give any details about what this work consists of (other than simply naming the title of one of Mill's most famous works) so don't even show that they fully understood Mill when they read him for school. A much better approach would be to say that you came across Mill's work while studying, but then wanted to take this interest further by reading more of his work and other material on the same subject to further increase your understanding.

Q52. How do you think we can know that something is right or wrong?

Good Answer: I think that we can never really *know* when something is right or wrong, but we can have an instinct about whether what we have just done was a morally acceptable thing to do. For example, when I give money to charity, I instinctively feel as though this was a morally acceptable thing to do, suggesting to me that it was a good thing to do. I think this feeling stems from the fact that giving money to charity helps someone other than myself, who is less fortunate than myself. On the other hand, if I were to steal money from someone, I would instinctively feel as though this was a bad thing to do, because it is taking something that isn't mine, therefore depriving someone else of something that belongs to them. I think that our moral instincts are quite strong and that we should listen to them when they respond to an action.

This answer recognises that it is very difficult to absolutely know whether an action is truly right or wrong. Instead, it provides a method through which we can generally judge our actions: reflecting on them using our moral instincts. Many philosophers take moral instincts to be a fairly good criteria against which to judge any moral theory and so appealing to this solution would accord with a lot of thinking in the field of moral philosophy.

Candidates should note here that the interviewer is not asking them to simply regurgitate an ethical theory that they have read about. Instead, they are asking them what *they* think about the question. A candidate might appeal to a theory that they've read about, but they should be prepared to justify why they agree/disagree with that theory. This shows the interviewer that they've actively thought about and engaged with what they've read, rather than simply taking it at face value (unlike the example of a bad answer).

Bad Answer: A utilitarian would argue that you can tell whether something is right or wrong by whether or not it brings about the greatest good for the greatest number of people. For example, when you are choosing an action, you should choose that action which brings about the greatest happiness in general society for you to have chosen the right thing to do.

This answer explains how someone else might determine whether an action is right or wrong, but it does not tell the interviewer what the candidate thinks. The interviewer isn't asking you to prove that you've read something about ethics – you might not have done! Instead, what they are asking you to do is to show that you can engage critically with a philosophical question, even if you haven't studied it before. It's much better to show that you have your own opinions and can support them with reason than to show that you've just read and remembered someone else's theory.

Q53. Consider the following case:

There is a train running down a track. There is a fork in the track a short way from where the train currently is. On the right-hand track at the fork there is tied one person. On the left-hand track at the fork there are tied five people. Currently the train will go to the left-hand fork. Whichever track the train runs down, anyone on that track will be killed by the train.

Should the train driver switch tracks so that the train kills one person rather than five people?

Good Answer: When we're talking about what the train driver "should" do, I'm going to assume that we're looking at what the right thing to do would be. The right thing in this situation will depend on whether you think that it's okay for the driver to actively choose to kill one person rather than choosing not to interfere with the current path of the train and allow five people to die. I'm going to assume that all of the six people who could die are identical so that their personalities or moralities don't need to factor into the decision. In my opinion, I think that the driver should choose to switch tracks and kill one person rather than five. This is because it is better to kill fewer people; this will result in the least pain caused by the action. This is also instinctively what I feel would be the best choice for the driver to make, even though it would be quite a difficult decision.

This answer clearly identifies what the problem is that they're being asked to solve and then reasons through their own personal response to the question. They give a justified answer and even bring in a control factor (making all the people who could die identical) so that they are just focusing on the particular moral decision that they are being asked to consider.

Bad Answer: Oh, I know this problem — it's a Trolley Problem Case. From what I've read, most people say that the driver should change tracks and kill the one instead of the five so that must be the right thing to do in this situation.

This candidate is demonstrating that they have done some further reading which is a good thing. However, they fail to provide a reasoned, personal response to the question that they are being asked. They could identify that this is a Trolley Problem Case (which it is) but then go on to work through their own personal response to the case. This would be a much better way of approaching the question, as it shows the examiner that the candidate is able to form their own opinions of things and approach questions with a critical eye, rather than just being happy to uncritically accept what they've read.

Q54. Consider the following case:

You are a Doctor with 5 patients who need immediate organ transplants; they have conditions which have been brought on by entirely natural causes. All patients have a very rare blood type, so they have been unable to find organ donors. A patient comes in to see you for a routine check-up. This patient has the same rare blood type as your other 5 patients but is otherwise entirely healthy.

The doctor could kill the healthy patient in order to donate her organs to the 5 patients. If the doctor did this, all 5 patients would live.

Do you think the case is different in any significant way to the Trolley Problem?

Good Answer: Yes I do think this case is significantly different from the Trolley problem. While we are dealing with the same numbers in both cases, here the doctor would have to actively kill the healthy patient in order to kill the 5. I think what is different here is that in the Trolley case, the train is the thing that would be killing the individuals in either case. That means that either the train kills one person or the train kills five people: it is simply a matter of which outcome would cause less pain and choosing that. In the case of the doctor, however, the doctor would need to choose to kill the healthy patient herself rather than letting the other 5 patients die from natural causes. It is interfering in the life of the healthy patient in a way that switching the train doesn't do in the Trolley case.

Therefore, I think that this case is different from the Trolley case and that here the Doctor would not be justified in killing the healthy patient in order to save the other 5.

This answer is good because it demonstrates what the candidate thinks is different between the two cases and how this makes a moral difference to the case. They then come to a moral conclusion based on their response. The candidate has identified that we are dealing with the same number of individuals in both cases, but then shows why they believe that there is a difference between the cases in spite of this similarity.

Bad Answer: Why would this be any different – it's just about numbers and the numbers are the same.

This answer also identifies the key similarity between the two cases (and why the case of the doctor might be so morally difficult when considered in conjunction with the Trolley Problem) but fails to even consider why there might be differences between the two cases, which is the key focus of the question. In order to improve here, the candidate would need to then consider why there might be differences between the cases but show that these are not relevant to come to the conclusion that the differences that exist between the two cases are not significant.

Q55. Do you think that you freely chose to apply to this PPE course?

Good Answer: I think at the time I made my application I would have assumed that I made the choice freely because that's how I tend to think about all of my choices – I think automatically I assume that I had free will in the situation unless I am being obviously coerced. However, I wonder whether something like my upbringing and school situation might have influenced my decision to choose to study PPE. For example, my parents have always encouraged me to take an interest in current affairs and politics, and the economics department was really good at my school which I why I decided to take it at A Level. If these things hadn't been the case then I might not have chosen to study politics and economics at A Level, so I might not have chosen to study PPE at university. I don't think, however, that this makes the choice unfree; I just think it means that there was a certain chain of events that led me to the moment of decision, but in that deciding moment I was the one who freely chose to study PPE. Therefore, I think that while the decision in which I made the choice to study PPE was influenced by my upbringing and surroundings, at the end of the day I am the one who made the choice to take that set of circumstances and study PPE as a result of that situation. So, yes, I do think that I freely chose to apply to this PPE course.

This is a nuanced and considered answer and directly responds to the question that the interviewer is asking. The candidate takes their initial assumption and critically considers it, looking at why their assumption might not have been right. They give examples to show that they have fully understand the case that they are considering. Then they logically work through the issue at hand and come to a justified conclusion. Finally, they round their answer off by giving a direct response at the end to signal to the examiner that they have understood and answered their question.

Bad Answer: I submitted my application form and no one else made me apply so I must have applied freely.

Here, the candidate has given a conclusion without giving any kind of justification for the conclusion. They haven't demonstrated that they have in any way considered why that choice might not have been free and have simply chosen the conclusion that comes most naturally to mind when we tend to think about whether we have free will or not. To make this answer better, the candidate needs to show that they have considered at least one reason why they might not have made the choice freely rather than simply assuming that they did. Furthermore, they need to justify why this is the right conclusion in the face of that other reason.

Q56. If humans don't have free will and knew that they didn't, do you think that would make any difference to how society functions?

Good Answer: Yes, I think it would make a lot of difference. If someone knows that everything they do is determined, then that suggests that they are not responsible for what they do. If someone isn't responsible for what they do, then they cannot be blamed or praised for their behaviour. As the people in this scenario know that they don't have free will, they would know that they cannot be justifiably blamed or praised for their actions. This means that people would stop thinking about what is the society acceptable action and instead do whatever they like, knowing that they can't be blamed for any of their actions. I think that people would start to act a lot more recklessly and society would become somewhat anarchistic.

The important thing to stress here is that the interviewer probably isn't concerned about what you say in response to this type of question. What they are looking at instead is how you argue for the conclusion you come to. This candidate has taken a clear position in response to the question and have given a reasoned explanation for how they come to that conclusion. The interviewer might disagree with them and try to find a flaw in their reasoning, but the candidate at this stage has done a good job of setting out their chain of reasoning and coming to a clear and definitive conclusion.

Bad Answer: I'm not really sure. I think maybe if people knew that they had free will it might make them think differently about themselves but I don't know what that would mean for society.

This candidate needs to be more confident in their reasoning and in coming to a conclusion. They have the beginnings of a good answer, identifying that if people know they don't have free will it might make them think differently about themselves and how they act. To turn this into a good answer they need to work through this chain of logic, thinking about what impact this would have on an individual's behaviour in society. They also need to remember that this type of question is really testing how you think and how you approach difficult concepts that you might not be familiar with. The interviewer wants to see that you can think on your feet and work through difficult problems, even if you aren't automatically sure what the answer should be.

Q57. Do you think that you can trust what your eyes are telling you?

Good Answer: Let me think about this. I wouldn't be able to trust what my eyes are telling me if sometimes what I think I see isn't actually what I see. In other words, I can't trust my senses if my senses sometimes deceive me. Sometimes when it's dark in my room I think that the pile of clothes on my chair looks like the outline of a person and I get worried that there's another person in my room. That tends to only happen when it's dark though. In this case, the dark can be classed as something that is interfering with my senses. Therefore, I think that I can trust what my eyes are telling me so long as there isn't something interfering with my senses.

This answer follows the structure of a premise and conclusion argument. It sets up what would be needed for the candidate to not be able to trust their senses and then considers whether this is possible. They give an example of when they can't trust their senses but conclude that this is an exceptional case. What makes this answer a good answer is that the candidate has clearly reasoned through the logic behind their conclusion, showing the interviewer exactly how they are approaching this difficult question. Their answer is justified and well-reasoned and they have come to a distinct conclusion, rather than giving a vague answer to try to get out of thinking the case through properly.

Bad Answer: Of course I can trust what my eyes are telling me – why wouldn't I be able to?

This candidate has themselves identified why this is a bad answer: they haven't thought about why they might not be able to trust what their eyes are telling them. It is okay to come to the conclusion that you can trust what you see, so long as this conclusion is reasoned and well thought-through. And the candidate needs to show the interviewer that they have actually thought it through, rather than just asserting their conclusion without trying to explain how they reach that point. To improve this answer, the candidate needs to explain their reasoning and justify why they can trust what their eyes are telling them, rather than simply taking this as a given.

Q58. Consider the following case:

Smith and Jones have both applied for the same job. The hiring manager for the job has told Smith that Jones will get the job. Smith has also counted the coins in Jones's pocket and has found there are 10 coins there. Based on this evidence, Smith makes the following assertion:

(1) The person who will get the job has 10 coins in his pocket.

As it turns out, Smith actually gets the job and has 10 coins in his pocket, although he didn't count these coins before he got the job. This means that (1) is true.

Do you think that we can say that Smith knew that (1) was true? (Gettier Case)

Good Answer: No, I do not think that we can say that Smith knew that (1) was true. This is because the evidence that Smith uses to support his claim of (1) isn't actually why (1) is true in the end. He has based his claim on false evidence – the fact that the hiring manager told him that Jones would get the job – and evidence which doesn't contribute to the truth of (1) – the fact that Jones had 10 coins in his pocket. Smith doesn't have evidence that he will get the job and he also hasn't counted the numbers of coins he has in his pocket at the time that he makes the assertion. In this case, he is just lucky that he happens to be right in asserting (1) so I do not think that we can say that Smith knew that (1) was true.

This answer identifies the problem in this case – that the evidence Smith bases his claim on does not contribute to the truth of (1) – and clearly relates it to the question of whether or not Smith knew that (1) was true. The candidate clearly sets out their chain of reasoning for the interviewer and comes to a justified and reasoned answer. The candidate doesn't rely on any additional reading that they may have done, although if relevant they could have brought in some wider reasoning if it would have helped them, but show that they are able to critically engage with challenging philosophical problems in a logical way.

Bad Answer: Yes, Smith must have known that (1) was true because he said it before it happened.

This answer has completely missed the point of the example and doesn't even try to reason through why Smith might not have known that (1) was true before he said it. A candidate might conclude this, but they would need to give strong and clear reasoning for this conclusion for it to be a good answer.

Q59. What do you think makes a strong philosophical argument?

Good Answer: A strong philosophical argument is one in which the conclusion is fully supported by the premises. There need to be no contradictions in the chain of reasoning and the chain of reasoning needs to lead clearly and securing to the conclusion that the argument is trying to come to. An example of this might be: I am an A Level student; I am a girl; therefore, I am a female A Level student. This is a very straightforward example but the conclusion is fully supported by the premises and there are no contradictions in the chain of argument.

This clearly sets out what criteria are required for a philosophical argument to be considered "strong". While a candidate might not know the term "Premises" they could still set out the second half of this response which shows the content of a strong philosophical argument and gives a clear and concise example to show the interviewer that they have fully understood what they are talking about. If possible, the candidate should then be able to give further examples of a strong philosophical argument if questioned further by the examiner.

Bad Answer: An argument that concludes in favour of a particularly important philosophical theory.

The candidate has here misunderstood what the interviewer is asking them for. In general, these types of defining questions will be asking about the methodology behind philosophy. It will be asking the candidate what they think is important in building a strong and important argument, rather than asking them to suggest what might support pre-existing philosophical theories. Here, the candidate could instead reverse the sentiments in their answer, replying instead that philosophical theories need strong philosophical arguments in order to support them and to make them convincing. From here, the candidate could then walk through the methodology that would make a philosophical argument convincing, such as the methodology given in the "Good Answer" to this question.

Q60. Can you see any problems with the following argument?

1: Samantha can't get a job where she's currently living.

2: Samantha got a job in London.

Conclusion: Samantha will move to London.

This question is testing skills similar to those tested in some of the verbal reasoning questions in the TSA. It is asking you to look at the answer and check whether or not the conclusion follows from the stated premises. The argument might be problematic if any of the following are true: (i) the premises contradict each other or the conclusion, (ii) the argument is relying on a premise that isn't explicitly stated, (iii) the conclusion doesn't follow from the premises. There is a problem with this argument, as the "Good Answer" below will set out.

Good Answer: Yes, I can see a problem with the argument. The conclusion doesn't follow directly from the premises, as there is nothing contained within the premises that states that Samantha will move for her job. A better argument would be as follows:

1: Samantha can't get a job where she's currently living.

2: Samantha got a job in London.

Conclusion: Samantha isn't currently living in London.

An alternative argument would be:

1: Samantha can't get a job where she's currently living.

2: Samantha will move to wherever she can get a job.

3: Samantha got a job in London.

Conclusion: Samantha will move to London.

Bad Answer: I can't see any problem with this argument.

Q61. Can you see any problems with the following argument?

1: All men are mortal.

2: Socrates is a man.

Conclusion: Socrates is mortal.

As above in Q21, this question is testing skills similar to those tested in some of the verbal reasoning questions in the TSA. It is asking you to look at the answer and check whether or not the conclusion follows from the stated premises. The argument might be problematic if any of the following are true: (i) the premises contradict each other or the conclusion, (ii) the argument is relying on a premise that isn't explicitly stated, (iii) the conclusion doesn't follow from the premises. This argument is valid as it does not fulfil any of these criteria, as the "Good Answer" below will set out.

Good Answer: To me, this argument looks strong. The conclusion seems to follow directly from the premises and I cannot see any flaw in the chain of reasoning. I also can't see that the argument relies on an assertion that is not explicitly identified. Therefore, I think that there is no problem with this argument.

Bad Answer: A bad answer here would be unable to identify that this is a strong argument. It might highlight a problem that doesn't exist, for example.

HSPS INTERVIEW QUESTIONS

Q1: How would you discretise the concepts of ethnicity and race?

Race and ethnicity are both highly complex topics. Your interviewer is not expecting you to be able dissect these or necessarily give a 'correct' answer. In society, definitions of 'race' and 'ethnicity' are not specifically discussed, because they are relatively nebulous concepts that are highly political. Therefore, the interview is interested in seeing how you think critically about this question, what experiences and knowledge that you draw upon, and how you can synthesise this into a coherent answer.

Because this question is highly political, you must be incredibly careful about the kind of language you are using. Interviewers will accept minor slip-ups in terms of terminology, but do not use racial stereotypes or discriminative language.

Good Applicant: Well, I'd like to first acknowledge that race and ethnicity are interrelated, and that I don't think it is possible for us talk about one without being aware of the other, because they are both so prevalent in discussions of identity. But, broadly speaking, I think the difference between race and ethnicity, is that race is mostly situated in physical aspects of who a person is, such as their skin colour, but also other biological aspects. In contrast, ethnicity is more closely tied to socio-cultural aspects of a person, where they were brought up, their language, nationality, and regional identities. I think there's also a difference in the histories of the two concepts. Whilst race has a deep past originating from colonial times and was often used to categorise, and thereby dehumanise, different people, as a concept, ethnicity is a more recent creation that is used to better understand the complexity of identity in the post-colonial and global era. I think ultimately both concepts are difficult to clearly define, and the boundaries between the differences are often blurred.

This response is structured well, it starts by stating the relationship that ethnicity and race, and how they both relate to identity. It then clearly cites two points contrasting how race and ethnicity are different, using broad examples to back up the points, without delving into potential slippery slopes that specific examples in talking about these topics might lead to. Finally, the answer makes it clear at the end that you don't have a firm opinion on what race and ethnicity are; it has critically engaged with the question whilst making it clear that you are open to further discussion.

A **poor applicant** could go one of two ways. Firstly, you might not be willing to engage in critical examination of the two concepts because you don't want to say something inappropriate, or you are unaware of exactly what the concepts might mean. Being cautious around these topics is important, but not answering the question asked at all also doesn't help. Secondly, a poor answer might rely upon stereotypes, or even use crude terms to discuss these two highly sensitive topics.

Q2: Would you argue that the society and the state are inseparable? If not, what separates them?

This question is a good opportunity to demonstrate your understanding of definitions of state, and how society fits into it, but also how a state is reliant upon society; they are different but often interconnected. As with many concepts in anthropology and political science, concepts and definitions are important for creating benchmarks for discussion, but are still nebulous and require open thinking combined with critical engagement.

Good Applicant: Fundamentally, I think that the difference between state and society relates to the way in which they are structured. The state is typically made up of formal structures and institutions to be maintained, and is reliant upon four key aspects: population, territory, government, and sovereignty. Now, each of these four aspects are themselves debatable in their definitions and parameters, but the key thing is they form the pillars upon which the state is established. In contrast, society is typically made of informal structures, and interpersonal and intergroup relationships. They are established and maintained through human behaviours, such as exchange of goods and ideas, and are typically highly flexible. With this in mind, state and society are also highly influential upon each other. The formal structures of the state can influence the way in which people in a society interact and their relationships, whilst the state is inherently dependent on the stability of society and the ability of people to cooperate and communicate.

This answer is structured well, making it clear that the applicant understands the question being asked, and that they are able to back up their argument with evidence and examples. Bearing in mind that these are difficult concepts to discuss in a single response, the answer does not go down a rabbit hole trying to wrestle with these ideas, but shows that they are able to engage with both concepts in the question, and draw contrasts between the two. The synthesis at the end also demonstrates that respondent is able to think beyond the basic question, challenge the assumption in the question, and demonstrate the relationships between the two concepts.

A **Poor Applicant** would become tied down with trying to define the two concepts and would run out of time before actually answering the question. Whilst it is important to demonstrate your understanding of the concepts, it is important to demonstrate that you are able to see the bigger picture and critically engage.

Q3: A Roman magistrate appears on your doorstep, and asks you to tell him about the United Nations – how would you compare it to his Empire?

This question is testing your ability to draw comparisons between two seemingly unrelated organisations, and interacts with international law. In order to answer this question, you need to be able to think creatively and accept that sometimes unconventional comparisons can sometimes change your perspective and are useful heuristics.

Good Response: Well, this is certainly interesting. I think one of the first points that I would compare is that both intentionally or unintentionally acted as peacekeeping bodies. In the case of the UN, this is through mediation, forums, and small peace-keeping forces, in the Roman empire, which I would argue did maintain a decent level of relative peace for 200 years at the outset of the empire (Romana Pax), 'peace' was achieved mostly through prosperity of the empire, fairly decent governance, and the violent crushing of any rebellions. Another point of similarity is the fact that power in the both the Roman empire and UN is actually held by a small number of stakeholders. In the empire this meant the emperor and a few others, and whilst the senate existed, their power was negligible. One could argue that a similar reality occurs in the UN; power is held by the Director General and the Security Council, much of the discourse carried out in the main house of the UN by its members do not carry with it much power, similarly to the senate. I think a third point of similarity are the UN's and the empire's goals around development. Both have or had missions of developing those areas under their influence, in the formers case through sustainable economic development and the latter through its building of grandiose architecture. A final point of similarity that I would draw would be between the multi-state nature of the two organisations; although the UN does not directly govern those states that make it up, unlike the empire, both had to deal with the complexities of multiple states.

At first glance, this is a challenging question, and indeed, as outlined in this answer, the similarities are not going to be perfect. One could argue that there are far more differences between the UN and the RE. Hence, this answer has done well here because it has found ways of drawing similarities between four different points of the UN and the RE through some creative thinking, which your interviewers will be impressed by.

A **Poor Answer** could very easily struggle to find similarities, and become bogged down by the fact that any similarities you can see aren't perfect. Equally, it would be very easy to begin by talking about the differences between the two as these are much easier to identify, and never really identify any points of similarity.

Q4: Some of us think that the poor live in poverty because they don't try hard enough – what would you say to people like that?

As with many Oxbridge interview questions, this question is intentionally challenging or jarring. Whilst it may be tempting to form a strong and subjective opinion one way or the other, you must endeavour to remain balanced, whilst still reaching a conclusion. Thus, you should present your arguments, and then conclude by making your opinion clear on the matter.

Good Answer: Well, to begin with, I can understand why this point of view may be so prevalent among neoliberals. I think that it is derived primarily from those in power and those who control big media outlets influencing the general public's thought. For instance, the fact that the Murdoch empire controls multiple media outlets allows it to hold great sway among the populace in the UK and other countries. Now, media moguls such as Murdoch have two primary objectives: manipulating people to agree with their way of thinking, and making money for themselves and those whose interests align with their own. One of the easiest ways for this money to be made is to push a neoliberal agenda, both in lobbying governments and convincing people through their outlets that this is good for them and their families.

In essence, this means creating the idea that people must be productive within the capitalist system, and that the amount you work will equate directly to your income. In reality, the neoliberal agenda is to deregulate markets and state involvement so that workers' rights and pay can be cut without repercussions. Alongside the propaganda that your worth is equal to how much you work, this creates an environment where the wealthy are able to monopolise the working and middle classes by making them believe that they can be successful, whilst using this as a front to extract wealth from them. In the end, the system crushes many people, especially when state safety nets have been removed, and become poor. Thus, the system is manipulated by neoliberals to make it seem like poor people are only poor because they don't work hard enough. In reality, I think that most of the time, poor people have been exploited by a system created by neoliberals who have simultaneously convinced people through media propaganda that it is the poor's fault for not working hard enough.

This is not an easy question to answer, and in part centres around unpacking what it means to be neoliberal. This answer is strong because it puts pressure from the start on the falsehood underpinning everyday neoliberals; that they are different from poor people. In fact, most neoliberals have been manipulated into their beliefs by moguls and the super rich, and their neoliberal belief system is actually perpetuating those falsehoods that are manipulating them. As well as demonstrating this issue, the answer logically works through the relationship between the political belief system of neoliberalism, the media, and the state. In the end, the answer draws together these lines of argument to answer the question and demonstrate that poverty is not a result of laziness, but instead a failure of state as result of the influence of money within politics.

A **Poor Answer** could react one of two ways. Someone who tacitly agrees with the notion of the question might argue positively, and agree with the question, whilst failing to challenge their own belief system, which would likely be picked up on the interviewer. On the other hand, it would be very easy to become personally offended by the question, as it is undoubtedly an insulting notion. Thus it is important to take the question apart and show that you are able to remain objective whilst still creating a forthright answer that takes a balanced approach.

Q5: What do you think lies behind the recent resurgence of Nationalism in Europe?

This question is testing several different aspects of your knowledge: your recent and deep historic understanding of nationalism within Europe, as well as how this plays out throughout the geography of Europe. In order to answer the question, it is important to highlight that nationalism is a broad idea that fluctuates over time and can mean different things to different people.

A **Good Answer:** I think first it is important to point a bit of an assumption within the question of whether nationalism ever really weakened in Europe. If we look at the history of Europe, really going back to the Roman conquests of Europe, when tribes of the different territories fought back to "protect their lands", we could argue that this is a kind of nationalism, or a kind of cultural or ethnic identity tied to the landscape. From there, throughout the history of Europe, I think that nationalism has always been bubbling under the surface in one form or another. Even when it may seem like nationalistic sentiment has diminished, there are always those factions within a state that advocate for nationalistic policies, and occasionally those with these sentiments achieve power and drive forward with those nationalistic attitudes.

With this in mind, it seems that we are in a time where people with nationalistic sentiments are gaining traction politically. I think there are a number of reasons for this. Firstly, nationalism in Europe is not isolated from the rest of the world, in the same way that nationalism within individual European countries is not isolated from other countries. To this extent, the election of Donald Trump, as well as other fascist leaders such as Jair Bolsanero, and Duterte to name just a couple, always have a knock-on effect elsewhere by emboldening other nationalists directly and indirectly (e.g., Trump's endorsement of Nigel Farage). Beyond just this, the migrant crisis, caused by the ongoing conflicts in the Middle East and North Africa, and exponentially exacerbated by Western and Russian interventions, has undoubtedly increased nationalistic sentiments in Europe as Europeans feel threatened by a sudden influx of people alongside some pretty incompetent policies and leaders unable to deal with this crisis. Finally, both of these issues are ultimately enflamed by the press, which is controlled by a small number of people who directly profit from the controversy that they drive especially around nationalistic sentiments in order to sell papers.

In summary, I think nationalism is an ever-present element of European sociopolitics, but that there are clearly events in the recent past and ongoing that continue to fuel nationalistic sentiments in areas of Europe.

This is a good answer because it shows that you are able to critically engage with the question, deconstruct and offer a foundational starting point by addressing the key assumption within the question. The answer is then structured well, outlining three key points that you feel has driven the strengthening of nationalism within Europe. Finally, it has provided a neat summary that synthesises everything you have tried to outline in your answer.

A **Poor Answer** might try to inherently question whether nationalism has strengthened at all in Europe. Whilst it is possible to play this as devil's advocate, it may inadvertently show that you have a poor grasp of current or recent historical events. Alternatively, it would be easy to become tied up in the deep history of nationalism in Europe, which whilst a useful point of comparison and grounding to your answer, would not address the idea of a recent development.

Q6. You're redesigning a map of the world, how would you go about deciding on national borders?

Whilst seemingly simple, in fact this question is seeking to have you draw upon your ability to synthesise several different disciplines, in reflection of the complexity of drawing of national borders, to answer the question. There is not necessarily a straightforward answer to this, thus you must instead draw upon your different subject knowledges, including history, geography, and politics, to demonstrate that you are able to bring together several different ways of thinking.

A **Good Answer**: At a basic level, national borders are drawn by the political or social bodies that control each side. However, the reality of the drawing of national borders is that there are often complex historical and geographical factors at play, alongside the political ones. For instance, geographical features such as mountain ranges or rivers, serve as physical boundaries that are used as straightforward and often practical borders, such as the Pyrenees separating France and Spain, or the Akagera river separating Rwanda and Tanzania. However, physical boundaries are not always a limiting factor to national borders and can even make the drawing of national borders more, not less complex. In the latter instance, take for example the occasionally conflicted border of India and China, which because of its size and location among the Himalayas, makes defining the border incredibly complicated.

Moreover, in historic terms, physical features have not always been a defining factor for drawing national borders. The invasion and colonisation of other countries, such as by the British or Mongolian empires, entirely betrayed the limitations of the English Channel and the Central Asian Steppe. Conveniently, this leads to consideration of the impact that historical events have on the drawing of national borders. In the post-colonial era, many of the national borders that still exist today are a direct result of colonial powers. Whilst these borders were still defined politically during their time between the colonial powers, it is interesting to examine how infrequently these borders are actually challenged by the modern nations that they affect. Overall, what I'm trying to elucidate, is that national borders are in fact incredibly complex and dynamic, and are affected by a whole array of factors on a case by case basis; almost no two borders are drawn in exactly the same way, and this is reflected in the way that they are drawn.

It would be very easy to write an entire thesis on this subject, as there are so many case studies that you could draw upon to provide examples and counter examples. Ultimately, this answer is strong because it is able to demonstrate that you have a wide understanding of the realities of the complexities of drawing national borders, and that it is perfectly fine, once you have outlined decent and varied evidence, as has been done here, to conclude that there is no finite answer to this question.

A **Poor Answer** would only rely upon examples that fit the narrative you create about how national borders are drawn. For example, it would be easy to argue that national borders are drawn as a result of conflict and upheaval, and then only illustrate this with one type of example, without considering the multitude of different realities involved.

Q7. Do you think that you have free will? Does free will as a concept relate to the notion of the state of nature?

This question is attempting to get you to think about what might normally be two unrelated concepts and understand how one can inform the other. This is a particularly pertinent question as it is a reflection of the kind of question that you might be asked to write an essay about during your time at the university. It should be noted that this question assumes your pre-understanding of the state of nature. If this is an unfamiliar concept to you, because you haven't studied a subject that considers it before, it is perfectly fine to say this to your interviewer, you will not be penalised. In many ways, it is better to acknowledge that you do not know everything, and ask for clarification, before attempting to answer it; interviewers are more interested in how you think than what you know.

A **Good Answer**: Well, thank you for clarifying for me what exactly the state of nature is. I think that the crux of this question centres around the idea that when the hypothetical state of nature existed, before the existence of societies, people would not have been constrained by social norms or rules, and whether or not this could potentially be defined as a time when we had true free will. In this context, I believe therefore, it is important to define free will as the ability to make decisions about your behaviour and life, unhindered by the actions of others or the rules of society. I think that this is a logical assumption to make, as so much of our modern behaviour is tied up in social contracts between people, and therefore free will in a true sense can rarely exist.

If this is case, then the issue becomes when do we consider that society actually started? If, for example, we look at other species that live in groups, such as chimpanzees, they still have social rules, ways of behaving in a group that are enforced by other members. Thus, in a sense, they cannot have complete 'free' will, because their behaviour doesn't exist in a vacuum; the things that they do have consequences for those around them. From this perspective, we could then analogously consider whether humans could achieve complete free will in a state where no groups, and therefore no social behaviours (i.e., societies) existed. However, there is an inherent problem in this assumption, and that is that the vast majority of humans do not exist in complete in isolation, nor would it be logical to assume that they ever have done, as we would have died out as a species. In reality, there will always be moments where people must interact - to have offspring etc. - and therefore, there will be moments where their free will is given up to the needs of the group.

Thus, to reiterate my original definition of free will, it is the ability to make decisions without anyone else's agency affecting or inhibiting those decisions. As I believe I've demonstrated, this kind of free-will can only exist in a hypothetical vacuum, because we as a species are never 100% isolated from the actions of others or from the effect of our actions on others. Based upon the reference I made to chimpanzees, even if there was a time before society when human behaviour was entirely 'natural', the reality is that living in any kind of group comes with implicit rules as a direct result of the agency of others. The relationship therefore between free will and the state of nature is only hypothetical, and whilst it might be easy to conclude that the state of nature was the only time when free will could have existed, as I have demonstrated here, I don't believe that even that would be possible due to our interdependent, group nature as a species.

This is by no means a straightforward question as it is dealing with two huge philosophical ideas. However, this answer is strong because whilst it would be impossible to fully elucidate the two ideas separately in an answer, it has achieved what the question is asking: for you to speculate about the relationship between the two concepts. As well as outlining generally the two ideas, it has used examples from primatology and made logical conclusions based upon your understanding of the two ideas. Ultimately, it synthesises the two ideas into a conclusion in order to answer the question.

A **Poor Answer** could become overwhelmed by the enormity of the two concepts that you are being asked to answer and get too caught up in trying to consider all the different interpretations of these ideas, without actually trying to draw a conclusion about their relationship. Equally, a poor answer might entirely focus on one or the other of these concepts, without paying heed to the other. In order to answer the question well, it is important to try to remain logical and bring each of your points back to how free will and the state of nature are related.

Q8. Do you think that primates, like chimpanzees, should be given the same rights as people?

This question hinges around two key points: how do we define 'human', and do chimpanzees sufficiently fulfil this definition. The easier option in this question is definitely to argue that chimpanzees are not human and therefore do not deserve human rights, however, there is definitely scope to make the argument that they do deserve rights. In some ways, the question can be considered: are humans unique in comparison to our closest relations, and how does this relate to rights?

A **Good Response**: Well, I think at a broad level, it is clear that whilst chimpanzees have a high level of intelligence, both social and emotional, that can be used to draw parallels with humans, that ultimately there is enough of a biological and cultural difference between humans and chimpanzees, that they probably shouldn't be afforded human rights. This being said, there is growing evidence that the 'uniqueness' of humans in comparison to chimpanzees and other animals is not as distinct as we first thought. For instance, in the Great Ape family, humans are often touted as unique due to our bipedality, but there is plenty of evidence now that whilst chimps are not habitually bipedal, they certainly have the ability to do so for extended periods. Equally, the argument that humans in general are the only species to have cumulative culture (behaviours and technologies that are passed down through generations with increasing complexity) is also being challenged by evidence from chimpanzees, with suggestions that complex behaviours, such as termite fishing, are passed between generations. I think these two examples are excellent challenges to the notion of human uniqueness, and thereby a challenge to whether human rights should be exclusively human. Based upon this kind of evidence, maybe we need to re-evaluate how binary human : animal rights are, and consider whether animals that display higher levels of culture should have different levels of rights. This is of course a slippery slope, but as more and more evidence comes in to play about the complexity of animal (and especially chimpanzee and bonobo) behaviour, these are going to become more complex debates.

Whilst this question may at first seem like a straightforward question to answer, as outlined here, once you start dealing with *why* humans are considered unique and how this plays into our ideas of human rights, the answer becomes complicated very quickly. Thus, this is a good response because it tries to take a balanced approach, suggesting at the beginning that there are obvious differences between humans and chimpanzees, before going onto elaborate how this discussion is not as binary as it may at first appear, outlining the growing evidence for the complexity of chimp behaviour. Finally, it acknowledges that there is not necessarily an easy answer to this question, and that evidence in the future may cause us to re-evaluate our position.

A **Poor Response** could quite easily dismiss this question out of hand, stating that chimps clearly don't deserve human rights. Even if one was unaware of the evidence around chimp behaviour, a basic awareness of chimps will tell you that they are clearly highly intelligent and that it is worth considering how what you know about their biology or behaviour may play into arguments for giving chimps human rights.

Q9. What do you think is one of the most fascinating facts about where you come from, what makes that so interesting?

This question is an opportunity for you to be reflexive and demonstrate to your interviewers your interest in the world around you. In anthropology, the ability to be self-reflective, to understand how your background - including your culture, personal upbringing, and the environment in which these occurred - influences your study of other cultures and societies is fundamental to acknowledging that we all have our own set biases, or constructed lenses, through which we see the world. Here, you could discuss aspects of material culture, architecture, behaviour, or pretty much anything that you feel confident talking about. Be creative!

A **Good Applicant**: Something that has always interested me about teenagers and young people in Great Britain are attitudes and behaviours towards alcohol. It has always amazed me how willing people are to get inebriated to the point of passing out in the street, or causing themselves bodily harm, and then repeating this behaviour the following week. It is this self-destructive aspect that particularly fascinates me; people are aware of how much damage that level of alcohol can cause (both directly and indirectly) to their bodies, but they do it anyway. I suppose that ultimately it comes down to a combination of cultural acceptance - both tacitly through people accepting that this behaviour is the 'norm' and pragmatically through young people's ability to access alcohol.

It is particularly interesting when you compare these kinds of behaviours to other young people in other cultures. For instance, I know that in America, alcohol is very difficult to access as a young person, but marijuana isn't, and therefore the latter is far more prevalent. In France, people are often introduced to alcohol at a younger age, and the culture around drinking has less of a tendency towards binge drinking, but then, a huge majority of French young people smoke which is in contrast to young people in Britain. I think that these comparisons and experiences of other cultures can be incredibly interesting as points of comparison. This is because they both allow us draw way markers in other cultures to help our understanding as well as give us an alternative lens through which to reflect on our own culture.

This is a good answer because it has chosen an aspect of your culture that has interested you. It doesn't necessarily have to be a positive thing, indeed, often some of the most interesting behaviours are those that seem in some way counter-intuitive or deviant. Hence, not only does this answer outline why you're interested in this particular thing, but it also demonstrates how you've thought about this issue or thing in other cultural contexts. Moreover, it has shown how one cultural understanding can inform another.

A **Poor Answer** could choose something that you find interesting, but then fail to explain why you find it interesting. Whilst this question seems open ended, in the context of which interview you are in, it is important to demonstrate that you understand that this question is about society and/or culture, and show that your interested is derived from that context.

Q10. Take a look at these cave paintings, how might you analyse them for meaning?

This question will be accompanied by pictures of cave paintings (you may be given one or more to look at). There are a whole range of cave paintings that we now know about from across the world and across a whole range of time periods. The most famous cave paintings come from Europe (mostly France and Spain), but archaeologists are discovering new cave art globally all the time. Equally, this is the kind of question where an interviewer might throw a curve ball, and for instance, show you modern "cave art" in the form of graffiti inside an urban building, for instance. Regardless, you could cover a number of topics when deciphering them: content (is it a clear shape(s) or is it abstract), colours used, medium (e.g., paint, ochre, blood), location (e.g. ceiling, floor), and finally what is it symbolic or representative of; does it have a purpose? For the sake of this question, the following answer is in response to the image in this article, from Lascaux https://medium.com/@stevechatterton/what-the-lascaux-cave-paintings-tell-us-about-the-nature-of-human-desire-4c8d06deef83:

Good Answer: In this picture, there are a number of different animals clearly depicted. There are three distinct kinds of image, a bull-like animal with horns, what appear to be two brown and black horses, and two entirely black horses. The parsimonious explanation is simply that the artists here were depicting the animals around them. If this was the case, we could speculate about whether they simply drew these animals as a kind of appreciation of their beauty or whether they represented the animals that they were hunting. If this is a literal portrayal of the animals, it is also interesting to note that they appear to be demonstrating a level of depth perception that might imply a multitude of animals such that they overlap in the image.

Alternatively, we could interpret these animals in a symbolic way, with the animals being metaphorical for different groups in a society. Perhaps the horned bull represents a leader and the horses their followers. If this was the case, then the blurring of the animals may in some way represent levels of relationships, such that the brown and black horses have a closer relationship with the bull, than the black horses do. Perhaps the physical blurring of the animals here even represents a psychological blurring of people that is similarly observed in some contemporary cultures, with boundary between self and other being indistinct, with each person's identity and personhood melting into one another.

There is no correct answer here, the interviewers are more interested in your thought process and ability to make inferences rather than finding the 'right answer' (debates about what cave art actually 'means' are infinite). Thus, this answer shows your ability to think about the cave art from different perspectives, and offers different interpretations from these. It considers both a literal and a metaphorical interpretation and tries to link our understanding of these ancient people to modern cultures.

A **poor answer** might simply describe what is you see before you, without considering its wider implications or potential inferences. Whilst there is nothing inherently wrong with using a literal interpretation as a starting point, a literal interpretation must still be used to draw inferences about the people who created these artworks and suggest potential conclusions about these people from studying them.

Q11. What is love?

This question is an opportunity for you to demonstrate your ability to synthesise the scientific and the quantitative, with the qualitative and phenomenological. That is, what science has to say about love, versus what we find first- and second- hand through the human experience. As is so often the case, there is no right answer here, instead it is more important for you to construct a clear answer and try to draw a conclusion.

Good Response: I think that this question can be approached from two different perspectives. On the one hand, we have what science tell us, that is, that love is a particular set of chemicals, hormones, and impulses throughout your brain and body that lead you to be profoundly connected to another person. This makes sense from an evolutionary perspective because evidence shows that primate groups with stronger social bonds - including what we call 'love' - provide more support to one another, protect each other more, and in general work together better.

Building upon this, in reproduction, love also makes sense as it draws people powerfully together, leading to copulation, and more often than not in heterosexual couples, offspring. Logically, it may also then play a role in keeping parents around. That is, love between the mother and the father may mean that offspring are raised together, reducing the workload for both parents. Even where love between the mother and the father doesn't occur long-term, the love between parent and child is, in the vast majority of cases, incredibly powerful, such that the parents are often willing to lay down their lives in order to protect their offspring. Thus, from this perspective what constitutes love is a set of evolutionary biological functions that serve a sociobiological function.

On the other hand, I think that there is a completely phenomenological element to love. That is, love is so much about the personal experience. To reduce love to a set of biological and evolutionary processes seems to do it an injustice. Indeed, when we look at all the things done in the name of love, whether it is war, poetry, sacrifice, or the construction of monumental architecture, there definitely is more to love than just chemicals. On that last point of monumental architecture, if you think about the construction of the Taj Mahal by Mughal emperor Shah Jahan as a tomb for his wife, then this is not something constitutes a biological or evolutionary process. That is, there was no way for him to produce offspring with his wife after her death. Yet, he still had built one of the most revered buildings in the world for love of her.

Hence, I think that there are definitely elements and viewpoints from biology that we can use to consider what constitutes love, but without an understanding of that qualitative, phenomenological, almost intangible element of the human experience that we call love, we would have only a small piece of all that constitutes love.

This is a strong answer because it is very structured. It first lays out the scientific evidence that is often quoted to comprise love, demonstrating your understanding of the different biological and evolutionary functions that love may comprise. The answer then goes on to demonstrate the sociological or social anthropological perspective, including an example that directly contradicts some of the reductionist arguments made from the scientific perspective. Ultimately, it concludes by synthesising these two perspectives and providing a clear answer to the question.

Q12. On the course we are introducing a new paper this year in which we can teach you about any part of the world you like – which part of the world do you think you will pick?

This is a question that allows you to show your wider interests in the world beyond your own nation and culture. This really is an opportunity for you to show a passion for studying other cultures, political structures, and people.

A **Good Response**: I would love to learn more about Central Asia, especially the steppe, including the history, archaeology, and culture of, for instance, Mongolia. I think part of the reason that I would want to learn more about this area of the world is first and foremost is because so little is known or taught about its history or culture outside of the area. Studying history at school, even though my IB course was pretty international, we focussed on Europe, East Asia, and America. And then in discussions of international support for other countries outside of Europe, there is a lot of research done in Africa, South East Asia, and South America, but so often it seems to me that Central Asia is not nearly as talked about. In fact, I think the only time Western media covers the area is of 'flashy' aspects of the culture, such as eagle hunting. This has always somewhat surprised me as the Mongolian empire was the second largest in history stretching almost the entirety of Eurasia, Genghis Khan has 16 million direct male descendants, and in some ways it was the greatest overall influence on the world certainly in the first half of the 2nd millennium AD, with arguable influence throughout the entirety of the millennium.

Beyond this, I'm aware that there is a deep past behind the Mongol empire, and the nomadic nature of those people really intrigues me, especially as so much of that behaviour continues to this day. And then finally, looking at the recent past of Central Asia and the culture there, I still know relatively little about it other than that China and Russia both have strong influence there, but I simply would love to learn more about the culture and people, and where they have come from.

This answer is particularly strong because it not only shows a passion for learning about the archaeology, anthropology, and political science of the area, but it also outlines specific examples that you would be interested in knowing about. It shows that you have an awareness of many of the potential areas and ways that areas of the world could be studied, and it provides a clear justification and answer to the question.

A **Poor Answer** might fail to elucidate exactly why you're interested in a particular area effectively. In reality, you could choose almost any area of the world, but it is important to show (especially in the context of applying for HSPS or Arch. and Anth.) how relevant disciplines might approach these areas of the world. Equally, a poor answer might inadvertently exotically describe another culture, almost fetishising it rather than offering a more objective and intrigue-based approach.

Q13. Can you think of anything happening in the news at the moment which you feel is a particularly good example of a larger significant issue?

This is an opportunity to show your broader understanding of political events in the world. This question allows you to show your ability to draw connections between micro and macro events, and is asking you to demonstrate your ability to inform a broad understanding from a focussed perspective.

Good Response: With the inauguration of US President Joe Biden, we have seen the almost immediate reversal of the damaging climate change denial and policies of the Trump administration of the last four years. Whilst it is seems true that Trump did not have a clear understanding of climate change, it does not entirely explain his actions. Indeed, some of his ulterior motivation was clear; America has been incredibly reliant upon fossil fuels both in terms of directly powering its economy and indirectly providing jobs. This latter fact is still true, and whilst Biden's policies could create a shift away from a reliance on fossil fuels whilst providing many jobs in the long term through renewable energy projects, there are plenty of Americans who will feel pain in the short term as a result of job losses. This friction between a need for a radical change in policy and practice, whilst protecting people's livelihoods is particularly indicative of a world issue.

In America, fossil fuel companies who have wielded significant wealth and influence in the last 150 years in America, as elsewhere, constantly lobby governments to allow them to continue exploiting the planet and accruing wealth. The reason that this current affair is particularly indicative of a world issue is because almost every country on earth is wrestling with these same issues. They know that change is needed and needed now, but they are under pressure on two fronts, both from those large companies that want to continue making money and their own people who are either reliant directly or indirectly on jobs and income from fossil fuels, and for finding and building alternative sources of energy. This current affair is even more indicative of many countries' situations as it is indicative of how a change in democratic power can lead to rapid changes in policy one way or the other.

This is a good answer because it has identified a well-reported current affair that is an ongoing issue. Moreover, it is an issue that affects every person in the world and every country. Not only is the complexity of dealing with climate change a world issue, but the situation in America is particularly indicative of the balance that many governments are attempting to strike between multiple issues.

A **Poor Answer** might choose a current affair that does not relate to a world issue. That is, it might be particular to specific context and wouldn't be easy to draw parallels with a world issue, or alternatively it might be irrelevant at the world level e.g., dog kidnapping in the UK.

Q14. You are an archaeologist in the year 2500, excavating Oxford – what material culture might you expect to find from my present?

Material culture includes everything in human reality that does not relate to behaviours. Thus, this question is an excellent opportunity to be creative and really show your thought process in your answer, which is ultimately what your interviewers are most interested in. For ideas you could talk about: clothing, food, furniture, architecture, computers, cutlery, or lightbulbs.

Good Answer: Well, I think Smartphones are an interesting piece of material culture in contemporary society. In some ways, smartphones represent the pinnacle of modern technology. What once required an entire room of computer hardware, can now be carried around in our pockets. Moreover, it is remarkable to think about how far the technology in smartphones has come since their inception in the 2000s. I think this is the result of two key aspects of contemporary society: a thirst for connectivity and convenience that smartphones facilitate at an unprecedented scale, and the competition between large companies to create the best product. Particularly, if you think that one of the unique aspects of being human is our cumulative culture over time, then the smartphone is an excellent example of how this operates in contemporary society.

Beyond just the developments of smartphones themselves, smartphones represent the accumulation of our communication and language abilities as a species. From when we first starting writing language, to postal and messenger services, to telegrams, to telephones, to emails, and now mobile phones. Not only this, but mobile phones in general and smartphones in particular are becoming more and more ubiquitous. Even in areas of the world where very little other technology exists, smartphones can be found, and they are more and more frequently being used in transformative ways for health and education purposes in contemporary society.

This is a strong answer because the object chosen is something that is highly indicative of contemporary society. Not only that, as illustrated in the answer, they have a clearly delineated history that is representative of how material culture changes over time and how it affects society. Moreover, it is a particularly nice example, because as demonstrated, not only are they a piece of material culture that are growing in prevalence throughout many societies, but they are also having a remarkable impact in peoples' lives.

A **Poor Answer** might choose an object that whilst a piece of material culture, fails to connect with the idea of contemporary society. For instance, if the answer had chosen a printing press, whilst this is undoubtedly a piece of material culture, it has almost no role in contemporary society other than as a historical object with very rare usage. It is important to be able to situate the object within that modern context.

Q15. Do you think that one's culture can shape one's perceptions? Is the way we see colour the same as someone from a different culture would?

The key to this question relies on understanding the difference between human perception and human categorisation. In order to answer this question appropriately, you need to first have a fundamental understanding that biologically and neurologically, humans are almost identical, and any differences occur within a relatively small standard deviation. This is particularly important, as any claims about the biological differences in humans, have in the past been used to oppress, dehumanise, enslave, and destroy other humans.

Good Answer: I think that the answer to this questions by how we define perception. Essentially, perception in relation to colour is the process by which light hits a surface, and different lengths of the colour spectrum are reflected into our eyes, which then pass information to the brain and are processed neurologically to identify certain colours. Now, irrespective of cultural influences, apart from people with conditions such as colour blindness, all humans process these colours in the same way. That is to say, that perception of colours is not culturally specific. That being said, what is culturally specific are the ways in which humans categorise colours. For instance, some languages have more than one word for slightly different shades of blue - in Russian, the word 'goluboy' is used to differentiate from the slightly darker 'siniy' - but if you showed these same colours to an English speaker, they would only use the word 'blue'. So in this instance, categorisations of colour are culturally specific, and the language that we use to talk about colours varies, whilst our actual perception is the same.

This is answer has a good structure, starting by breaking down the question to get to the heart of what is being asked, and demonstrating a clear understanding of this, before answering the question. This answer is particularly strong, because it then extends the response by showing how colour is categorised differently, whilst being perceptually the same, using a well-known example to back this up. It finally ties the extended part of the answer back to the original question.

Q16: What areas of Philosophy are you interested in?

[Extremely clear-headed] Applicant: I am interested in theories of the state. Many thinkers have attempted to tackle this issue throughout history, ranging from Plato, through Hobbes and Rousseau, to Marx. They all have very different visions of what an efficient political system should look like, whether the human being is inherently good or bad, and who should have the right to rule. What is interesting in this area of Philosophy is that the thinkers have often actually affected the reality.

The writings of Marx are the best example of this phenomenon since they have been used and abused by activists in many countries, leading to the October Revolution in 1917 and the establishment of the USSR, one of two systems dominating the international system for decades. I think that there are many interesting questions in this area of Philosophy. Is it possible to design a system which would be applicable to any setting and society? Do philosophers have a responsibility over how their writings are understood and used?

A good candidate will show both a certain degree of knowledge and of genuine interest in the topic of his choice. He will identify some of the big questions related to the field.

A poor candidate might give an exhaustive list of areas of Philosophy without going into depth on any of them. Alternatively, he could try to demonstrate his extensive factual knowledge of the writings of a single author, without engaging with the wider question on the area of Philosophy.

HISTORY

Law interviews can take several different formats as each college has their own way of conducting them, and they can include questions which go beyond Law directly, and are more about your thinking skills. We've provided interview questions from history subjects as additional preparation for you.

It may be the case that you have prepared extensively for one aspect of your interview, but aren't given a chance to draw on that preparation. For example, they might not ask you about anything on your personal statement, even if you are very keen to talk about it. If this happens, try not to let it rattle you. The interview process can be unpredictable, so try to remain as calm and flexible as you can.

Draw on the work you have done at school to answer these questions, but be prepared that the conversation might go beyond your syllabus. Avoid saying things like 'we haven't covered this in school yet' – just try your best to answer each question.

The interviewers will also have read your personal statement (and your SAQ form, if you applied to Cambridge). They are likely to ask you questions about the academic sections of it, for law applicants this can often overlap with questions from history, and we hope these provide valuable insight into the way you should think about interview questions.

WORKED QUESTIONS

Below are a few examples of how to start breaking down an interview question, complete with model answers.

Q1: Does the study of history serve any practical purpose?

Applicant: This question covers quite a lot of potential areas, so I will start by looking at the study of history in the context of university/higher education as that seems most relevant. Firstly, I will evaluate a few potential arguments. Studying history at university serves many practical purposes, both for the student and society as a whole. The student gains many skills such as research and formulating an argument. Society gets to benefit from these skills when they graduate. But these benefits are not unique to history alone as this description could also cover other humanities subjects such as Classics or Sociology.

The other argument is that **history teaches lessons**, without which history would simply repeat itself and humanity would go on making the same 'mistakes'. This is also not a particularly convincing view in my opinion. Though, there can be similarities between different historical events as all historical events are unique, which I believe undermines the idea that history constantly repeats itself. I think this idea is based too much on hindsight as it is easy to see similarities between events after they have happened.

Instead, I think that historical causation (what makes events happen) depends above all on the context in which those events take place. This means that we cannot necessarily learn specific practical 'lessons' from history to apply in the future because the context of the future will be completely different.

However, this does not mean that history does not serve any practical purpose. Even though I don't think one can learn concrete 'lessons' from history, being able to understand how a certain problem came about can make it easier to find a solution. This means that the **skills gained by studying history can have a positive practical impact** on policy-making. Aside from that, the study of history also serves to educate and entertain the public. Most historical works are written by historians at universities and TV documentaries are usually made with the input of historians.

Analysis: You will not be expected to answer questions as fully as this. This answer is an indication of some of the things you might be expected to talk about in response to a question like this, but the interviewer will help you along the way with additional questions and comments. The merit of the answer is that it **breaks down the question** into manageable chunks and proceeds through an answer while signposting this process to the interviewer. These are good skills for you to try to develop, but remember that the interviewer is there to help get the best out of you.

Poor applicant: A poor applicant could begin by saying "we haven't studied this in class", and make no effort to further the conversation. He or she might then, if pressed, express a vague opinion that history serves a practical purpose in that it teaches people lessons for the future. As discussed, this is not a very strong interpretation because historical events depend on a specific configuration of circumstances. It would be difficult to gain a concrete and specific 'lesson' from one historical situation that could be applied in another historical situation as no two historical situations are the same.

A **poor applicant** may also respond to this question by saying that there is no practical purpose to history at all. Unless you have a very good argument to back this up, this would be a bad answer to this question because it would overlook the practical benefits that a historical perspective can bring to various areas of public life. It would also be a bad answer because it would imply that there is no practical purpose to the career to which your interviewers have dedicated their lives, as well as the degree to which you are applying.

Q2: Is it ever possible to find out 'what really happened' in the past?

A **good applicant** will recognise the complexity of this question. Throughout school, one is encouraged to assume that every statement written in a history book is a statement of fact. But at university level, it becomes clear that sources are subjective, historical interpretations are subjective, and the idea that history is just a series of events and facts seems a little simplistic. With a question like this, a good way to break it down is to focus first on one side of the argument and then on the other before coming to a conclusion. If you do this, you might choose to say to the interviewer, "first I will look at the idea that it is not possible to find out 'what really happened' in the past", so they know your approach.

Then you might choose to discuss the fact that you can never really know whether a source is telling the truth because **historical sources are inherently subjective**. A diary entry or letter about a certain event is only written from one person's perspective and they might not have had a full understanding of events or may be recording them in hindsight, having forgotten some of what happened. Even official documents are subjective; they might have an agenda behind them or be subject to censorship. When it comes to more distant historical events, the source material is necessarily subjective because it depends on a large extent on what has survived.

So, in many ways, it may be impossible to find out 'what really happened' in the past – there are too many obstacles in the way and history is only ever an interpretation of past events, rather than an objective statement of fact.

On the other hand, however, it would be unfair to say that this means all interpretations are equally invalid. While historical sources are subjective, it is possible to come to a reasonable interpretation of past events by using a wide variety of sources that corroborate each other. If all available sources say the same thing about a certain event, we can be reasonably sure that this is correct. This is how we can determine certain facts that are beyond interpretation. For example, the French Revolution occurred in 1789. Therefore, it is possible to find out some aspects of what really happened. Even though sources and interpretations are subjective, **history is not fiction**.

Q3: Is history increasingly the study of ordinary people?

In many ways, the answer to this would be quite straightforward. Yes, history does seem to be moving away from the study of great men to that of ordinary people – whereas in the early 20th century, 'history' was almost synonymous with **'political history'** and focused largely on politicians and generals. History seems to have democratised in recent decades. Scholarship in recent years appears to have focused more than ever on people who had not been represented by historical studies before such as women, ethnic minorities, the working classes, etc.

A good answer may, therefore, challenge this obvious response in a few ways. While all of the above is true, it would be worth mentioning that some **parts of history still focus disproportionately on 'great men'** rather than 'ordinary people'. Political history still occupies a big part of university history curricula while 'popular history', such as TV documentaries and historical bestsellers, are more often than not focused on 'great men' (or great events or occasionally, great women such as Elizabeth I) rather than 'ordinary people'.

A good answer would also recognise the secondary question implicit in this question – **Why** *is history moving away from the study of great men to that of ordinary people?* Answers to this would perhaps include a discussion of how minority rights movements often initiate new historical interest in minorities or a discussion of the democratisation of education in recent decades (e.g. African-American civil rights or second-wave feminism).

Q4: How would a biography of a major political figure written during their lifetime differ from one written after they had died? Which would be more accurate?

This type of question is a great one to get as it gives you a lot of scope to be creative and to bring in your own knowledge. The interviewers may ask this in response to a political biography you have listed in your personal statement, which would allow you to speak about a topic you are familiar with and passionate about.

However, assuming you are asked this question hypothetically without a specific biography in mind, there are **several ways** to approach it- even if you are not familiar with any biography of a major political figure yourself.

First, it would be sensible to tackle the first part of this question in isolation and leave the additional question (*"which would be more accurate?"*) for later in the discussion. A biography of a major political figure written during their lifetime would be likely to differ significantly from one written after their death.

The biographer may have had **access to meetings with the political figure** or the biography may even have been written with the input of the political figure. This may make the text richer in its detail, but may also mean that it is coloured by the politician's political agenda and desire to manage his image and reputation. A biography written after the politician's death may have access to **newly released sources** not available during the figure's lifetime. There are many possible answers to this question.

In response to the second part of the question, a **weak candidate** may have a strong opinion on this, saying something like "a biography written during their lifetime would be more accurate because the biographer would know the politician, so they would tell the truth" or alternatively, "a biography written after their lifetime would be more accurate because the biographer would have the benefit of hindsight". Both of these answers fail to take the complexity of the situation into account.

A **stronger candidate** would investigate both options more fully and would not take too dogmatic a view on what is a complicated question without a clear answer. After considering the merits and weaknesses of each type of source, a stronger candidate may conclude that one cannot deem either type of source more accurate than the other. This is because it would depend entirely on the specific biography and biographers in question, or may conclude that it would be best to draw upon both sources to get the most accurate depiction of the politician in question.

Q5: Do you think that we should be careful when examining colonial history in a postcolonial world?

Postcolonialism is the study of the legacy of colonialism, particularly the ways in which empires made an impact on colonies that still have ramifications today. You will generally only be asked questions on specific topics which you have mentioned in your personal statement or which the interviewers will expect you to have studied based on your UCAS form.

Good Applicant: Studying colonial societies is a complex task for postcolonial academics, especially those who come from a region that was a previous enforcer of colonialism. No study of colonial societies cannot acknowledge the flaws of empire, the exploitation of natives and the appropriation of their cultures. Therefore, recognising former mistakes is an uncomfortable process that postcolonial scholars have to undertake. Western perceptions of ex-colonies today are usually shaped by the legacies of Western imperialism. It is necessary not just to reverse this process, but also celebrate the individuality of ex-colonies before they were assimilated into various empires.

Poor Applicant: Postcolonialism creates a lot of problems because the history of colonialism and imperialism does not reflect well on the Western world. Most people are offended by the mistakes made during the colonial era and many choose to protest against them so that they can be remembered in a more condemning way. Colonialism is very divisive, and therefore it is a difficult thing to study in the present day.

The first applicant's answer is stronger because they display a more nuanced and sensitive understanding of the question. They note how postcolonial studies inevitably reflect badly on Western societies, but that reflection is necessary for giving them a better reputation in the modern day. They also acknowledge how there are several processes that must occur to truly reconcile with the colonial past, including a greater recognition of former indigenous cultures.

The second applicant's answer addresses the same issues but is too vague. Statements such as 'most people' and 'colonialism is very divisive' could benefit from **greater precision and clarity.**

To show even more confidence when discussing this topic in front of interviewers, candidates could make reference to some of the most influential postcolonial theorists, such as **Franz Fanon**, a strong critic of colonialism, or **Edward Said**, who introduced the term Orientalism into the colonial discourse.

Q6: Can you think of any examples of a student protest having a significant impact on the path of history?

A candidate may or may not have studied some form of student uprising before, but regardless of if they have or not, it encourages them to think openly about how people of their own age have in the past tried to influence history.

Good Applicant: I think student uprisings are hugely important because they force governments to take serious notice of the causes they are protesting for or against. Young individuals studying at universities and other institutions are the next generation to take power, and they often voice concerns that older politicians are blind to or unaffected by. For example, many campaigns in the United States in the 20th century – civil rights, women's rights', anti-Vietnam protests – became radical and violent over frustrations with the incumbent political regime. Students used their platform as a means of taking the action, provoking the US government to respond.

Poor Applicant: Student uprisings have a big role in history because governments have to listen to them. If they show too much violence against the students, they could be made villains in the media and become very unpopular.

The first applicant has though carefully about **why** students have had such an influential role in history and what makes them a particularly powerful demographic in times of protest. The example they provide, although broad, is well chosen and perhaps opens up grounds for future discussion in the interview. The poor applicant has made a valid point – that students have a certain leverage due to the sympathy they can often get from the media – but has not supported it with a specific example.

Q7: Do you think that historical eras have tangible meaning, should the 'Progressive Era' be capitalised?

Good Applicant: I think this is very important that these eras are distinguished from the widespread usage of these terms. The Progressive Era in the US, for instance, refers to a specific period of history that was marked by social activism and political reform. It was particularly concerned with the issues that were arising from industrialisation and uncontrolled immigration. Whilst the changes that the reformers were pushing for would certainly be regarded as 'progressive', the use of capitalisation helps define it as an entire era of American history rather than as a general wave of progressive reforms. Other periods of American history, such as the Civil War, Reconstruction or Great Depression, are all capitalised, so the Progressive Era should be no different.

Poor Applicant: We should use a capital letter for these eras because they refer to actual periods of history. Therefore, we must distinguish, say, the Romantic Era, from other romantic movements in history.

The first applicant has been <u>successful in making a point and then supporting it with a well-chosen example</u>. Importantly, they have shown that the Progressive Era (1896-1916) refers to an entire period of American history, and it is concerned with far more than the 'progressive' reforms that were a part of those years. **Periodisation** is incredibly important for historians, and this candidate will impress the interviewers for exploring how it can be used.

In contrast, the second applicant has not demonstrated this same level of sophistication with their example of the Romantic Era. They should have explored what exactly was 'romantic' about the Romantic Era, and therefore why it is remembered as such in historical periodisation.

Q8: Should we exclusively teach British history in British schools?

In 2013 the then-Educational Secretary Michael Gove redrafted the history curriculum to provide a greater emphasis on world history in lieu of some traditional British topics. This process is far from complete however, and interviewees may tackle this question by addressing the gaps in Britain's current educational system.

Good Applicant: Personally, I think that British students should be learning about British history, but we are currently learning about the wrong topics. A greater emphasis should be placed on periods and themes that have a greater relevance today. For example, we should learn more about imperial Britain and its involvement in the colonies. This is important because it helps us understand Britain's role in the slave trade and how we should remember it today, while also placing British history in a more global context. Learning about monarchy and politics, as is traditionally common, is still important in understanding how our current form of government has come to be. Particularly important is how the British monarch has gone from being an absolute ruler, to a constitutional one in the 17th century, to an almost ceremonial one today. However, students should have a greater flexibility and choice over the aspects of British history that they study.

Poor Applicant: I think that British students should continue to learn British history. It is incredibly important to learn about the country to live in, and understand how present-day institutions and traditions have ended up as they were. Teachers are familiar with the topics and it would be disruptive for them to learn new things. British history does interact with many other countries as well, so students get a sense of Britain's position.

The first applicant's answer is strong because they have been explicit about *how* they would change the British historical curriculum. Both candidates have made the point that British history is important to learn as it helps us understand Britain today. However, only the first candidate has shown how there are some aspects of British history that need to be visited more thoroughly in order to get the complete picture.

The second applicant's claim that teachers should not need to learn new topics is fairly contentious, and an issue that the first applicant raises. The historical curriculum should constantly change over time so that it properly reflects on the society in which it is learnt.

Q9: Can you learn real history from films and television programmes?

Historical films and dramas often come under criticism for taking artistic license and failing to accurately represent the historical events that they showcase. However, surely it is the role of documentaries to provide the 'accurate' renditions of history on our screens? Candidates could answer this question with reference to any film or TV show that would shed light on this issue.

Good Applicant: In my opinion, historical films and TV shows have a much more important function than accurately providing the truth. Because of their cinematography, storylines and quality of acting, historical dramas attract a much wider audience than historical documentaries, and are an established part of the entertainment industry. People would go to the cinema to watch a historical film, but not a documentary. Although the truth is often distorted, historical dramas often promote interest in the watcher to then learn more about that particular part of history, through documentaries and books. 'The Crown', a TV show which has been criticised for inaccuracy, has in my opinion, had a crucial role in promoting recent interest about the history of the royal family and the major events of the 20th century through their lens. By bringing topics to a wider audience, they can encourage viewers to investigate about the past themselves.

Poor Applicant: TV shows and films about history are important because they bring history to the wider audience. Not everybody wants to read books about history, so the screen provides a more accessible format for learning. The average watcher is not concerned about the specific details that historians pick up on. They are more interested in a general idea of what was happening during the time that the film or show depicts.

Both responses argue along the lines that historical films and TV shows are the most accessible form of history for popular consumption, even if they are sometimes far from accurate. What makes the first candidates answer stronger is that they have drawn a link between the different ways in which people learn about history, and specifically the ability of mass media to inspire even casual enthusiasts to become invested in historical issues. In many ways, the very inaccuracies of some historical films and shows actively encourages watchers to do more research in order to find out the truth.

Q10: Do you think that it's possible to learn lessons from history?

This question is addressing the practical application of history and candidates could argue either for or against. They could provide circumstances when the 'lessons' of history are useful and when they are not.

Good Applicant: I think we ought to be careful about using the lessons of history. The problems we face today have arisen from radically different circumstances compared to those of the past. For example, warfare as a means of resolving political conflict is far more dangerous now than it was in the medieval era due to the increased militarisation of countries across the globe, not to mention the nuclear capacity of some nations. However, history can be useful when we remember its general patterns and lessons, rather than specific case studies of how to deal with problems. The lessons of overreaching, autocratic monarchies and states teach us to be wary of emerging dictatorships today.

Poor Applicant: I do not think we can learn 'lessons' from history as they are not applicable to the present day. In our modernised, democratic world there is no benefit from learning about the fates of flawed ideologies and institutions, such as absolute monarchy, since they already declined, and we have found better solutions to our problems.

The first applicant's answer is stronger because they provide a more **balanced** response to the question. They provide a reason why we should be cautious about using the lessons of history, before explaining how they could be useful as broad frameworks that could shed light on current situations. The poor applicant could have considered *why* our current systems and institutions have survived and others have failed, and what lessons we can draw from their success.

A great (and short) book on this topic is **Will and Ariel Durant's "The Lessons of History"**, which looks at long-term patterns and continuities from several perspectives such as race, religion, war, or government.

Q11: Do you think that the concept of race is useful for historians?

This question is looking at how historians approach their study of the past. Racial history has not always been a focus for scholars, but has only become more prevalent with various Civil Rights movements in the 20th century and our study of international slave trades. Interviewees could think about the role that race has played in history, especially when race was not discussed.

Good Applicant: I think race is an incredibly valuable concept for historians. We must think carefully about how humanity has gone from being ambivalent about race - evident in the monogenesis preached in the Bible - to institutionalised, scientific forms of racism during the time of the slave trade, to repudiating racial discrimination altogether in the modern day. Race is a social identity that intersects and challenges identities of kinship, nation, and religion. Countries have established deep-rooted injustices on racial grounds, such as the eugenics movement of the Nazi regime, or of Apartheid in South Africa. In no other field perhaps, have ideas and values changed so radically over time, so studying racial history is crucial to truly understanding the prejudices of the past.

Poor Applicant: Race is very important for historians. History has often focused on the role of white men and this is not representative of the past as a whole. Many past indigenous and native societies are lost in a Western-centric narrative. Race is essential to understanding events such as the Civil Rights movement in America, or the Apartheid regime in South Africa.

The first applicant has provided a complex understanding of what race is and how it can be used by historians. The **broad timeline** of racial thinking that they provide, from the Bible to the modern day, is an effective way of framing just how much assumptions surrounding race have changed, even only in the last 100 years or so. They also place race within the wider framework of social identities, and their examples are well chosen.

The second applicant has argued along the same lines, focusing on how race should be revisited by historians due to the previous suppression of non-Western cultures. Unlike the first candidate however, they have not explained *why* their examples are such important moments in racial history. To improve their answer, they could have mentioned the necessary changes in the Civil Rights movement – to mass organisation and more active forms of protest – necessary for political change.

Q12: Can you identify patterns or cycles in history?

Candidates may be familiar with some theories of historical recurrence. A very famous one, by David Hackett Fischer, proposes that European history repeats itself every 200 years. Machiavelli analysed the waves of 'order' and 'disorder' in 15th century Italy. However, candidates could equally answer this question with ideas of their own.

Good Applicant: To say that history repeats itself is too sweeping a generalisation. No events repeat themselves exactly, usually because an event results in structural change purposed to prevent that same event from happening again. However, historical events spread across large periods often bare similarities because over time the conditions for that type of event resurface, as the past is gradually forgotten. An example of this is the history of financial crises. A financial crash is usually followed by stricter economic policies, but increased deregulation over time makes the market once again susceptible to speculation and at risk of collapsing.

Poor Applicant: History cannot repeat itself because everything that happens is unique. Each event has its own causes and consequences, its own actors, and therefore should not be seen as a repeat occurrence. It is our tendency to draw similarities from events that took roughly the same form, but these are often quite forced.

The first applicant's answer is strong because they have used an example that illustrates their point very effectively. Their argument – that history is capable of repeating itself once the 'repeated event' becomes forgotten and its lessons unlearnt – is well contextualised within economic cycles of boom and bust.

The second applicant has argued that repetition in history is forced by the historians and political figures who are actively seeking to draw comparisons to their own benefit. This point could benefit from a specific case study. To use the first applicant's example, did The Great Recession of 2008 have the same causes as The Great Depression of the 1930s, or have their structural similarities been exaggerated in the interests of proving that history has repeated itself in the US?

Q13: Define 'revolution'

Questions like this are not necessarily looking for a precise definition of what a 'revolution' is, or at the very least might expect you to reach that definition after a thorough exploration of revolution as a concept. A response could discuss different types of revolution, and illustrate these with case studies, or provide a broader, conceptual definition.

Good Applicant: Revolutions take many different forms. The question of whether things like the Industrial Revolution were really just that is still being debated today. If we want to think about revolutions as a period of drastic change, or a 'Paradigm Shift', then we can say that a revolution is an instance or a set of processes in a defined set of time which result in a drastic change in one or a number of systems on a national or global level. However, for a lot of people, revolution is synonymous with revolt, often armed. Notions of technological revolutions then become more like a catchphrase that has been coined, rather than representative of the truth, and the only revolutions one can really see in history are like the French and Russian revolutions. Both approaches have advantages, but for me I think revolution is about more than a regime change, it is about a drastic shift in the way in which things are done, or the ways which people live – this definition of revolution would allow an historian to draw comparisons between political and technological revolutions, and that kind of comparative work is fascinating to me as an aspiring historian.

Poor Applicant: A revolution is when a government is overthrown by another group, usually the army or an opposition party. It typically involves violence and mass riots and protest, like in the French Revolution when the monarchy was kicked out.

The first applicant has thought creatively about the question, considering not just political revolutions (which would have been a perfectly acceptable assumption to make) but revolutions in other fields. They have also strengthened their answer by suggesting which view of a revolution is more appealing to them and why, and tied that in to their own ambitions for university.

The second applicant has given a narrower, although not incorrect, definition, and has supported it with a good example. Their answer could benefit from considering if this definition applies to *all* political revolutions. Was the French Revolution unusually more bloody and violent than other revolutions? What are the differences between the French Revolution and the various 20th century coups that occurred in African nations?

Q14: Do you think that ideology exists in history?

Good Applicant: Yes, I think so. I think that ideology is an incredibly valuable concept for historians. It is the fusion of philosophical ideas with practical application. Most political movements, protests and revolutions will have an ideology behind them. For example, people in the 19th century who had a liberal philosophy believed in free markets, the extension of franchise, and constitutional limits on state power. Whilst groups and individuals can operate without an ideology and have purely practical beliefs, it is often from a philosophical base that most movements originate from.

Poor Applicant: There is definitely a concept of ideology. An ideology is a set of ideas that any person or group has, that serves to explain their actions. No one in history has acted without motivations, therefore every historical event can be explained by an underlying ideology.

Both candidates have attempted to **define** the term 'ideology', and either of their responses are acceptable approaches. However, the first applicant has supported their definition with a **specific example** that highlights both of their points; that ideologies exist as both theory and application.

The first applicant has stated that not everything can be explained by an ideology, whereas the second applicant has argued the opposite. Both of these views could have been better supported with examples. The first applicant could have continued their 19th century theme and refer to peasant and working-class movements that might not have had an ideology of their own but were influenced by a small handful of leaders. This raises a second issue that has not been addressed by the candidates; does ideology have to originate from the doctrines of philosophers and political theorists? Or can it emerge in more colloquial, folkloric forms among the illiterate classes?

Q15: How can we ever really know what people in the past thought or felt?

This is a broad and widely disputed question, with no definitive answer. However, since it is not topic specific it allows candidate to discuss whatever they are confident about. This sort of question might provide a springboard into a wider conversation or might even take the form of a mini debate between the student and interviewer.

Good Applicant: It is very difficult to understand exactly how people thought because of the limited evidence we possess of past societies. The further you go back in time, the fewer videos, audio recordings and written documents we have to reconstruct the past. Many societies had an entirely oral culture and we therefore have no official records at all. However, we can learn a great deal from interpreting interesting documents such as court cases, pamphlets, or sermons. For example, judicial records from the 17th century in England - a period I studied for my A-Level - can help us understand how people were so fearful of witchcraft at the time, a crime punishable even by death. It can be hard to relate to radical beliefs of the past due to our present-day standards, which is why it is important for the historian to try to empathise with the past.

Poor Applicant: We cannot go back in time so we will never truly understand the past. Our understanding of the past is mostly interpretations and approximations based on the limited sources we have.

The first applicant's response is strong for several reasons. Firstly, the candidate has been cautious when approaching the question; they have acknowledged the problems that historians face when trying to understand the past. Secondly, unlike the poor applicant, they have then provided a solution to the problem. It is important to always **answer the question clearly**, otherwise the interviewers will not be convinced as to whether or not the candidate understood what was being asked of them.

Thirdly they have provided a relevant example to help back up their points. This will impress the interviewer as it shows that the candidate has thought critically about their A-Level course and is able to apply their knowledge to more general, conceptual questions about history. To go further, another example could be provided, either to further support their point, or provide a counterexample of where past records and documents can be misleading.

Q16: Do you think that class is valuable as an analytical tool for historians?

Class refers to the hierarchical distinctions between individuals or groups within a society. It is typically associated with the work of Max Weber and Karl Marx. Candidates should think about the advantages and disadvantages of using class as a social category.

Good Applicant: In my opinion, class is a flawed but useful concept for historians. It divides people into groups that they may not identify with. Identities of race, language and gender exist within classes, and it is very debateable as to whether members of a class had a 'class consciousness' as Marx believed. However, it can be valuable for historians in categorising groups of people within a historical society, and trying to establish general trends. For example, in Medieval England there was no contemporary notion of class, but it is useful for historians to understand how the peasants, gentry or nobility acted as a collective group. It is also important for historians to see how class intersected with those other social identities, and in evaluating which ones created the most cohesive collective groups.

Poor Applicant: Not massively, history was written by the rich, so we only really have one class to ever look at.

The first applicant's answer is stronger for several reasons. Firstly, they have also acknowledged some the flaws of class as a social category, and have made a good reference to one of the disputable claims of Marxist history. Secondly, they have provided a useful example, since it is an era before class was a concept it highlights the way in which historians have used it retrospectively. Lastly, they have shown the relationship between class and other identities, arguing that class, like most concepts, should not be studied in isolation. The second applicant fell down because their answer was too short, limiting opportunities for the interviewer to maintain a conversation through it, and because it showed the candidate isn't particularly open minded or experienced with the diversity of sources available to historians.

To improve even further, the first applicant could have considered whether some class models are more useful or relevant than others. Marx and Weber's theories were followed by US sociologist William Lloyd Warner's six-tier hierarchy, and candidates may want to think if some class approaches are more useful than others. There are also unique hierarchies found in India, China, and Japan, providing good international comparisons.

Q17: Do you think historians should just tell the story of the past in the plainest terms, or should they add their own input?

Candidates should think here about the role of the historian and the ways in which they present their historical findings. Is it their job to simply tell the past as it happened? Or should they provide interpretation and analysis?

Good Applicant: I think that narration is a perfectly valid way of approaching the past, but it should be recognised as only one of the ways in which the past can be retold. Narrative history is useful because it is often chronological, and event driven. There are clear chains of cause and effect, and events are often given a focus according to their magnitude and impact. For learning simply about what happened, the narrative approach is most valuable. However, more interpretative histories also have their place, either in explaining why things happened, or by placing the narrative within a wider context. Analytical approaches can address themes and trends in non-chronological order, or approach the past from a particular angle, such as class or gender. I believe that both types of history are equally important.

Poor Applicant: I think we should narrate the past because it is the most accurate way of understanding what happened. A story-based approach is very accessible and provides the most honest recollection of what order events occurred in. We need a narrative history, with all the facts laid out, before we can even begin to think about interpreting the past.

The first applicant has successfully shown how narrative history is an effective, but not exclusive, way of interpreting the past. They have not only defined both narrative and interpretative history as two distinct categories of historical writing, but they have also explored the advantages of each.

The second applicant has, to a lesser extent, done the same. They have stated that narrative history must come before more analytical history. Their claim that narration is the most accurate form of retelling the past could be challenged, however. Adding interpretation to events can often provide greater clarity, especially if they seem contradictory or even out of place at first in the greater narrative. Both candidates could have thought about how narrative history is written. Does the historian, as a storyteller, have to sacrifice accuracy for narrative technique and literary style? This question might be picked up by interviewers in the ensuing discussion.

Q18: Do you think that religion remains important for historians of the modern world?

Religion is present in almost any society the historian studies, but modern historians tend to deal with more secular, centralised states in which the Church has lost much of its political power. Candidates should think about how religion continues to be an important social concept, and could provide examples of modern history in which religion has still been able to play an integral role.

Good Applicant: In my opinion, the study of religion remains important regardless of the period the historian is studying. National churches have become less important, particularly after the Enlightenment and rise of scientific thinking. However, especially in the lower, rural classes, religion remains an integral part of an individual's worldview. Furthermore, many modern issues are dictated more so by religion than any other factor. The Arab-Israeli conflict of the 20th century was partly caused by the growth of Zionism among Israelis and of Arab nationalism among Muslim groups. This is a reminder that opposing systems of belief can still drive wedges between people of the same nationality or ethnicity, and can escalate into political, territorial conflict.

Poor Applicant: Religion is important because a lot of what happens in the world can be blamed on religion. We need to make sure that we study it to help shed light on the damage it can cause and clarify its role in human history.

The first applicant's answer is strong because they have provided two clear reasons for the continued importance of studying religion in modern history; its ideological and political influences remain important. The second applicant has failed to interact with the 'modern' part of the question, and seems to be attaching their own value judgements to the response, which can quickly demonstrate a lack of understanding and thought.

Q19: What do you think are the values of gender-history?

Candidates answering this question should think about why a gender-orientated approach is crucial to history, particularly in reinterpreting old assumptions about gender roles. It is important not to assume that 'gender history' means 'women's history', although undoubtedly one of the main functions of gender history is to revisit male-centric histories that have suppressed the contribution of women.

Good Applicant: Gender is an incredibly important approach to history because it tells us about the ways in which gender and gender difference have been incredibly influential in the past, and are often forgotten in political, economic, and religious narratives. Gender history involves revising deep-rooted narratives with fixed assumptions about patriarchy and masculinity. Gender as a category invites a more social approach to history, looking not just at state institutions but at household structures, the radically wide-ranging gender dynamics in different parts of the world, and changing identities. It amplifies and reinterprets the human past.

Poor Applicant: Gender history is important because it has previously been forgotten by historians. Most history is the history of men, specifically leading men. Gender history can try to undo that, but the chances of it working are slim due to the lack of material.

The first applicant has discussed gender in terms of both the roles of men and women, as well as the relationship between them. The intricate dynamics between genders is a key aspect of gender history, especially when considering how this dynamic has changed over time. Their answer could be improved by giving an example of where a gender approach to history is incredibly useful, like women in labour movements.

The second applicant has argued that gender history is important because it rebalances the exaggerated role of men in history with none of the nuance such a statement requires, and the student is pessimistic about the success of the endeavour. A better response here would have, like the first applicant, thought about the relationship between genders. A lot of 'great man' history does not necessarily think about these men in terms of their gender, rather they focus on their actions as political figures.

An article worth reading on gender history is **Joan Scott's "Gender: A Useful Category of Historical Analysis" (1986)**

Q20: How do you think people were able to justify slavery on the grounds of the economic benefits?

In modern debates about the history of slavery, it is clear that racial thinking has changed considerably since the height of European imperialism. However, the use of enslaved Africans for manual labour was also justified on economic grounds – to serve the interests of industrialising Western nations. Even if unfamiliar with the topic, applicants could think creatively about the evolution of the plantations in the colonial era.

Good Applicant: Aside from racial justification, slavery was adopted on the grounds that in was more economically profitable than its predecessor, indentured servitude. Unpaid labour and longer, more demanding working hours meant that slaves produced a greater output of resources such as sugar or tobacco, and needed less of an input themselves. In the North American and Caribbean colonies, land was abundant, but labour was dear, and therefore it made sense – in contemporary thinking – to export African slaves to the plantations in the Americas so that this land could be exploited. Goods sent home to Europe could hasten the speed of industrialisation and promote long-run economic development.

Poor Applicant: Slavery was a system that exploited Africans in a way that could not be done with white workers. Since they were not paid and could be treated worse, greater profits were made in the running of plantations. These profits could be used on other things, such as economic change back in Europe.

Both these responses outline the process by which slavery was adopted in the colonies. They are both able to identify the shift from indentured servitude to slavery and the reasons behind it.

The first applicant's answer is better because they display a more intricate understanding of the relationship between slavery and economic growth. It was not just increased 'profits' that enabled European countries to develop themselves, it was the greater quantities of raw materials than were being sent to her industrial centres that truly accelerated industrialisation.

To improve their answers, the candidates could have addressed which European powers were most successful in exploiting the advantages of slavery. Britain, for example, saw the advantages of industrialising first and monopolised on manufactured products by the 18th century.

Q21: How do you think we should commemorate the Great War?

The First World War is well commemorated annually in most of its participants. In the UK at least, the focus is on both celebrating the Allied victory, but also paying respects to those who lost their lives. Candidates could think about this question from the perspective of Britain, an ex-Axis power, or multiple nations in order to make comparisons. They could also think about the political, social, and territorial legacies of the War.

Good Applicant: I think we should remember World War One both through commemoration and reflection. We should continue, as we do in the UK, to show our gratitude every year on Remembrance Day for the fallen soldiers of all Allied nations. However, we should also think about the impact the War had on our longer-term future. Conflict abroad meant that the government was under increased scrutiny at home, enabling pressure groups to seek reforms. The War led to women enfranchisement, an extension of democracy, the regeneration of urban areas, the birth of the welfare state, and was part of the downfall of Empire. Dramatic social and political change often occur in periods of war, and the years 1914-1918 were no different.

Poor Applicant: We should remember World War One because it is a significant moment of British history. It represents a major victory both militarily and of national solidarity. We should commemorate it every year to reinforce our universal identity. It should also be remembered because it led to considerable change in Germany. Arguably it laid the foundations for the birth of the Third Reich and the Second World War.

The first applicant's answer is well-constructed. It tackles the question from two different directions, namely the importance of memory and commemoration, and the long-term impacts the war had on Britain. They end their answer with the interesting observation that change is accelerated in times of war, and perhaps could have explored this further. Why exactly is this the case?

The second applicant has focused more on the commemorative aspects, but have also introduced the notion of national solidarity. The interviewer may challenge this view on the grounds that not every societal group will be able to identify with the victory of World War One. The candidate could also have more thoroughly explored the relationship between the two World Wars.

Q22: Should economic history be purely quantitative?

Quantitative research involves the collection of measurable data, whereas qualitative research encompasses non-numerical information. Economic history calls for a greater use of statistics than most historical approaches. Candidates should think about whether quantitative data alone provides sufficient answers to questions in economic history.

Good Applicant: I think that economic history must be both quantitative and qualitative, in order to get the most complete picture of events. The quantitative aspect provides reliable and measurable statistics, that can be presented in tables and graphs. From these we can spot trends and identify anomalies. However, qualitative research is necessary for the historian to explain the data, especially to contextualise it within the historical period. For example, a graph might show British GDP increase over the 19th century. But the historian must have knowledge of the political decisions that enabled structural change, or of the creation of new industrial centres that stimulated economic growth. Without a historical narrative, raw quantitative data lacks meaning.

Poor Applicant: In my opinion, economic history can be studied with just quantitative methods. Economic history concerns the changes in a country's wealth and development over time. These changes are best represented with concrete data. While qualitative details can help explain any fluctuations or surprises in the data, they are not essential for the historian to make an argument.

The two candidates have argued both sides of this issue, with the first applicant suggesting that economic history cannot be purely quantitative, and the second applicant proposing that it can. The first applicant's answer succeeds in explaining the relationship between the two types of data, and argues that they are dependent on each other. One question an interviewer might ask, is whether multiple quantitative data sets could help explain each other. For example, understanding GDP growth over time could benefit from quantitative data on population growth, urbanisation, literacy rates and many other variables. The second applicant could have benefitted on making that very point, in order to defend their view that qualitative data is not 'essential' for drawing historical conclusions.

Q23: What could you learn about a past society from a pair of shoes?

This question encourages candidates to think outside the box about an unusual aspect of the past. It is unlikely that they will have studied or read about the history of shoes in any detail! Here, historical imagination and a creative use of topics covered at school are far more important than a specific knowledge of the history of shoes.

Good Applicant: Shoes can teach us a lot about the society from which they belonged. Different types of shoes may have been worn by different social groups, so we can get a sense of class hierarchies based on who had enough wealth to buy studier, more bespoke footwear. We can learn about the professions of individuals given how shoes of manual labour and agriculture take such different appearances to shoes of fashion and leisure. They can teach us about the geography of a region too, and which members of society spent more time travelling. This could be interesting in considering European migration patterns in the 19th and 20th centuries, and which lower classes were required to relocate following industrialisation, whereas larger landowners were able to stay put. Comparisons can be drawn between people for whom shoes were mostly practical and functional, and for those whom they were fashionable.

Poor Applicant: Shoes can teach us about specific individuals from the past. We can learn of their rank in society, their profession, and how rich they were. We can learn about the changes made to footwear over time and the designs that were less successful and therefore do not exist anymore.

The applicants explore some of the many things we can learn from the footwear of the past. They both mention class, wealth, and travel as things that we can infer from people's choice and availability of shoes. The first answer is stronger <u>because they engage more critically with the question</u>. Rather than simply accepting there were differences in footwear they seek to explore some of the context behind these differences, using the example of rural Europe to illustrate his point.

Q24: What separates a terrorist and a patriot?

This question addresses a very relevant issue today, especially in the post-9/11 world. The USA PATRIOT Act (2001) expanded the definition of terrorism to include "domestic" as well as "international" instances of terrorism. The distinction between the terms 'terrorist' and 'patriot' is also brought up in debates about the IRA. Those are just two of the potential directions that candidates could take this question in.

Good Applicant: Patriots are individuals who strongly support their country and its national values. By this definition, most terrorists are also patriots. However, terroristic behaviour differs greatly from purely patriotic behaviour in my opinion. While both are prepared to participate in protests and riots, terrorists show a disregard for the civilian life around them. They are willing to use tactics of coercion, kidnapping, assassination and mass destruction in order to achieve their goals. Often, these occurrences serve to further their own interests; 9/11 for example, or the IRA bombings in Britain, were deliberately purposed to strike fear into their opponents. It is worth considering as well the extent to which terrorism can be separated from other kinds of direct conflict – if widened sufficiently, is an invading or occupying power participating in terrorism? For this to not be the case I think we would also have to argue that terrorism cannot be directly sponsored by the state, and that throws our existing understanding of terrorism into considerable doubt. Perhaps, then, the separation between a terrorist and a patriot is terror itself. If you are seeking to affect others through a climate which is intimidating or dangerous, you are a terrorist. If you do not seek these goals, but maintain the other aspects in common, you are a patriot.

Poor Applicant: The difference is just about whose side your on. In my opinion, one person's patriot is another person's terrorist and vice versa.

The first applicant's answer is stronger because they have better explored the relationship between the two terms, going as far to say that terrorism is a subset of patriotism. This is an interesting approach, and could have been taken further by exploring differences in ideology within the IRA. Some of its members were less convinced about the violent direction the faction was taking.

It would be worth taking a look at how the USA PATRIOT Act defines terrorism: (https://www.aclu.org/other/how-usa-patriot-act-redefines-domestic-terrorism)

Terrorism is a fairly modern concept. How can we apply it to historical examples? An interesting case to explore would be the Reign of Terror (1793-94), a period of excessive violence that caused many to become disillusioned in the ideals of the French Revolution.

Q25: If you could invite someone from the past to dinner, who would you choose and why?

This is a classic interview question that gives the candidate a great deal of freedom. It is important to **take your time** before launching into an answer, as it is likely that you will be made to explain and defend your decision in some depth.

Good Applicant: I would most want to have dinner with Martin Luther King. Firstly, I would love to hear about his experiences, how he was able to rally protesters on such a large-scale and cause such drastic change to the status of African Americans over the 20th century. Secondly, I think his skills of rhetoric, leadership and persuasion make him such a fascinating individual, and I would love to ask him about his methods and how he decided to tackle the challenges he faced. Finally, I would like to hear what he thought of other key individuals within the Civil Rights Movement, particularly those who had more radical, nationalistic views than his own.

Poor Applicant: I think Winston Churchill would be a really interesting person to have dinner with. He was such a great leader and was so important during the Second World War. He was a great speaker and as Prime Minister I think everyone had great respect for him. I am sure he would have many great stories about his career that he could share with me.

The first candidate's response is strong as they provide several reasons for why King would make such a fascinating dinner guest. They not only show an interest in *what* he did, but *how* he did it and how he perceived his own role within the Civil Rights Movement.

The second candidate has not done as effective a job of **empathising** with Churchill's position and the society he was a part of. An improved response might have included a reference to Churchill's colonial past, since that has a strong resonance in the current day and would provide a more two-sided portrayal of him. There is no historical individual who *could not* be an interesting person to have dinner with, but stronger answers will display an interest in really wanting to dig deep into the character of the person they have chosen.

Q26: What is a nation?

This is a classic historical issue that has been widely debated by historians and political theorists over the last 200 years, when many new nations were being formed across Europe. Interviewers are not looking for a short and perfect definition, but a more discursive response that begins to think about the aspects of a nation that best define it from other state entities.

Good Applicant: I believe that a nation is held together by two key features. Firstly, a clear territory with well defined borders. Secondly, a shared history or myth that all its members can identify with. Nations are not formed through all its inhabitants having a common language, race, or religion, for example, Switzerland was and still is a multi-ethnic, multi linguistic nation. A national myth is a binding tale that becomes part of a shared memory, it enables all members of the nation, regardless of their ethnicity, to identify within it. Because they have a shared past there is a common interest to further the progress of the nation in the future.

Poor Applicant: A nation is a state that binds people together, based on their common interests. They are able to operate independently of other nations, having their own government, economy, and culture. The people of a nation pursue national interests, but also cooperate internationally.

Both applicants have provided a succinct definition of the 'nation' and have expanded upon them. However, the first applicant has more persuasively supported their point of view. Their argument, that nations are multi-ethnic and are held together by a shared past, is well supported with the example of Switzerland. By making a distinction between 'history', and 'myth' – but acknowledging the significance of either – they have demonstrated to the interviewer that they have thought carefully about the question.

The second applicant successfully argued that nations are defined by other nations, and that each nation has interests that are specifically unique to them. However, they could have provided more clarity as to exactly what 'common interests' tend to bind a nation together.

Defining the 'nation' has long been a topic of interest for historians. Candidates might want to read **Ernest Renan's "What is a Nation" (1882)** as a starting point, and compare his views to those in **Benedict Anderson's "Imagined Communities" (1983)** and **Ernest Gellner's "Nations and Nationalism" (1983)**

Q27: Does nationalism have negative connotations?

Nationalism generally refers to a support for one's own nation, particularly at the expense of other nations. Nationalism can often be viewed negatively due to the actions of far-right racist parties such as the English Defence League, or due to its association with Nazism. However, candidates should think more widely about what constitutes a nationalist ideology, and if strong exclusionary policies are a necessary component of it.

Good Applicant: Personally, I believe that nationalism should not have negative connotations. Many forms of nationalism are about a passionate belief in the ideals of one's own nation, and a desire to continue to pursue those interests. Nationalism does not have to be ethnically homogenous or dangerous; this was evident during the growth of French nationalism after the Revolution. Nations can continue to embrace multiple languages and races as long as they have some form of coherent ideology based on a common past or mythology. Radical, far-right nationalisms are an exception rather than the rule, and they are more interested in excluding outsider groups rather than promoting their own national interests.

Poor Applicant: I think that nationalism deserves its negative connotations. Patriotism is largely benign, but nationalist policies look to exclude other groups and impose hierarchies. It often betrays liberal or democratic ideals that a nation is founded on. Germany was unified in 1871, but very quickly it adopted a discourse about the superiority of the Teutonic race and the inferiority of Jews.

The first applicant's response is effective because they have distinguished between different forms of nationalism. Dissecting a question like this is often a better approach than providing a catch-all answer. They have shown how most nationalisms are not ethnically exclusive and therefore should not be viewed negatively. Their distinction between patriotism and nationalism is a useful way of giving their answer further clarity.

The second applicant has argued the contrary and has provided a well-chosen example to support their view that nationalism is exclusionary and hierarchical. However, they could have benefited from confidently dismissing the counterargument, or at least acknowledging its presence. Interviewers may ask why such strong racist discourses did not emerge in newly unified Italy, or in Hungary when it achieved more independence from the Austrian Empire. A strong point of view in an interview is not a bad thing, but applicants must be prepared to defend their arguments and justify their choice of examples.

Q28: You're transported back in time with one goal – stop Hitler. How do you accomplish this?

This is a good opportunity for candidates to show their hypothetical skills, and this question is open to several interpretations. One could say how they would have ended the Second World War earlier, or how they would have prevented Hitler from rising to power at all.

Good Applicant: I believe that the best opportunity to stop Hitler would be to prevent him from consolidating his power as Chancellor in the Spring of 1933. Before then he was too inconspicuous, and afterwards too powerful. I think that the easiest way to topple him would have been through the use of the German Trade Unions. The power of the strike was evident in 1920, when the Unions almost singlehandedly prevented the Kapp Putsch coup from succeeding. Mass strikes would have forced Hitler to rely on the support of the national army, and would have undermined the capabilities of his own military force, the SA. If this happened, I do not think that Hitler would have been able to become as powerful and independent of government as he did.

Poor Applicant: I think Hitler could have been stopped if countries from across the world reacted more urgently and comprehensively to the growth of Fascism and anti-Semitism in Germany. These ideologies should have been alarming to nations and a clear threat to international stability, and military intervention could have ousted Hitler from the Chancellorship well before the war.

The first applicant's answer here is a more convincing response to the question. He provides greater **detail**, with accurate dates and facts. He uses a historical precedent (the failed Coup) to support his argument that the Trade Unions could have defeated Hitler, which makes his hypothetical approach more persuasive than the second applicant's. The second applicant's answer would benefit from similarly precise detail. They suggest that international intervention could have easily toppled Hitler, but this is very easy to say with hindsight. Was the threat of Fascism evident on a global scale in the early 1930s?

Q29: How might history be written by the loser?

"History is written by victors" – a quote typically attributed to Winston Churchill but has doubtless been used throughout history. This question raises several interesting issues. Who are the losers of history? Aside from military or political defeats this is not always clear cut. Secondly, is the 'losing' side of history getting greater attention today through revisionist movements?

Good Applicant: Everyone writes history, but it is the winners who get to keep interpreting it and mould the stories that get remembered by future generations. In World War One for instance, members of both sides kept diaries, memoirs, letters of correspondence and battle plans, meaning that there was plenty of source material. Yet since the Allies won, it was their sources that were shaped into sympathetic histories, whilst many documents on the Axis' side were suppressed, censored, or destroyed. However, revisionist historians who revisit the past that give the losers a greater voice. Field Marshal Haig was villainised for his carelessness in the immediate aftermath of the war, but biographers such as John Terraine or Sir John Davidson have restored his reputation as a military leader. A 'loser' was turned a 'winner' by revisionist historians.

Poor Applicant: Losers do not get to write history because their version of events is suppressed by the winners. Those in power get to influence the media, write positive histories about themselves and tell their versions of the past. The losers of history do not have the same platform to achieve this and so they become forgotten.

The first applicant has given a detailed answer crystallised around the example of World War 1, showing how both the losing side and 'losers' within the winner side can easily become condemned or lost in history. The revisionist case of Haig is well-chosen, a reminder of how history is not simply events that have happened, but events that can be constantly reinterpreted.

The second applicant has somewhat failed to answer the question. They have stated why winners often get to write history, but have not even considered how losers might find a way of writing their own narratives. A fascinating medieval example is how the Anglo-Saxon monks, although 'losers' to the invading Vikings of the 8th to 11th centuries, were the writers of history because they were the literate group. This shows that there are other factors at play when it comes to deciding who writes history.

Q30: Why did Europe not follow America's example and form a USE?

Good Applicant: I think this question is best answered if one considers why the United States of America was formed in 1776. Whilst fighting the British during the Revolutionary war, the American colonies needed to form a sense of collective identity in order to inspire purpose and unity among its members. It also provided Americans with a sense of what they were fighting for. The Declaration of Independence created a shared myth that has become the backbone of the American identity ever since. In contrast, every country of Europe has its own national myths and identities, and there is less of a need for a collective one. That is why there are confederations such as the EU, but no United States of Europe.

Poor Applicant: I think that Europe is too divided to become a United State. Europe has too long a history of internal conflict and there is little to bind all Europeans together. In contrast, the American colonies had all had a similar experience during British imperial rule and therefore were able to obtain a collective identity more easily.

Both answers have focused on the importance of a sense of collective identity in forming a United State. The first applicant's response benefits from greater precision in their reasoning. They have clearly outlined how the United States of America was formed, and in showing the specific circumstances in which it emerged, have proven why there is no European counterpart. They finish by stating that Europe only needs the EU, and this idea could be expanded further. They could think about what the EU, a mostly political and economic union rather than an ideological one, provides in comparison to a United State, and why those features are well suited to the needs of many European countries.

TEXT/SOURCE-BASED INTERVIEW

If your college decides to give you a text- or source-based interview, you will be given a piece of **academic text to look at before the interview**. You may also need to write a summary or commentary; the Admissions Office will tell you if this is the case. It is likely that the text you are given will be unfamiliar to you, on a topic or area of history you have not studied before. Do not be daunted by this – you are not expected to have any detailed factual knowledge related to the text.

The interview will then be based on the contents of the extract, and the issues surrounding it. Things to keep in mind:

- When reading the text in advance, **pay attention to the author, the date of publication, and the nature of the work**. It may be a historical source or an extract from a work of historiography by a theorist such as E.H. Carr or Richard Evans. It may be an introduction from a history book on a topic you have never encountered before.

- Try to pick up on aspects of the publication that are unusual or revealing (e.g. was it written anonymously? Is it a revision of an earlier text? Is it clearly written in response to another text or another writer's view? Who is the intended audience?)

- When reading the text, pay attention to the argument it is making. Is it a strong argument or a weak argument and why? Can you think of any counter-arguments?

- Does the text relate in any way to any other area of history and historiography that you -are familiar which can be drawn upon in the interview?

WHAT QUESTIONS MIGHT BE ASKED?

For this type of interview setting, the interviewers will ask questions about the text and the broader historical issues that the text raises. Questions about the text directly will range from content comprehension (what is the author arguing? What does the author mean by X?) to interpretation (do you agree with the author's characterization of X?) to questions of historical methodology (why has the author approached this subject in this way? Is the author's method valid?)

The thing to remember when answering these questions is not to panic! **The questions are designed to be difficult** to give you the chance to show your full intellectual potential. The interviewers will help guide you to the right idea if you provide ideas for them to guide. This is your chance to show your creativity, analytical skills, intellectual flexibility, problem-solving skills and your go-getter attitude. Don't waste it on nervousness or a fear of messing up or looking stupid.

Q31: You are given an extract from an introduction to a historical work that is based entirely on oral sources, such as Robert Fraser's 'Blood of Spain'.

Can one ever understand a historical event from oral history sources alone?

This question is asking you to evaluate a particular type of source. A good way to approach a question like this would be to look firstly at the ways in which this type of source can help to understand an event, then to look at the **weaknesses of this type of source**, and then to come to a conclusion. There are lots of aspects of a historical event that could be understood through oral history sources alone. Using the example of the Spanish Civil War, oral history allows one to understand what the war was like in terms of lived experience, as in a fairly decentralised state with low levels of literacy and high levels of censorship. Oral history can bring a perspective to the war that is lacking in other types of sources and official documents.

Furthermore, seeing as oral histories are generally collected in interviews after the event in question, this type of source allows the historian to understand not only the event itself but also its aftermath and long-term effects on those who lived through it.

However, there are several drawbacks to oral history. While it is a useful way to understand what it was like to live through an event, it only shows the perspective of those interviewed, which may not be representative of the people of Spain as a whole. It also would not take into account political, economic or international factors influencing the course of events, which can only be illuminated by other types of sources. Oral history is also fallible, in that people are interviewed about events that happened years or even decades earlier. Therefore, **recollections of events may not be entirely reliable**.

A good conclusion to this question would be that while certain aspects of historical events could be understood from oral sources alone, no one type of source is comprehensive enough to encapsulate every aspect of an event. For the best understanding of the Spanish Civil War, it would be necessary to use as wide a variety of sources as possible, including oral history.

You may be given an extract from an introduction to a history book on a very specific topic about which you know very little about, and asked to comment on the historian's proposed method. For example, it may be an extract from a work that looks at Georgian England from a woman's perspective, such as Vickery's Behind Closed Doors: At Home in Georgian England.

Q32: This work looks at Georgian England from a feminist perspective. Do you think it is acceptable to analyse a period through the lens of a concept that didn't exist during the period under study (i.e. feminism)?

This would be a difficult question to be presented with at an interview. It is important to stay calm and be open-minded, and **the interviewers will help guide you to an answer**. It would be useful to analyse both sides of such a question before coming to a conclusion. You might start by looking at the drawbacks of analysing a certain period through the lens of a concept that was not contemporary to the period you are looking at.

There are several problems with analysing Georgian England through a feminist framework (for example). Many historians argue that it is better to analyse the past through terminology that was in use in the period under discussion.

By looking at Georgian England through a feminist perspective, you may be imposing ideas onto the past that are incompatible with the period under study. You could argue that **this is not so much history as sociology**, as it is putting more of an emphasis on the modern concept (feminism) than on the period you are supposed to be studying (Georgian England).

However, there are also benefits to this type of historiography. Part of the purpose of history is to look at the past through a new perspective. Even if this perspective would not have been understood by the people who lived in the period under discussion, it may still illuminate aspects of the period that have not yet been covered by the scholarship.

You may be given an extract from a work about a certain aspect of historical theory, such as Niall Ferguson's Virtual History or Richard Evans' Altered Pasts, both of which deal with counter-factual history.

Q33: What, if any, is the value of studying counter-factual history?

Counter-factual history is the history of *what if?* It challenges the historian to consider what would have happened had something else occurred. A common counter-factual investigated by Ferguson is '*what if Great Britain had never entered the First World War?*'

A good answer to this question would **reflect on the merits and limitations of this type of history** and the basis of the information given in the source.

There are several merits to studying counter-factual history. It allows one to focus on crucial turning points in historical events. You may only really be able to understand the consequences of a certain event (such as Britain entering the First World War) if you have gone through the process of imagining how things might have turned out if this one event had gone differently. It may also help in thinking about causation in history. You may come to the realisation that a certain factor was a key cause in a certain event only by considering whether the event would have gone ahead without the factor. *What If?* History can also be entertaining and engaging and may be a good way of inspiring interest in history.

However, there are also problems associated with studying counter-factual history. Many counter-factual hypotheses (such as *'what if Britain had not entered the First World War?'*) can be taken too far. It's one thing to reflect on such a question in order to analyse the importance of what did happen and the consequences of Britain's entry into the war. It's another thing to imagine a complete parallel universe in which a hypothetical scenario (Britain staying out of the war) is extrapolated into a completely different historical narrative. Perhaps **counter-factual speculation** is a useful historical tool when used in moderation but can easily slide into fiction.

ESSAY-BASED INTERVIEW

Some colleges at Oxford and Cambridge will ask you to submit one or two essays with your application. The details for this will be made clear in the application process. One of your interviews may, therefore, be based in part on the contents of your essay. This is a chance for you to demonstrate your detailed factual knowledge about an area of history you are familiar with, as well as to show your passion for the subject.

The interviewer may open by asking for a summary of the piece of work, of the methodology behind it, and the conclusion reached. They may then ask some follow-up questions related to the work or the subject matter. This part of the interview will be very individual and depend on the nature and subject of the work submitted. Here are some things to keep in mind if you are submitting essays as part of your application:

- Ensure that any work you are submitting is your own. You will not be able to justify an argument you make in an interview if that argument was written by your tutor or teacher. The interviewers will be able to tell if this is the case.
- Ensure that any work you are submitting is on topics that you feel comfortable talking about in detail (e.g. something you have studied at AS-level, rather than something you have only just started studying)

- Of course, ensure that the work you submit is of a high standard that you believe reflects your academic abilities. If it is a piece of work you are proud of, you will better be able to defend it in your interview.

- Re-read the essays you have submitted before the interview so they are fresh in your mind.

- While it is good to remain flexible and open to revising your arguments, **try not to disagree with your own essay**! If the interviewer asks about a certain aspect of the essay and you respond by saying "I wrote this ages ago, I don't think it's very good", that won't come across well. On the other hand, if you have a very solid reason for revising your argument, this is something you can bring up in your interview.

EXAMPLE QUESTIONS

These questions are likely to be **tailored to the individual essay you've submitted**, so it is likely that the answers given are not relevant to the topics covered in your own essay. However, it is useful to read them anyway and think about the *types* of questions you might be asked.

The questions are likely to build on the essay you have written or they will prompt you to investigate an aspect of the topic your essay has not covered fully. A candidate who has written an essay on the topic 'Did Napoleon bring an end to the French Revolution' in which he/she has argued in the affirmative could be asked the question:

Q34: "When did Napoleon bring an end to the French Revolution?"

A good answer to a question such as this should firstly **acknowledge the complexity of the question**. In this case, this would require recognising that there are many potential answers to the question. One could argue that Napoleon ended the French Revolution in 1799 when he became First Consul, or in 1802 when he declared himself Consul for life, or in 1804 when he made himself Emperor. You may have a strong opinion in favour of one of these interpretations, but before making your case, it would be good to show that you are aware that there are many possible arguments that could be made.

If you believe that the French Revolution ended when Napoleon made himself Emperor in 1804, you would need to explain why. In this type of question, factual detail and a command of the material is crucial as the topic on which you have written an essay should be one with which you are very familiar. You may, for instance, talk about this event from a constitutional perspective and argue that this is the point at which leadership of France technically returns to the type of monarchical system the Revolution had aimed to overthrow. You may mention that the Pope takes part in Napoleon's coronation ceremony, showing that the anti-Catholic nature of the Revolution has been reversed. Whatever you decide to argue, you must show clear factual evidence to back up your interpretation.

A **poor candidate** may respond to this question in a number of ways. The most obvious mistakes to be avoided would be to reply, "I don't know" or to say "1804" and refuse to explain your answer. It would also be unwise to reverse the argument you originally made in your essay by saying "Napoleon didn't bring an end to the French Revolution" (unless you have very good reason, for example, new research to back up this revision).

Q35: A candidate who has written an essay on the Enlightenment could be asked a question such as "Why do you write '__the E__nlightenment' in your essay, rather than 'enlightenment'?"

A **good answer** will recognise the complexity of the question. It is not a question about grammar and formatting at all. Instead, it highlights the issue of whether the Enlightenment (or enlightenment) can be seen as a movement that was clear and homogeneous enough to warrant being labelled with a proper noun (The Enlightenment) rather than a vaguer descriptive term (enlightenment).

A good answer would then talk this through with the interviewers, with reference to factual evidence you are familiar with. You could talk about how the Enlightenment was a very diverse movement, encompassing ideas as varied as Rousseau's *The Social Contract* to enlightened absolutism in the Habsburg monarchy. This might, be better characterised through a descriptive term rather than a proper noun as The Enlightenment makes these ideas seem more uniform than they were in reality. However, you might on balance argue that it should still be categorised as The Enlightenment because many of its thinkers referred to themselves in these terms.

A **weaker candidate** may simply say "My teacher said it was The Enlightenment" or "My textbook says The Enlightenment" and refuse to engage with the topic. A weak candidate may also say "I had never really thought about it" and leave it at that. If you have genuinely never considered an idea that you are presented with in the interview (which is very likely to happen), it is fine to say so. But then do go on to engage with the idea critically, e.g. "I had considered that but it's a very interesting point".

READING LIST

The obvious way to prepare for any Oxbridge interview is to **read widely**. This is important so that you can mention books and interests in your personal statement. It is also important because it means that you will be able to draw upon a greater number and variety of ideas for your interview.

- **Make a record** of the book, who wrote it, when they wrote it, and summarise the argument. This means that you have some details about your research in the days before the interview.

- Reading is a passive exercise. To make it genuinely meaningful, you should **engage with the text**. Summarise the argument. Ask yourself questions like how is the writer arguing? Is it a compelling viewpoint?

- **Quality over quantity**. This is not a race as to how many books you can read in a short period of time. It is instead a test of your ability to critically analyse and synthesise information from a text – something you'll be doing on a daily basis at university.

LAW

- Glanville Williams: Learning the Law
- Richard Susskind Tomorrow's Lawyers: An Introduction to Your Future
- Tom Bingham: The Rule of Law
- Anthony King: The British Constitution
- Nicolas J McBride: Letters to a Law Student: A Guide to Studying Law at University
- Helena Kennedy: Just Law

FINAL ADVICE

BEFORE YOUR INTERVIEW

- Make sure you understand your curriculum; your interview will most likely use material from your school courses as a starting point.

- Remind yourself of the selection criteria for your subject.

- Read around your subject in scientific articles and books, visit museums, watch documentaries, anything which broadens your knowledge of your favourite topics while demonstrating your passion for your subject. They may ask you at the interview which articles you've read recently to check you are engaged with the subject. Scientists should try New Scientist's online articles to start you off; TED talks are also a great way to be quickly briefed on cutting-edge research, and it's more likely you will remember the name of the researcher, etc.

- Practice common questions or sample questions – this is better done with a teacher or someone you are less familiar with or who is an experienced interviewer.

- Make up your own questions throughout your day: Why is that flower shaped like that? Why is that bird red-breasted? Why does my dog like to fetch sticks? What did I mean when I said that man wasn't 'normal', and is this the criteria everyone uses? How do I know I see the same colours as others?

- Re-read your personal statement and any coursework you are providing. Anticipate questions that may arise from these and prepare them in advance.

- Read and do anything you've said you've done in your application – they may ask you about it at the interview!

- Check your interview specifications – what type of interviews you will have for which subjects, how many there will be, where, when, and with whom they will be so there are no surprises.

ON THE DAY OF YOUR INTERVIEW

- Get a good night's sleep before the big day.

- If you are travelling from far away, try to arrive the night before so that you're fresh in the morning. Getting up early in the morning and travelling far could tire you out and you might be less focused whilst being interviewed. Many colleges will provide you accommodation if you're travelling from a certain distance away.

- Take a shower in the morning and dress to your comfort, though you don't want to give a sloppy first impression – most opt for smart/casual

- Get there early so you aren't late or stressed out before it even starts.

- Smile at everyone and be polite.

- Don't worry about other candidates; be nice of course, but you are there for you, and their impressions of how their interviews went have nothing to do with what the interviewers thought or how yours will go.

- It's OK to be nervous – they know you're nervous and understand, but try to move past it and be in the moment to get the most out of the experience.

- Don't be discouraged if it feels like one interview didn't go well – you may have shown the interviewers exactly what they wanted to see, even if it wasn't what you wanted to see.

- Have a cuppa and relax, there's nothing you can do now but be yourself.

> ## The Most Important Advice...
>
> - Explain your thought processes as much as possible – it doesn't matter if you're wrong. *It really is the journey; not the destination that matters.*
> - Interviewers aren't interested in *what you know*. Instead, they are more interested in *what you can do* with what you already know.

✗ **DON'T** be quiet – even if you can't answer a question. How you approach the question could show the interviewer what they want to see.

✗ **DON'T** rely on the interviewer to guide you every step of the way.

✗ **DON'T** ever, ever, ever give up.

✗ **DON'T** be arrogant or rigid –you are bound to get things wrong, just accept them and move on.

✗ **DON'T** expect to know all the answers; this is different than school, you aren't expected to know the answer to everything – you are using your knowledge as a foundation for original thoughts and applications under the guidance of your interviewer.

✗ **DON'T** think you will remember everything you did/wrote without revising.

✗ **DON'T** be afraid to point out flaws in your own ideas – scientists need to be self-critical, and the interviewer has already noticed your mistakes!

✗ **DON'T** be defensive, especially if the interviewer is hinting that your idea may be on the wrong path – the interviewer is the expert!

✗ **DON'T** get hung up on a question for too long.

✗ **DON'T** rehearse scripted answers to be regurgitated.

✗ **DON'T** answer the question you wanted them to ask.

✗ **DON'T** lie about things you have read/done (and if you already lied in your personal statement, then read/do them before the interview!).

✓ **DO** speak freely about what you are thinking and ask for clarifications.

✓ **DO** take suggestions and listen for pointers from your interviewer.

✓ **DO** try your best to get to the answer.

✓ **DO** have confidence in yourself and the abilities that got you this far

✓ **DO** be prepared to discuss the ideas and problems in your work.

✓ **DO** make many suggestions and have many ideas.

✓ **DO** show intellectual flexibility by taking suggestions from the interviewer.

✓ **DO** take your time in answering to ensure your words come out right.

✓ **DO** research your interviewers so that you know their basic research interests. Then ensure you understand the basics of their work (no need to go into detail with this).

✓ **DO** prepare your answers to common questions.

✓ **DO** answer the question that the interviewer has asked – not the one you want them to!

✓ **DO** practice interviews with family or teachers – even easy questions may be harder to articulate out loud and on the spot to a stranger.

✓ **DO** think about strengths/experiences you may wish to highlight.

✓ **DO** visit www.uniadmissions.co.uk/example-interviews to see mock interviews in your subject. This will allow you to understand the differences between good and bad candidates.

Afterword

Remember that the route to success is your approach and practice. Don't fall into the trap that *"you can't prepare for Oxbridge interviews"*– this could not be further from the truth. With targeted preparation and focused reading, you can dramatically boost your chances of getting that dream offer.

Work hard, never give up, and do yourself justice.

Good luck!

This book is dedicated to my grandparents – thank you for your wisdom, kindness, and endless amounts of love.

Acknowledgements

I would like to express my gratitude to the many people who helped make this book possible. I would like to thank *Dr. Ranjna Garg* for suggesting that I take on this mammoth task and providing invaluable feedback. I am also grateful for the 30 Oxbridge tutors for their specialist input and advice. Last, but by no means least; I am thankful to *David Salt* for his practical advice and willingness to discuss my ideas- regardless of whether it was 4 AM or PM.

About Us

We currently publish over 85 titles across a range of subject areas – covering specialised admissions tests, examination techniques, personal statement guides, plus everything else you need to improve your chances of getting on to competitive courses such as medicine and law, as well as into universities such as Oxford and Cambridge.

Outside of publishing we also operate a highly successful tuition division, called UniAdmissions. This company was founded in 2013 by Dr Rohan Agarwal and Dr David Salt, both Cambridge Medical graduates with several years of tutoring experience. Since then, every year, hundreds of applicants and schools work with us on our programmes. Through the programmes we offer, we deliver expert tuition, exclusive course places, online courses, best-selling textbooks and much more.

With a team of over 1,000 Oxbridge tutors and a proven track record, UniAdmissions have quickly become the UK's number one admissions company.

Visit and engage with us at:

Website (UniAdmissions): www.uniadmissions.co.uk
Facebook: www.facebook.com/uniadmissionsuk

Printed in Great Britain
by Amazon

33021635R00201